J. M. Coetzee & the Ethics of Reading

J. M. Coetzee &
the Ethics of Reading

Literature in the Event

DEREK ATTRIDGE

The University of Chicago Press : *Chicago & London*

DEREK ATTRIDGE is professor of English at the University
of York. He is the author or editor of numerous works, including
*Peculiar Language, Joyce Effects, Meter and Meaning, Poetic
Rhythm,* and *The Singularity of Literature.*

The University of Chicago Press, Chicago 60637
The University of Chicago Press, Ltd., London
© 2004 by The University of Chicago
All rights reserved. Published 2004
Printed in the United States of America

13 12 11 10 09 08 07 06 05   5 4 3 2

ISBN: 0-226-03116-0 (cloth)
ISBN: 0-226-03117-9 (paper)

Library of Congress Cataloging-in-Publication Data

Attridge, Derek.
    J. M. Coetzee and the ethics of reading : literature in the event /
Derek Attridge.
        p.   cm.
    Includes bibliographical references and index.
    ISBN 0-226-03116-0 (cloth : alk. paper) — ISBN 0-226-03117-9
(pbk. : alk. paper)
        1. Coetzee, J. M., 1940–Criticism and interpretation.
2. Modernism (Literature)–South Africa.   3. Difference
(Psychology) in literature.   4. South Africa–In literature.
5. Ethics in literature.   I. Title.
    PR9369.3.C58Z53   2004
    823'.914–dc22

                                        2004009713

In memory of

Peter Kerchhoff
1934–1999

A good person . . . in dark times

: CONTENTS :

In the late 1970s I was staying with a friend for a short holiday on the west coast of the United States. One evening he placed a slim hardback into my hands, saying, "This is something by a South African writer you might enjoy." (We were both voluntary exiles from South Africa; both, as it happens, students of Renaissance literature.) The book was entitled *Dusklands*; it was a novel (of sorts) by an author with a recognizably Afrikaans surname whom I had not come across before, and had been published in South Africa a few years previously. I did enjoy it, albeit with a certain degree of bafflement: it was quite unlike any other fiction emanating from South Africa that I had read, although its affinity with the modernist tradition of European and North American writing was evident. I decided to look out for more novels by J. M. Coetzee.

It turned out that a second work, *In the Heart of the Country,* had already been published, this time in the United States and Britain as well as South Africa, but had not made a great splash. Its numbered paragraphs and unreliable narrative were probably too overtly modernist, too "intellectual," to win an extensive public, and its setting—the Karoo semi-desert of the Western Cape—perhaps too locally specific. The novel that did attract wide international attention was Coetzee's next one, *Waiting for the Barbarians,* a less overtly antirealist and less identifiably South African work that appeared in 1980. (Its success led to the publication of *Dusklands* for the first time in the U.K. and the U.S.A., in 1982 and 1985 respectively.) *Waiting for the Barbarians* was followed in 1983 by *Life & Times of Michael K,* which won for Coetzee the first of his two Booker Prizes.

As these novels appeared, I read them with intense involvement and admiration, but had never thought of expressing my responses to them in a public forum. That changed when, shortly after the publication of *Foe* in 1986, I was invited to participate in a conference panel devoted to twentieth-century British literature and entitled "Canonical Reconsiderations: Class, Colonies, Gender." Apart from the impropriety, which I rather relished, of a South African writer's appearance in an event dedicated to British literature, *Foe* suited the panel perfectly. It gave me the opportunity to address not only the novel's powerful, and in my view justified, claim to be considered part of the twentieth-century canon of great literature in English, but also its own exploration of the processes of novelistic canonization, as they might have operated in eighteenth-century England, with gender and race playing a significant part. An extended version of that paper appears as chapter 3 of this book.

Having once tried to articulate my strong and complicated response to a newly published Coetzee novel, I found each new work thereafter demanding a similar attempt at articulation. *Age of Iron* (1990), *The Master of Petersburg* (1994), *Boyhood* (1997—a memoir), *Disgrace* (1999), *Youth* (2002—the sequel to *Boyhood*), and *Elizabeth Costello* (2003): every one of these, while it undeniably gave immense pleasure, seemed to break new ground and to call for a fresh thinking-through of significant aesthetic, ethical, and political issues. Often the pleasure was mixed with a feeling of dismay, as Coetzee, rather than following the easy path of repetition and conformity, ran risks and ignored sensibilities. In every case, I felt the need to put into writing something of my response. I also revisited the earlier fiction, to consider afresh its challenges and rewards. Alongside the novels and memoirs, I read and re-read Coetzee's many essays and rather fewer interviews.

My purpose in summarizing the genesis of the chapters that make up this book is to draw attention to an element present in all of them: the attempt to do justice to the singularity and inventiveness of a work that has recently come into existence. This is not just a matter of expatiating on their aesthetic brilliance and emotional scope, or attempting to explain their historical significance and political effectiveness. The importance of Coetzee's books, I believe, lies not only in their extraordinary ability to grip the reader in proceeding from sentence to sentence and from page to page, to move intensely with their depictions of cruelty, suffering, longing, and love, to give pleasure even when they dispirit and disturb, but also in the way they raise and illuminate questions of immense practical importance to all of us. These include the relation between ethical demands and political decisions, the human cost of artistic creation, the exactingness and uncertainty of confessional autobiography, and the difficulty of doing justice to others in a violent society. Each work has pushed in a different direction (sometimes going beyond, and thus challenging, its predecessors), and that feeling of bafflement that accompanied my early reading of *Dusklands* has never been absent from the experience of my initial encounter with a new book by Coetzee. This is not to say that the bafflement has entirely disappeared with re-readings and the passage of time, but in coming to know each work better I have found myself coming to understand the crucial role of that experience of bewilderment in its achievement as a work of art.

What I offer in each chapter is an argument necessarily focused on only one aspect (or cluster of related aspects) of the particular work or works that form its subject, an aspect which was peculiarly important in my coming to terms with its power and its uniqueness. There remains a certain degree of arbitrariness in this choice: any of these topics could have been the subject of an entire book on Coetzee, in which the significance of the topic in question for each of his works would have been made evident. However, my interest is as much in the specificity of each work as in the generalizations we might make about Coetzee as a writer, and I leave it to the reader to make further extrapolations across the entire oeuvre. In the case of the four early works, my commentary was, as I've explained, written retrospectively rather than on the works' first appearance, though my own initial encounters with them remain vivid in my memory. The chapters on the later works are based on essays written when they were published, but I have revised them to take account of the books that followed where it has seemed appropriate to do so—seeking always to preserve something of the sense of challenge which each new work produced at the time of its appearance. Just when I thought I had finished, *Elizabeth Costello* appeared, bringing together a number of pieces I had read in diverse publications but also adding significant new material; and a few weeks before I let go of the manuscript Coetzee was awarded the Nobel Prize and used the occasion to give a remarkable address I felt I had to respond to.

My hope is that this book will serve as an introduction to Coetzee's writing for those beginning to engage with it, provide increased enjoyment and a stimulus for thought for those who know it well, and raise for all readers a number of far-reaching questions about the place of literature in our lives, individual and social. An implicit claim in every chapter is that the impulses and acts that shape our lives as ethical beings—impulses and acts of respect, of love, of trust, of generosity—cannot be adequately represented in the discourses of philosophy, politics, or theology, but are in their natural element in literature; and this is not so much because literary works are capable of mimicking our daily existence and the choices it presents us with, but rather because they are capable of taking us through an intense experience of these other-directed impulses and acts. The inventive literary work, therefore, should be thought of as an ethically charged event, one that befalls individual readers and, at the same time, the culture within which, and through which, they read.

The aim of the various chapters, then, is to follow Coetzee's lead in exploring a number of issues that have a bearing on our lives as readers of literature and as members of various communities, issues such as interpretation and literary judgment, responsibility to the other, trust and betrayal, creativity and artistic commitment, confession and truth to the self. In every case, my interest is in the *literary* exploration of these issues, and in what "literary" might mean in such a statement. Clearly, no answers or recipes or programs emerge from these readings, but my claim is that what gives literature its peculiar importance is precisely that issues such as these are staged rather than argued (even in something as argumentative as Coetzee's Costello pieces); we perform them, and they perform us, as we read. A literary work is not an object or a thesis; literature *happens* (and not only in the texts we call "literary"). The event of the literary work can have powerful effects on its readers, and through them, on the cultural and political environment; but these can never be predicted in advance.

It is precisely this unpredictability, however, that gives literature its ethical force: in doing justice to a literary work, we encounter the singular demands of the other. Coetzee's works both stage, and are, irruptions of otherness into our familiar worlds, and they pose the question: what is our responsibility toward the other? The characters who encounter such irruptions evince a responsibility that is also in question in the novels' own responses to otherness, including that which is other to the tradition of fictional writing in Western culture, and in our own responsibility as readers, as citizens, as living beings. (Coetzee speaks of the fiction writer's sense of "responsibility toward something that has not yet emerged" [*Doubling the Point*, 246], suggesting that the process of creation is subject to a similar obligation.) The discomfort often produced by Coetzee's novels is an aspect of this otherness, one to which I have tried to do justice in this book.

These readings of Coetzee's works were developed coincidentally with my writing of a book entitled *The Singularity of Literature,* in which I elaborate on the understanding of literature's specificity that I have just sketched. Getting to grips with Coetzee's novels and memoirs played an important role in the thinking that went into that book—indeed at one point I imagined, unrealistically, that I was writing a single study switching between readings of Coetzee and more general arguments. For fuller theoretical developments of some of the questions about literature raised briefly in the chapters that follow, the reader is invited to turn to the companion volume.

In engaging with an author as demanding as Coetzee, it is a great boon to be able to discuss his work with others who are similarly engaged. I have benefited immensely from conversations, in various media, with a number of friends over many years, and can thank only a few by name here: David Attwell, Rita Barnard, Rachel Bowlby, Jacques Derrida, Samuel Durrant, Kai Easton, Rosemary Jolly, Mike Marais, Hillis Miller, Margot Norris, Benita Parry, Graham Pechey, Nicholas Royle, Mark Sanders, and Gayatri Spivak. Co-editing a special issue of *Interventions* on *Disgrace* with Peter McDonald was a pleasurable enterprise from which I learned a great deal, not least from my co-editor. Numerous audiences in the U.S.A., U.K., Canada, Sweden, Belgium, France, and South Africa have listened patiently to talks on many of these works and have been probing and generous with questions. A graduate class on Coetzee at Rutgers University enhanced my sense of the richness and provocativeness of his work. The anonymous readers for the University of Natal and University of Chicago Presses gave positive and helpful advice. For financial support at various stages of this project, I am grateful to the National Endowment for the Humanities, the Camargo Foundation, the John Simon Guggenheim Memorial Foundation, and the Leverhulme Trust. My thanks to Jonathan Crewe for introducing me to Coetzee's fiction. Two special debts can only be hinted at here: to my family—Suzanne Hall, Laura Attridge, and Eva Attridge—who never let me take my writing too seriously, and to John Coetzee, who, in true friendship, kept his reservations to himself.

Earlier versions of chapters, or parts of chapters, have appeared as follows. The editors and publishers are gratefully acknowledged. Chapter 3: in *Decolonizing Tradition: New Views of 20th-Century "British" Literature,* ed. Karen Lawrence (Champagne/Urbana: University of Illinois Press, 1991), 212–38, copyright © 1992 by the Board of Trustees of the University of Illinois; chapter 4: in "The Writings of J. M. Coetzee," ed. Michael Valdez Moses, special issue of *The South Atlantic Quarterly* 93 (1994): 59–82, copyright © 1994 by Duke University Press; chapter 5: in *Applying: To Derrida,* ed. John Brannigan, Ruth Robbins, and Julian Wolfreys (London: Macmillan, 1996), 21–40, reproduced with permission of Palgrave Macmillan; chapter 6: in "South African Writing at the Crossroads," ed. Nahem Yousaf and Graham Pechey, special issue of *Critical Survey* 11, no. 2 (1999): 77–93, copyright © Critical Survey and Berghahn Books, 1999; chapter 7: in *Novel: A Forum on Fiction* 34, no. 1 (2000): 98–121, copyright © Novel Corp 2001. Some paragraphs of chapter 1 were first published in "Literary Form and the Demands of Politics: Otherness in J. M. Coetzee's *Age of Iron,*" copyright © by Derek Attridge as reprinted from *Aesthetics and Ideology,* ed. George Levine, copyright © 1994 by Rutgers, The State University, and are reprinted by permission of Rutgers University Press.

CHAPTER ONE

Modernist Form
and the Ethics of Otherness

Dusklands and *In the Heart of the Country*

: I :

During the years in which Coetzee's first six novels were written—from *Dusklands* (1974) to *Age of Iron* (1990)[1]—there were few places in which the writing and reading of literature was more tested by political exigencies and expectations than South Africa. The demand that the production and judgment of art be governed by its immediate effectiveness in the struggle for change (or occasionally in the resistance to change) was immensely powerful, and in many discussions of South African literature this demand gave rise to a suspicion of anything appearing hermetic, self-referential, formally inventive, or otherwise distant from the canons and procedures of the realist tradition.[2] The cultural climate in the country

---

1. For convenience, I shall refer to the twin novellas published under the title *Dusklands* as a "novel."

2. For one example among many, see Karen Press's discussion of these pressures in contemporary South Africa ("Building a National Culture"). Press argues in favor of the construction of a "national culture" which allows for the intrinsic unpredictability of art, and against calls for a "people's culture" serving a specific political program; but since the only art she considers acceptable is art that identifies itself with a Marxist approach (a "historical materialist understanding of society" [36]), the important question of unpredictability is posed under rather severe restraints.

has altered greatly since the end of formal apartheid and the institution of democratic government in 1994 (an event which coincided with the publication of Coetzee's seventh novel, *The Master of Petersburg*), and conditions for the reception of work that transgresses the norms of realist fiction are now more favorable.

However, the questions raised by the strong opposition that work of this kind provoked during the apartheid years remain ones that need to be addressed. Despite the problems inherent in the assumptions that literature can and should serve preexisting political ends and that there is no space for other kinds of work alongside the popular and overtly political, the challenge which such demands direct at "elite art" and its claims is one that cannot be ignored. Lessons learned in South Africa have often proved valuable elsewhere, and the predicament literature found itself in during the struggle against apartheid has implications which extend to writing and reading in less politically fraught contexts.

Because of its use of nonrealist or antirealist devices, its allusiveness, and its metafictional proclivities, Coetzee's fiction is often adduced as an example of "postmodernism."[3] It would be more accurate, I believe, to characterize it as an instance of "late modernism,"[4] or perhaps "neomodernism";[5] Coetzee's work follows on from Kafka and Beckett, not Pynchon and Barth. However, these labels do not in themselves get

3. Linda Hutcheon is one of many who regard Coetzee as a postmodernist (see *A Poetics of Postmodernism*, 77–78, 107–8, 150, 198–99, and *The Politics of Postmodernism*, 51, 76); another is David Ward in *Chronicles of Darkness*, chap. 15. See also David Attwell's nuanced discussion in *J. M. Coetzee*, 20–23. *Foe*, in particular, is frequently taken to typify postmodernism; see for example, Peter de Voogd "La femme naufragée" and Annamaria Carusi, "Post, Post and Post," and many of the contributions to the special issue of the *Journal of Literary Studies* on *Foe*, edited by Marianne de Jong.

4. In a *Doubling the Point* interview, Attwell proposes the term "late modernism" as a label for Coetzee's fiction, and although Coetzee's response is guarded—he suspects (incorrectly, as Attwell assures him) that there is an implicit "merely" before "late modernism"—he doesn't reject it (198–201).

5. Neil Lazarus identifies the resistance offered by the fiction of Coetzee and some other white South African writers with modernism, as that term is defined by Adorno—that is, as a discourse in opposition to the instrumentalizing pressures of modernity (see n. 12 below). Stephen Watson, too, associates Coetzee's fiction with modernism and with modernism's resistance to the coercions of modernity ("Colonialism and the Novels of J. M. Coetzee"); and in writing of a "quasi-religious impulse" (372), a privilege of "being over against becoming" (385), in modernism and in Coetzee, he may be responding to the same qualities of the fiction that I am responding to in this chapter, though I would not use his terminology. Attwell has expressed agreement with Lazarus and Watson on the affinity between Coetzee with modernism ("The Problem of History," 130 n. 11). I must admit to some hesitation in

us very far in dealing with the relation between form and politics in his writing, given the wide disagreements about their scope and significance. "Modernism" can be a catch-all term for art that is governed by aestheticism, formalism, traditionalism, and political quietism (or reaction), or it can refer to an art of innovation, self-questioning, and the radical displacement of traditional verities. The term "postmodernism" is even less securely defined. There are some who see it as the final de-historicizing of an already anemic modernism, and others for whom it is a historically and politically responsible development of modernism; it is perceived sometimes as a pushing of modernism's claims to a new extreme and sometimes as an undermining of modernism's claims by the application of a version of its own methods.

The picture becomes even more complicated if we introduce the question of related theoretical discourses. The academic expression of modernism is often held to be New Criticism, with postmodernism having as its theoretical wing post-structuralism; but there are also strong grounds for arguing that post-structuralism is a derivation from and extension of modernism (in the work of such writers as Joyce and Mallarmé), in which case postmodernism either awaits a theoretical model, is its own theorization, or escapes theorization altogether.[6]

Clearly, different people are talking about different things here. If you conceptualize modernism as a cultural object hammered out on the forges of New Criticism, then postmodernism inevitably comes, hand in hand (or hand in glove) with post-structuralism, to explode that object and the

---

using a phrase such as "late modernism" since it implies a narrative in which contemporary uses of modernist methods are merely survivors, soon to be eliminated altogether; my sense of the future, and—as will emerge later—of modernism's relation to the future, is more open than this. However, I'm not sure that the resonances of "neomodernism" are quite appropriate either.

6. One of the most influential characterizations of modernism as apolitical aestheticism (in contrast to the avant-garde) is Andreas Huyssen; see, in particular, *After the Great Divide*. Huyssen follows through some of the implications of Peter Bürger's characterization of the 1920s avant-garde (in *Theory of the Avant-Garde*) as a critique of what he terms "aestheticism." Among the more prolific and prominent commentators on postmodernism, Fredric Jameson, in *Postmodernism*, sees it as a replacement of history by historicism and nostalgia, while for Hutcheon it is a rejection of modernism's refusal of history. Brian McHale (*Constructing Postmodernism*) begins to sort out the confusion by usefully delineating two current models of modernism, a "conservative" and a "radical" one, based on two different selections of works and giving rise to two different ideas of postmodernism (see, in particular, his discussion of *Ulysses* in chapter 2).

assumptions—transcendentalizing, universalizing, aestheticizing, and so on—that underlie it. If, on the other hand, modernism is viewed through the lens of the post-structuralist theory for which it functioned as the preeminent exemplar, postmodernism is likely to appear less a break with than an intensification of modernism's own detotalizing pressures—unless, that is, it's seen as a betrayal of modernism's radical ideals through capitulation to the marketplace.

Much of the dispute about the relation between modernism and postmodernism would disappear if there were less compulsion to define, in a totalizing and positivistic spirit, diverse contemporaneous cultural practices. Nevertheless, the question of the relationship between today's most influentially innovative art and the equivalent art of the decades between the wars remains an important and ill-understood one. It becomes particularly important when one is considering, as I am here, an artistic practice operating under intense political pressures. Do the techniques of modernism belong to a moment of capitulation and self-reflexiveness which offers the worst possible model for the politically responsible artist? And if so, is postmodernism, insofar as it continues along the modernist path of formal experiment and exposure of its own conventions, inescapably apolitical? Or is modernist innovation a possible source for a political art that recognizes the dangers of a merely instrumental artistic practice—and postmodernism, in some of its manifestations at least, the working out of such a practice?

Whether Coetzee's work should be labeled "modernist" or "postmodernist" is a significant question only insofar as it raises further questions about the practice of formal innovation and disruption that begins in the modernist period (though of course it has antecedents and foreshadowings in earlier periods). My argument, briefly, is that what often gets called (and condemned as) the self-reflexiveness of modernist writing, its foregrounding of its own linguistic, figurative, and generic operations, its willed interference with the transparency of discourse, is, in its effects if not always in its intentions, allied to a new apprehension of the claims of otherness, of that which cannot be expressed in the discourse available to us—not because of an essential ineffability but because of the constraints imposed by that discourse, often in its very productivity and proliferation.[7] Since the modernist period proper, there have continued

7. As Astradur Eysteinsson puts it in *The Concept of Modernism:* "Even though realism may be highly critical of capitalist reality (as many nineteenth-century realists were), it evinces a tendency to reproduce the narrative structures and the symbolic order that form

to appear works with this kind of responsiveness to the demands of otherness, achieved by means which, whatever their specific differences, are clearly related to one another in their general strategies.

This modernism after modernism necessarily involves a reworking of modernism's methods, since nothing could be less modernist than a repetition of previous modes, however disruptive they were in their time. An instance of such a tendency to repeat would be the work of another contemporary South African novelist, André Brink, whose series of novels (fifteen at the time of writing) constitute an impressive record of engagement with the political conflicts of his native country, yet whose use of modernist (or postmodern) techniques contributes much less to the success of his fiction than the essentially realist storytelling they sometimes mediate.[8] Thus Brink's 1982 novel *A Chain of Voices* utilizes the Faulknerian device of short personal narratives out of which a larger story gradually shapes itself, without the emergence of a totalizing and adjudicating central voice. It's a powerful novel, but its power derives not from an apprehension of otherness, as one might expect from its subject matter (a slave rebellion on a number of Boer farms in the Cape in 1825), but from the illusion of empathy and understanding that the intimate individual disclosures produce. *States of Emergency* (1988) is another novel by Brink that exploits the self-reflexivity characteristic of some modernist practice, staging very directly the conflict between political engagement and the exigencies of literary creation as the central character, a novelist, attempts, at a time of political crisis in South Africa, to write a love story, and life and fiction turn out to be mutually transformative. The overall effect, however, has a slight air of modernism-by-numbers, whatever the intensity of individual sections as representations of the impact of political urgencies on personal lives.

---

the basis of this society and its ideology. As a mode of cultural resistance..., modernism seeks to distance itself from this symbolic order" (208). For a related argument to mine, focusing on the work of Kafka, Beckett, and Witold Gombrowicz, see Ewa Ziarek, *The Rhetoric of Failure*.

8. That it should be members of South Africa's privileged white group who pursued innovative fictional modes during the apartheid era is, of course, not fortuitous; given their upbringing, education, and cultural situation, such writers were more likely to feel the need, and possess the means, to engage with literary (and critical) developments in Europe and North America. It should be added that the most accomplished and politically responsible of successful white novelists—I am thinking in particular of Coetzee, Brink, Nadine Gordimer, and Breyten Breytenbach—show an acute consciousness of the limits imposed upon them by their position in South African society.

J. M. Coetzee, I want to argue, does not merely employ but extends and revitalizes modernist practices, and in so doing develops a mode of writing that allows the attentive reader to live through the pressures and possibilities, and also the limits, of political engagement.[9] To make this claim is not to deny what has often been powerfully demonstrated: that a large part of modernist writing was insensitive to the otherness produced by patriarchal and imperialist policies and assumptions. My argument is merely that within what is called modernism, technical resources— and a certain attitude to the operations of language and discourse—were evolved that would make possible a new openness and alertness to such modalities of otherness. It is true that, with some notable exceptions, only in later developments of modernism have these resources been exploited in conjunction with a thematic interest in gender, race, and colonialism. Nor am I claiming that modernism alone uses the formal possibilities of literary writing in this way; the larger reaches of this argument, which I do not intend to enter here, extend to the question of the specificity of literature as a cultural institution and practice during a much longer epoch of Western culture.

It seems likely that the formal singularity of Coetzee's works is an important part of their effectiveness as literature; what I wish to argue here is that this effectiveness is not separate from the importance these works have in the ethico-political realm, but rather that to a large extent it constitutes that importance. Furthermore, I believe that this importance is considerable. Coetzee's handling of formal properties is bound up with the capacity of his work to engage with—to stage, confront, apprehend, explore—otherness, and in this engagement it broaches the most fundamental and widely significant issues involved in any consideration of ethics

---

9. My reluctance to call Coetzee's work "postmodern" or "postmodernist" stems in part from one aspect of the cultural configuration to which these labels are often applied: its tendency to reduce otherness to sameness (in the globalization and commodification of cultures, the pursuit of rapid gratification, etc.). Some accounts of postmodernism would, of course, exclude exactly these practices on account of their failure to resist hegemonic pressures; these accounts would more easily accommodate Coetzee's work, since their "postmodernism" comes close to what I am calling "modernism." Simon During, for example, depicts "postmodern thought" as a discourse which resists the reduction of otherness to sameness that characterizes what he calls postmodernity, as a general term for our cultural dominant ("Postmodernism or Post-colonialism Today"). Jameson's description of the depthlessness of postmodern cultural forms is another way of figuring its homogenizing drive, but his totalizing language leaves little room for an oppositional discourse of the type identified by During.

and politics.[10] I also believe that what happens in Coetzee's work, and in responses to it, is only a more intense version of the processes involved in all successful literary uses of the formal properties and potentialities of language, processes I discuss in *The Singularity of Literature*.

One consistent aspect of Coetzee's technique as a novelist is to deny the reader any ethical guidance from an authoritative voice or valorizing metalanguage. We are left to make the difficult judgments ourselves, on the Magistrate's mixed-up humanism, on Michael K's strategy of withdrawal, on Susan Barton's attempts at self-promotion, on Mrs. Curren's clinging to—and letting go of—the truisms of Western democratic liberalism, on David Lurie's sexual predatoriness and adoption of a changed way of living. (It is one of the weaknesses of the novellas of *Dusklands* in comparison with the later works that we experience little difficulty in passing judgment on their central figures, Eugene Dawn and Jacobus Coetzee.) At the same time, we remain conscious of these narrating figures as fictional characters, as selves mediated by a language which has not forgotten its mediating role, a language with a density and irreducibility which signals its rhetorical shaping, its intertextual affiliations, its saturatedness with cultural meanings. For both these reasons, we can never remove the aura of something like irony that plays about these representations of human individuals—though by the same token we can never determine its strength.

It is this uncertain irony that makes the protagonist of *Life & Times of Michael K*—a figure of otherness to most in the society through which he moves—a figure of otherness to the reader as well, even though we are privy to his mental processes and his emotional life. To treat Michael K as a representative of the author, as is sometimes done, is to bring him prematurely within the circle of the same, overlooking the stylistic movements that keep him constantly opaque.[11] And this permanent possibility of irony, this resistance to closure, is, once again, achieved by modernist

---

10. I am not attempting in this chapter to make a distinction between ethics and politics, but am treating the political as one domain in which the ethical makes its demands; for further discussion see chapter 4 below. Coetzee himself, however, contrasts the two terms in *Doubling the Point*; see, for instance, pp. 200 and 337–38, where the political is more narrowly associated with mass action and the use of violence.

11. For further discussion, see chapter 2. This identification of Michael K with a position held by Coetzee is characteristic of critiques of the novel that find fault with its "rejection of politics." Thus Stephen Clingman can write: "For him, it becomes clear, any form of systematization—including political systematization—is a form of control" ("Revolution and Reality," 48), and mean by "him" not Michael K but Coetzee. Through the character

techniques; it is itself a kind of trust, a kind of wager—an act of writing that signals its own limits and its own dangers, while opening itself to a future of unpredictable readings. Instead of an aesthetics of the static and the essential, preserving its form across time and cultural difference, Coetzee's fiction opens the possibility of an ethics of unique acts, rooted always in the here and now, yet acknowledging a deep responsibility to the otherness of elsewhere, of the past, and of the future.

The issue of otherness and its political ramifications is, of course, particularly acute in colonial and post-colonial writing, and has been the subject of much discussion. However, the link between this question and the formal practices of literature—and in particular the practices we label "modernist"—has not been given sufficient consideration.[12] The reason for this is obvious: the category of form is closely associated with a tradition of literary (and more generally, artistic) commentary we can call "aestheticism" (recognizing, as we do so, that the term covers a wide variety of works and theories). And aestheticism—with modernism often adduced as a major example—is regarded as being defined precisely by the avoidance of political responsibility, by the vaunting of an artistic autonomy that has little interest in modes of otherness in cultural and political life. Yet the importance of form to literature needs no demonstrating; it is at the heart of every writer's practice, and any account of literature's difference from other textual activities and products—however guarded or problematized—must involve some version of it.

In order to bring the issue back to the center of discussion, what we need is a way of talking about form (or of that aspect of the literary that has prompted the longstanding use of the term) which avoids the simple opposition with content or meaning that characterizes traditional aesthetic

---

of Michael K, the novel certainly constitutes a test of conventional politics, but this is not a rejection of politics; the ethical issues it raises could scarcely be more fundamental to political life.

12. One interesting exception is Lazarus's discussion of contemporary white South African writers in "Modernism and Modernity." But the view of modernism which Lazarus takes from Adorno is not one that valorizes an opening onto otherness; for instance, his categorization of Coetzee's writing as modernist rather than postmodernist is based on its being "*ethically* saturated, ... *humanistic* in its critique of the established order, ... concerned to *represent* reality, and ... *rationalistic*" (148; emphases in original). The modernism with which I am aligning Coetzee involves a questioning of just these qualities, at least as self-evident values (even "ethical" is rendered problematic, as we shall see). Using McHale's terms (see note 6), Lazarus's Adornian modernism is "conservative" modernism; mine—and, I am contending, Coetzee's—is radical modernism. For further discussion, see chapter 4.

discourse. As long as this conceptual opposition dominates our thinking about art, form will be considered either as a property to be admired and enjoyed in itself, or as merely a means to a political, ethical, historical, or other more "substantial" end. In *The Singularity of Literature,* I have argued that the literary use of language involves the *performing* of meanings and feelings, and that what has traditionally been called form is central to this performance. The literary work is an *event* (though an event that cannot be distinguished from an act) for both its creator and its reader, and it is the reader—not as free-floating subject but as the nexus of a number of specific histories and contextual formations—who brings the work into being, differently each time, in a singular performance of the work not so much as written but as a writing. The meaning of a literary work, then, can be understood as a verb rather than as a noun: not something carried away when we have finished reading it, but something that happens as we read or recall it.[13] And that happening occurs only because the language is shaped and organized, an active shaping and organizing that we re-live as we experience the literariness of the work.[14]

In order for a literary work to take place, the act of reading must be responsive to its singularity. This is hardly a new or controversial assertion, but what is less easy to grasp is that singularity in this sense exists not in opposition to generality. The literary work is constituted, that is, not by an unchanging core but by the singular fashioning of the codes and conventions of the institution of literature, as they exist and exert pressure in a particular time and place. Its singularity is a uniqueness derived from a capacity to be endlessly transformed while remaining identifiable—within the institutional norms—as what it is. A response that might be called "responsible," that simultaneously reenacts and brings into being the work as literature and not as something else, and as *this* work of literature and not another one, is a response that takes into account as fully as possible, by re-staging them, the work's own performances—of, for example, referentiality, metaphoricity, intentionality, and ethicity.

---

13. An emphasis on reading literature as an event which does not aim at truth or meaning is, of course, more common in discussions of lyric poetry. Thus Altieri, in "Taking Lyrics Literally," proposes that we "treat the lyric as resisting the very idea that 'truth' is a workable ideal for literary productions," and that if we learn anything from lyrics it has nothing to do with the concept of knowledge we inherit from the Enlightenment (260).

14. This argument has implications for the other arts too, of course, but they are not to be discovered by a simple process of extrapolation. I should make it clear that I am assuming that literature is not a transhistorical and transcultural category but an institution and a practice with historical and geographical determinants and limits.

What I am trying to counter is the common view of the literary work (implicit if not explicit in much discussion of literature) as a static, self-sufficient, formal entity which, while it may be the product of historical processes and the occasion for various interpretations across time, is itself a fixed linguistic structure without a temporal or performative dimension—or, at most, a simple linear one derived from the necessary sequentiality of reading.[15] This view is usually attended by a sense of reverence for the formal object that is the literary text, whereas I am arguing for an engagement with the text that recognizes, and capitalizes on, its potential for reinterpretation, for grafting into new contexts, for fission and fusion. At the same time, I do not want to suggest that literariness is merely a bogus category foisted on an undifferentiated body of texts by a certain ideology;[16] there seems to me to be a real difference between a text that functions—in a given reading—as an object to be interpreted (whose raison d'être *is* that final interpretation) and one which exists only in, and as, an event uniting a reading with a writing, between the presentation of truth and the performance or production (which is also a kind of suspension) of truth. That a single text (whether conventionally classified as "literary" or not) may be both of these—and both of these in a single reading (which is never in fact single)—is not, as I see it, a major problem.

15. This hypostatization of the work—usually the poem—as a voice moving steadily from the moment of the beginning to the moment of the conclusion is, to borrow Derrida's terms, a phonocentric representation which overlooks the importance of the *writtenness* of literature; it remains idealized and, in a sense, static. The more overtly static, spatialized view of the literary work as object that I am describing also fails to take account of writing in Derrida's sense, of the work as act, staging, or performance.

16. A large part of the inspiration for current views of literature as an illusory cultural category produced entirely by ideological operations comes from Foucault, and it is interesting to see him struggling with this issue in a 1975 interview: having answered "I don't know" to the question of whether literature is defined by criteria internal to the texts, and having explained that his interest is only in how nonliterary texts enter the field of the literary, he valorizes the writing of Bataille, Blanchot, and Klossowski for its ability to put philosophy in question ("The Functions of Literature," 309–13). Derrida, who values literature for the same ability, is more certain that "Potentiality is not hidden in the text like an intrinsic property" but that *within* a given context, certain literary texts have potentialities which are "richer and denser" ("This Strange Institution Called Literature," 46–47). Since our apprehension of a text is always contextualized, as Stanley Fish has demonstrated eloquently in a number of essays, the question of an absolute, "intrinsic" difference between literary and nonliterary texts does not arise.

The singularity of the literary work is produced not just by its difference from all other works, but by the new possibilities for thought and feeling it opens up in its creative transformation of familiar norms and habits: singularity is thus inseparable from *inventiveness*. And the singular inventiveness of the work is what constitutes its *otherness*—not as an absolute quality, but one that is meaningful only in relation to a given context; otherness is always otherness *to* a particular self or situation. In order to be readable at all, otherness must turn into sameness, and it is this experience of transformation (which is a transformation of the reader's habits, expectations, ways of understanding the world) that constitutes the event of the literary work. A reading that does justice to what is literary in a literary work—in *The Singularity of Literature* I develop this claim at some length—is one that is fully responsive to its singularity, inventiveness, and otherness, as these manifest themselves in the event or experience of the work.

There is thus an ethical dimension to any act of literary signification or literary response, and there is also a sense in which the formally innovative text, the one that most estranges itself from the reader, makes the strongest ethical demand.[17] But of course ethics concerns persons and not texts, and this may sound like a rather cheap metaphorical point; if, however, the literary text is an event of signification (which is to say human signification),[18] the demands it makes—to respect its otherness, to respond to its singularity, to avoid reducing it to the familiar and the utilitarian even while attempting to understand it—may be ethical in a fundamental, nonmetaphorical sense. Formal innovation (of the sort that matters in literature) is innovation in meaning, and is therefore a kind of ethical testing and experiment. Indeed, ethics may be the wrong word, implying as it does a philosophical conceptualization which the demands

17. This may sound like a devaluation of the realist tradition, but it is a critique only of a certain way of reading that tradition—a reading, it is true, which realist authors often invited, but not one that is inevitable. To respond with full responsibility to the act of a realist work is to respond to its unique staging of meaning, and therefore to its otherness. It could even be said that the realist work is more, not less, demanding than the modernist work, in that its otherness is often disguised, and requires an even more scrupulous responsiveness on the part of the reader.

18. This at least is our current conception of the literary. The "human," however, is a category whose self-sufficiency and superiority is being challenged in many quarters, literature being one of them. For references to Coetzee's and Derrida's discussions of the human/animal distinction, see chapter 7 below.

of otherness disturb.[19] Whatever else the "modernist" text may be doing (and all literary texts function as a number of things besides literature), it is, through its form, which is to say through its staging of human meanings and intentions, a challenge that goes to the heart of the ethical and political.

: II :

Otherness, then, is at stake in every literary work, and in a particularly conspicuous way in the work that disrupts the illusions of linguistic immediacy and instrumentality. Among these works are some in which otherness is thematized as a central moral and political issue, and in these works modernist techniques may play a peculiarly important role. Coetzee's novels are cases in point. They can be read as a continued, strenuous enterprise in acknowledging alterity, a project which is at once highly local in its engagement with the urgent political and social problems of South Africa—no less urgent since the end of apartheid in 1994—and widely pertinent in its confrontation of the ethical demands of otherness, and its investigation of the relation of otherness to language, culture, and knowledge.[20] Figures of alterity recur in these novels, usually as members of a subordinated group perceived from the point of view of a dominant "first-world" culture (though one whose claim to any kind of "firstness" is frequently put in question). Instances are the Vietnamese "enemy" and the native South Africans in the two novellas of *Dusklands;* the farm servants in *In the Heart of the Country;* the barbarians in *Waiting for the Barbarians;* Friday in *Foe;* and Vercueil in *Age of Iron.* (*Life & Times of Michael K* is an interesting case, since the main figure of alterity in this novel is also the individual whose inner life is presented in detail; we shall

19. It is for this reason that Derrida, following Heidegger, tended for a long time to avoid the term "ethics." As he explains in a transcribed commentary, "It is not as a sign of protest against morality that I don't use the word 'ethics,' but this word is heavily loaded with a history, with a historical determination; it seems to me that one has to begin by tracing the genealogy of an ethical discourse before settling into it" (Derrida and Labarrière, *Altérités,* 70 [my translation]). Derrida goes on to speak of a responsibility that is not intrinsically ethical, but which makes demands in a manner that is even more imperious.

20. A critic who has consistently read Coetzee's work as an engagement with otherness, understood in the terms proposed by Levinas and Blanchot, is Michael Marais; see, for instance, "'Little Enough, Less than Little: Nothing,'" "The Possibility of Ethical Action," and "Literature and the Labour of Negation."

consider this peculiarity in the following chapter.) It is noteworthy that Coetzee does not stage the alterity that arises from the systematic subordination of women within first-world culture in the same way: although the disadvantaged position of women is often dramatized with great power—one has only to think of Susan Barton and Mrs. Curren—there is no sense that female narrators present a problem for a male author. One might hazard the proposition that in the conflicts that have scarred South Africa's history it has been the racial and class inequalities that Coetzee feels have most effectively excluded him, as a white middle-class writer, from an easy understanding of large numbers of his fellow humans.

The task Coetzee seems to have set himself is to convey the resistance of these figures to the discourses of the ruling culture (the culture, that is, which has conditioned the author, the kind of reader which the novels are likely to find, and the genre of the novel itself) and at the same time to find a means of representing the claims they make upon those who inhabit this culture—who, for the sake of simplicity, I shall call "us." Such claims, however, are not to be understood in traditional humanist, Enlightenment, or Romantic terms: it's not simply a question of sympathy for a suffering fellow human-being, or of the equal rights of all persons, or of the inscrutable mystery of the unique individual. The demands these figures make upon the culture which excludes them are also demands made upon all these familiar discourses, which thereby come under pressure to abandon their universalizing pretensions and to recognize their historical origins and contingent existence. The novel can succeed in making these claims felt only if its representational methods convey with sufficient force and richness that alterity, an alterity that makes demands on us not by entering into dialogue with us—something which is ruled out in advance—but by the very intensity of its unignorable being-there. And my hypothesis is that it is thanks to his allegiance to certain aspects of modernism that Coetzee succeeds to the remarkable extent that he does.

In engaging with the political and social issues rending his native country, most obviously colonialism and its legacy of racial, sexual, and economic oppression, Coetzee has used a variety of formal devices that disrupt the realistic surface of the writing, reminding the reader forcibly of the conventionality of the fictional text and inhibiting any straightforward drawing of moral or political conclusions. Consequently, as we have seen, his work during the apartheid years was often found wanting when judged as a response to the South African situation, while Coetzee's own comments on his fiction and on the responsibility of the novelist sometimes added fuel to the fire.[21] It would be possible to focus a discussion of this issue on any one of a number of self-reflexive traits in Coetzee's works, such the use of an existing literary classic to generate a fiction about its origins in *Foe* and *The Master of Petersburg,* or the impossible epistle that makes up the text of *Age of Iron,* or the thematizing of the idea of storytelling in *Michael K,* but the most flagrant challenge to the tradition of the realist novel (still, we must remember, scarcely questioned in South African writing in English in the 1970s) are the narrative contradictions in his first two novels, *Dusklands* (1974) and *In the Heart of the Country* (1977).

Dusklands is made up of two novellas, "The Vietnam Project" and "The Narrative of Jacobus Coetzee," which present forceful indictments of the brutal inhumanity that marked two historical events: the American bombing of Vietnam and Cambodia in the 1960s and early 1970s and the journeys into the interior of South Africa by white hunter-adventurers in the eighteenth century. In the first novella, Eugene Dawn, assigned to produce a report on the potential of broadcast propaganda in the war with the Vietcong, ends instead by dismissing propaganda as a military strategy and passionately urging a massive chemical attack on the earth of the enemy country itself.[22] The crazed note struck at the conclusion of

21. Coetzee's most inflammatory comments on this subject were made in an address given in Cape Town in 1987, subsequently published as "The Novel Today," in which he observed that "in times of intense ideological pressure like the present, when the space in which the novel and history normally coexist like two cows on the same pasture, each minding its own business, is squeezed to almost nothing, the novel, it seems to me, has only two options, supplementarity or rivalry"—and advocated the position of rivalry (3). The debate surrounding Coetzee's fiction and its relation to South African politics is sketched in the opening chapters of Susan VanZanten Gallagher's *A Story of South Africa* and of David Attwell's *J. M. Coetzee.* Like his book, Attwell's essay "The Problem of History in the Fiction of J. M. Coetzee," is a valuable discussion of the questions of realism and referentiality in relation to Coetzee's work. Perhaps the best-known critique of the political implications of Coetzee's fiction is Nadine Gordimer's review of *Michael K,* "The Idea of Gardening."

22. Oddly, commentators have tended to overlook Dawn's rejection of psychological warfare and his fervent advocacy of relentless destruction as the only path to victory. Thus Attwell sees the "ultimate application of his mythography" not as a physical attack on the earth but as "the broadcasting of radio propaganda that manipulates the psychic reflexes built into traditional Vietnamese culture" (*J. M. Coetzee,* 43), and Gallagher states merely that "Dawn argues that the United States should concentrate on forming a counter-myth to the current Vietnamese myth" (*A Story of South Africa,* 57). Yet the "report" is perfectly clear: section 1.6, "*Victory,*" includes the comment "I dismiss Phase IV of the conflict [in which propaganda plays a significant part]. I look forward to Phase V and the return of total air-war" (28), and imagines an "assault on the mothering earth herself" preferably by means of the soil poison PROP-12 (29).

the report is continued into the growing insanity of actions that follow its completion, as Dawn decamps with, and then injures, his young son, and is finally institutionalized. Jacobus Coetzee, from the start of his "narrative" in the second novella, exhibits the prejudices of the eighteenth-century Dutch frontier-dweller in South Africa, prejudices that allow him to treat the native inhabitants of the country as an inferior, and if necessary expendable, species. These attitudes are most graphically manifested when, having been deserted by several of his servants on his elephant-hunting expedition to the territory of the Great Namaquas, he makes a return visit to punish them with the utmost savagery.

The question I want to pose is this: if the primary value of these works lies in their exposure of the cruelty that characterized these historical moments, as is often claimed, what are we to make of their references to their own fictionality, their disturbances of the readerly involvement in the narrated world? Do these references, drawing attention as they do to the fact that we are not reading trustworthy historical accounts but made-up stories, weaken the force of the critique and hence diminish the achievement of the novels? Or does the merit—and readers' enjoyment— of these works lie in something other than the moral and political critique they ostensibly offer?

Both works make a claim to be documentaries of sorts, the first an auto-biographical account by an expert in psychological warfare that includes verbatim the report he has written for the American military, in numbered sections, and the second a scholarly publication translated from Afrikaans and Dutch by one J. M. Coetzee. Yet this documentary pretense is undermined at several points.[23] On the first page of "The Vietnam Project" we become aware that a textual game is being played, for we learn that the narrator's supervisor is called Coetzee, and by the end of the novella the first-person present-tense narrative has become an impossibility, telling as it does of events that could not by any stretch of the imagination coincide with the recording of them. As if this were not enough, our attention is drawn to this impossibility in a classic metafictional comment by the putative narrator: "A convention," he suddenly tells us while describing

---

23. It is interesting that in *Youth*, Coetzee's memoir of the years 1959 to 1964, the origin of "The Narrative of Jacobus Coetzee" is presented as a desire, awoken by reading the works of William Burchell and others, to create a fictional travel book about an early ox-wagon expedition in the Karoo that will have the "aura of truth" (138). If we are to take this as an autobiographical account, the project of simultaneously undermining the aura of truth must have been a later development.

the moments just before he stabs his son, "allows me to record these details" (42). Reading on to "The Narrative of Jacobus Coetzee," we find a text that is at once both more thoroughgoing in its documentary trappings and more subversive of them, in, for instance, the glaring inconsistencies among the three accounts of Jacobus's expeditions:[24] the main "Narrative," the "Afterword" (supposedly by the translator's father, S. J. Coetzee), and the "Deposition" (presented as Jacobus's recorded statement).[25] Another example of the undermining of documentary verisimilitude is the unlikely philosophical speculation of the frontiersman, including—to give just one example of the challenges to realism—an unacknowledged and anachronistic citation from William Blake.[26]

Although both novellas contain passages of characteristic Coetzean intensity, it is the second that carries the greater weight and presages more fully the achievements to come. One of its central concerns is a specific version of the self-other nexus that was to be developed further in several later works: the relationship between master and servant. The representation of Jacobus's relations with his Hottentot (Khoi) servants, and particularly with the foreman on his farm, Jan Klawer, is the first of many treatments in Coetzee's fiction of the master-servant dynamic; later instances include Magda and the coloured servants in *In the Heart of the Country*,[27] Susan Barton and Friday in *Foe*, Mrs. Curren and Florence

24. To avoid confusion among the various Coetzees, I shall refer to Jacobus Coetzee as "Jacobus," though this should not be taken to imply that he has endeared himself to me . . .

25. The status of the main narrative (within the fiction, that is) is left vague, although its use of the first person together with the assertion that it has merely been "edited" by S. J. Coetzee give the impression that it has some historical validity. Yet there is no evidence that it is anything other than an imaginary reconstruction, expressing S. J. Coetzee's fantasies and prejudices. We also have to bear in mind that the "translator" of these documents, S. J. Coetzee's son J. M. Coetzee—an equally fictional character—may have been less than dutiful in his filial labors. For an account of the relation between the text as written by the real J. M. Coetzee and the historical documents it utilizes and parodies, see Attwell, *J. M. Coetzee*, 44–46.

26. "How do I know that Johannes Plaatje, or even Adonis, not to speak of the Hottentot dead, was not an immense world of delight closed off to my senses?" (106), asks Jacobus, echoing Blake's "How do you know but ev'ry Bird that cuts the airy way, / Is an immense world of delight, clos'd by your senses five?" (*The Marriage of Heaven and Hell*, plate 7).

27. For readers unfamiliar with the racial classifications of apartheid South Africa, it may be necessary to point out that "coloured" here and throughout this book refers to the "mixed-race" inhabitants of the country, and more particularly to the Afrikaans-speaking community traditionally known as "Cape Coloureds." I use the South African (and British) spelling to distinguish the word from its American equivalent, which has different connotations. (A valuable discussion of the place of the coloured community in South Africa's recent cultural and political development is Zoë Wicomb's "Shame and Identity.")

in *Age of Iron,* and the Luries, David and Lucy, and Petrus in *Disgrace.* The Magistrate and the barbarian girl in *Waiting for the Barbarians* are a kindred pair, though the girl's status as servant is less important than her status as tortured ex-captive. Servants are also a significant and puzzling presence in *Boyhood* for the young John, and the older John in *Youth* is deeply troubled by the presence of a Malawian nanny when house-sitting. In every case, the dominant figure is white, and owes his or her power over the racially different other largely to that fact. And in every case, the language and the consciousness through which the servant's world is mediated is the master's.

Racial alterity is thus combined with the alterity of the servant, giving a particular complexity to the question posed by much of Coetzee's writing: is it possible to do justice to the otherness of the other in the language and discursive conventions that have historically been one of the instruments ensuring that this other is kept subordinate? This question—which is a question both for the novelist and for the characters who find themselves in the role of the master—applies to all attempts to represent or respond ethically to an individual who has been classified, or traditionally thought of, as inferior by virtue of race; but when this individual is *also* the servant of the character through whom we perceive the events of the novel, a number of additional issues are raised, among them trust, intimacy, and dependence.

Bruce Robbins, in *The Servant's Hand,* has shown how the figure of the servant in the tradition of realist fiction seldom conforms to the demands of realistic representation, and tends to puncture the naturalistic surface of the novel with tropes and commonplaces derived from Roman, Elizabethan, and Restoration comedy. But he stresses, too, following Foucault, that realistic representation is not the only way to do justice to the lives of servants—indeed, it may be a particularly ineffective way to achieve this goal, since it conceals the "powers and interests by which this signifying practice is traversed" (7). If the language by means of which the life of the servant has traditionally been depicted by the master has been one of the instruments for the perpetuation of mastery, and realism does not offer a satisfactory alternative, a different literary practice, willing to reveal its own dependence on convention and its own part in the exercise of power, may be less repressive. Such a literary practice is what I am calling Coetzee's "modernism."

Coetzee provides some indication of the tradition he is resisting by means of his reliance on the resources of modernism in a chapter of his study *White Writing* entitled "Simple Language, Simple People: Smith, Paton, Mikro." Here he discusses the language ascribed by two white

South African writers, Alan Paton and C. H. Kühn (who wrote, in Afrikaans, under the pen-name Mikro), to nonwhite characters.[28] The example he chooses from Mikro's fiction is the coloured shepherd known as "Toiings" ("Tatters"), a name given to him by his white master, Baas Fanie.[29] Coetzee shows how even the language in which Toiings's thought is represented is that of his master, and how it repeatedly declares the servant's subservience—Toiings mentally refers to himself, for instance, by the derogatory racial denomination *hotnot,* and to coloured men and women by the Afrikaans terms reserved for this racial group alone, *jong* and *meid* (129–35).

It is, of course, possible to avoid supremacist presuppositions in one's depiction of racially other servants without going as far as Coetzee in disrupting the illusion of realistic narrative. One example would be Nadine Gordimer's novel about master-servant relations in an imaginary future South Africa, *July's People:* while utilizing the familiar techniques of realist fiction, Gordimer avoids any attempt to relay the thoughts of July, the (ex-)servant on whom Maureen Smales and her family have become entirely dependent. It is only at the very close of the novel, when Maureen runs toward the sound of a helicopter landing, that we are made conscious of the author's control over her fiction and thus of its necessary limits—not by any self-reflexive gesture of a Coetzean type, but by the willed act of textual closure which denies, forever, knowledge of the future that this ending ambiguously portends.

Coetzee signals the author's power and powerlessness more continuously than Gordimer, and never again as flagrantly as in "The Narrative of Jacobus Coetzee." It is best to approach this aspect of the work not as a technical feature to be assessed and interpreted, however, but rather as a moment in the reader's experience of the work. I have stressed already the importance of acknowledging that the literary work has its being as an event, an event that takes place when the work is read, or, to use the term I suggested earlier, performed, and in the next chapter I shall develop some of the implications of this point. The most appropriate way of proceeding, therefore, given the limitations of space, is to examine a single passage, bearing in mind that we come to it in the unfolding process of reading or rereading, and that this process always occurs in a richly determined context, including the context of the reader's situation and personal history.

28. The interest of Coetzee's first example, Pauline Smith, lies in her attempt to evoke Afrikaans speech while writing in English.

29. Interestingly, given his rewriting of Defoe's first novel in *Foe,* Coetzee compares this act to Robinson Crusoe's naming of Friday (*Doubling the Point,* 132).

In Jacobus's descriptions of Jan Klawer many of the clichés of the "faithful servant" are recognizable; these are the age-old formulae discerned by Robbins in *The Servant's Hand*. Klawer is an "old-time Hottentot" (62), one of "the breed, now dying, of the old farm Hottentot" (67)—it always seems to be the case that the current generation of servants is inferior to the previous one—and not once but twice called "good, faithful old Jan Klawer" (75, 92). Level-headed under pressure, willing to fight for justice, yet capable of regularly performing the most intimate of services for his master (supporting him while he empties his bowels into a gourd [77], cleaning the pus from his anal boil [82, 84]), he seems the model servant. Even his peccadilloes are conventional, and treated in a conventional way: Jacobus finds him one morning asleep, after a night of revelry, with a fat Namaqua woman, and instead of punishing him for failing to bring breakfast, merely teases him, with man-to-man sexual raillery (88). When Jacobus waxes philosophical to Klawer the servant excuses himself for not understanding: "'He was only a poor hotnot,' he said" (81). (We might note that Coetzee chooses here one of the words used by Mikro to convey the servant's internalization of his master's discourse and prejudices—although in this instance there are reasons to believe that Klawer is acting a part.)[30]

Klawer remains loyal when the other servants desert Jacobus, and the two of them set off on the arduous journey home. Reaching the river which Jacobus has named the Great River (later to become the Orange River) they tie themselves together and attempt a crossing. Klawer accidentally steps into a hippopotamus hole and is swept into deep water:

> With horror I watched my faithful servant and companion drawn struggling downstream, shouting broken pleas for help which I was powerless to tender him, him whose voice I had never in all my days heard raised, until he disappeared from sight around a bend and went to his death bearing the blanket roll and all the food. (94)

We may recognize as we read this sentence yet another instance of the familiar discourse of the trusty servant, and as at many other points in the novella (and in the report within "The Vietnam Project"), parody seems on the verge of losing its critical edge and giving way to something

30. This moment might be compared with a significant episode in Ishiguro's *Remains of the Day*, another recent fictional exploration of the role of the servant: the butler Stevens (again one of the old school), posed complex questions about the politics of the day by a guest, answers three times, "I'm very sorry, sir, but I am unable to be of assistance on this matter" (195–96).

more like pastiche (a shift Coetzee avoids in his later novels). What is hard not to experience as parodic, however, is the rapidity with which Klawer is dispatched, a rapidity which the formulaic bids for pathos fail to mitigate. "Companion," after all, is part of the self-deceiving rhetoric of mastery, and the parenthetical comment about Klawer's voice a further sentimentalization of an exploitative relationship. And highly comic parody certainly reasserts itself at the end of the sentence, when the natural climax on "went to his death" is succeeded by a further clause registering what appears to be of greater concern to the narrator, the loss of the bedroll and the food. But whatever the hints of authorial mockery at Jacobus's self-deceiving rhetoric, the narrative unfurls smoothly enough, and we willingly go along with the rehearsal of events, perhaps barely aware of the highly conventional nature of the language.

The next paragraph begins:

> The crossing took all of an hour, for we had to probe the bottom before each step for fear of slipping into a hippopotamus hole and being swept off our feet. But sodden and shivering we finally reached the south bank and lit a discreet fire to dry our clothes and blankets. (94)

The shock of this negation of what we have just read is all the greater for the lack of any preparation (notwithstanding all the peculiarities of the work up to this point, no flat contradictions in the unfolding of events have occurred), or of any stylistic signal that something strange is happening to the narrative. (There are stories of early readers returning the book with complaints about a misprint.) The style remains resolutely normal, yet every word seems wrong. We cannot read these sentences in the way we have been reading up to now—sharing the thoughts and feelings of a recognizable (if repugnant) human being, letting ourselves be impelled onward by the successive events of the story—but have to read them as sentences in a crafted fiction, sentences constructed by selecting from the treasury of conventional phrases associated with the adventure tale. (Only the "hippopotamus hole" is startlingly precise.) We may try to naturalize the contradiction—hallucination on the part of Jacobus Coetzee? imperfect revision on the part of S. J. Coetzee? malicious mistranslation on the part of the fictional J. M. Coetzee?—but it remains a powerful disturbance in the hitherto relatively smooth operation of the reality effect, a breach of the contract between author and reader from which we may not, as readers of *Dusklands* and perhaps as readers of Coetzee, recover.

From the vantage point of this paragraph, the familiar discourse of the servant by means of which we have come to know Klawer is exposed, in retrospect, in all its conventionality: Jacobus's claims to know his servant through and through are revealed as worse than false, since the very terms in which such claims are made are barriers to knowledge. We read on, more alert than we have been, perhaps, to the multiple and simultaneous threads of the work—the mimetic tracing of the mental processes of an eighteenth-century colonial adventurer, the displacements of that mimesis by anachronisms and parodies, the successive stages in the narrative of discovery, survival, and revenge, the tonal and stylistic surprises. What follows is a different death for Klawer, this time from illness, and again the clichés come thick and fast. Here is a selection:

> If he had believed in me, or indeed in anything, he would have recovered. But he had the constitution of a slave, resilient under the everyday blows of life, frail under disaster. (94)

> "Klawer, old friend," I said, "things are going badly with you. But never fear, I will not desert you." (94–95)

> "No, master," said Klawer, "I cannot do it, you must leave me." A noble moment, worthy of record. (95)

> "Goodbye, master," he said, and wept. My eyes were wet too. I trudged off. He waved. (95)

Having promised to come back within a week by horse, Jacobus leaves. He is soon exulting almost insanely in his solitude, his freedom from "watching eyes and listening ears" (95). There is no further mention of his promise to Klawer, and few readers can be surprised: the final dialogue between master and servant sounds, as we say, as if it came out of a book.

: III :

The first thing the reader of *In the Heart of the Country* notices is that every paragraph is numbered. This simple device announces from the outset that we are not to suspend disbelief as we read, that our encounter with human lives, thoughts, and feelings is to take place against the background of a constant awareness of their mediation by language, generic and other conventions, and artistic decisions. It is testimony to the power of fictional narration that it is not difficult to forget the numbering as we read; after all, the division of virtually all novels into chapters or sections is not something that interferes with the illusion of immediacy, and in every one of his novels Coetzee's intense prose can produce a readerly involvement that overrides all markers of fictionality. It is, however, always possible to shift our attention to the numbering and to its antirealist implications. The device also encourages the reader to treat each paragraph as having more self-sufficiency than is usually the case with fictional prose: each one a little mini-narrative or speculation or diary entry, something like the stanzas of a long poem.[31]

The novel exists in two forms, the 1977 British and American version (differing only in the title—the American publisher preferred *From the Heart of the Country*) and the 1978 South African version.[32] The latter presents the reader with another defamiliarizing surprise: the dialogue is in Afrikaans. For most South African readers, the shift into Afrikaans would not hinder comprehension—there is nothing very complex in the utterances—but to encounter the juxtaposition between the two languages is to be made aware of the main narrative's mediation via English, and via the European fictional tradition. This mediation becomes particularly evident when Magda on two occasions (paras. 203 and 226) addresses one of the servants in what are effectively soliloquies, and provides both English and Afrikaans equivalents for many of her phrases—usually the English first, as if this were the language that comes naturally to Magda, then the Afrikaans, as if for the benefit of her ostensible addressee. Thus, to give a short example:

> But that is not the worst, dit is nie die ergste gewees nie. Energy is eternal delight, I could have been another person, ek kon heeltemal anders gewees het, I could have burned my way out of this prison, my tongue is forked with fire, verstaan jy, ek kan met 'n tong van vuur praat. (para. 203)

The question of the use of English and Afrikaans—is Magda really an English speaker, for whom Afrikaans is a necessary instrument in practical matters?—is, however, never addressed in the text. (It becomes an important issue in *Boyhood*, reflecting Coetzee's own complicated linguistic

---

31. Coetzee himself has related his use of discrete paragraphs to the influence of film on modernist writers, who discovered that they could omit a great deal of "scene-setting and connective tissue" (*Doubling the Point*, 59) to speed up the narrative. However, the use of numbers is not a characteristic filmic device (except rarely, as in Peter Greenaway's *Drowning by Numbers*). As Coetzee himself observes, *Dust*, Marion Hänsel's film of *In the Heart of the Country*, makes little attempt to find an equivalent for the numbered paragraphs.

32. Because the two editions have different pagination, I shall refer to the text by paragraph numbers.

background.) Yet the question of language choice is foregrounded toward the end of the novel, when Magda, alone on the farm, hears voices speaking what she is convinced is Spanish, although her lack of Spanish doesn't prevent her from understanding them, and we read them as English. (In fact, we have already heard about her "voices" and been given an example—a sentence, in English translation, from Rousseau's "Discourse on Political Economy" [para. 76]. We might notice, too, that the Blakean proverb in the soliloquy just quoted, "Energy is eternal delight"—once again from *The Marriage of Heaven and Hell*—remains untranslated.) A final surprise is the speech of reminiscence Magda addresses to her father (with whom she has always used Afrikaans) near the end of the book: it is in highly conventional "literary" English (para. 262).

For the reader of the British and American versions of the novel, however, there is no switching of languages to disturb the process of comprehension. The disquieting unreliability of the first-person narrative is, however, something that emerges for all readers in the very first paragraph. The narrator (whom at this stage we do not know as Magda) gives two alternatives for the animals drawing her father's dog-cart—a horse or two donkeys—as it brought him and his new bride back to the farmhouse earlier in the day,[33] and two alternatives for what she was doing when they arrived—reading or lying with a towel over her eyes. So the statement in the middle of the paragraph, "More detail I cannot give unless I begin to embroider," already reads ironically. In any case, it turns out in paragraph 36 (after Magda has apparently murdered both of them in their bed) that the father in fact arrived back without a bride (at least, if we give the second version priority over the first, as we are encouraged to do), and when the same words are used in paragraph 38 to describe the arrival back on the farm of Hendrik, the coloured servant and *his* new bride Anna, we remain uncertain whether this arrival will be confirmed or retracted in our further reading.

What transpires is that Hendrik, like the father, lives on to play an important role in the strange narrative that follows. But once having read paragraphs 1–35 in the good faith of the novelistic consumer, only to find them a fantasy, we can never quite achieve the same confidence in the scenes presented to us thereafter. The question "What *really* happened?" becomes unanswerable, and, in a sense, unaskable, since we have been

---

33. In the South African version of the text, the bride, unlike the other characters in the novel, is imagined as speaking English (para. 11); and later Magda discovers a love-letter written to her father in English (para. 121).

made conscious of what we usually keep out of our minds as we read: that novels, unlike histories, do not tell of what happened.[34] (Similarly, it makes no sense to ask of "The Narrative of Jacobus Coetzee": "How did Klawer *really* die?")

Unlike "The Narrative of Jacobus Coetzee," however, we do have an escape route that keeps us within the bounds of the realist tradition (apart, that is, from those numbered paragraphs): we can ascribe the inconsistencies and impossibilities in the narrative to Magda's disordered state of mind, and treat the unaskability of the question of what really happened as the inevitable result of a discourse that proceeds entirely from a mind that is breaking down. This is, of course, a common readerly or critical ploy in dealing with problematic fictions—Gregor Samsa, in Kafka's *Metamorphosis,* is held to be suffering from hallucinations, or the peculiarities of *Finnegans Wake* are explained away by calling the whole thing a "dream"[35]—but it's one that we fall back on only at some cost: if everything we read could be the product of fantasy or insanity, the novel loses *any* grip on the real, and thus much of its narrative drive and engagement with the very real issues of family, gender, racial, and master-servant relations.[36] A more satisfactory approach is to assume, as we normally do in reading fiction, that the words are to be taken as referring to real events unless there is good reason, in a particular section of the novel, to take them as the outcome of fantasy or psychological derangement.

Of course, "real events" in fiction may go beyond the norms governing the world we are familiar with. "Magic realism" is based on this premise; and in the later stages of the novel, when Magda hears, delivered to her from aircraft passing overhead, her "Spanish" voices uttering quotations from European literature and philosophy, we might consider that Coetzee has entered this realm.[37] Fantasy or mental disorder on Magda's part

34. Dominic Head provides a lucid account of the uncertainties of reference in the novel; see *J. M. Coetzee,* 56–58.

35. I have discussed the problems raised by this common interpretive strategy in dealing with Joyce's last work in *Joyce Effects,* chap. 11.

36. In *Doubling the Point,* Coetzee—for all his reluctance to comment on his own novels—is clearly unhappy with the idea that Magda is sometimes taken to be mad, and stresses instead the intensity of her passion, a passion allied to the love for the country and its people which he feels has been lacking among white South Africans (60–61).

37. Yet a comparison of *In the Heart of the Country* with, for example, Etienne van Heerden's *Ancestral Voices* or *The Long Silence of Mario Salviati*—fine South African examples of magic realism, which has flourished especially in Afrikaans writing—forces the acknowledgment that Coetzee's fiction has little in common with this mode.

seems out of the question now, as there is no suggestion that she could have read Hegel, Blake, Pascal, Spinoza, and Rousseau.

Coetzee's use of modernist techniques is just as prominent in this novel as in *Dusklands*, then, although the richer evocation of a mental world makes it easier for the reader to experience the mimetic power of narrative, the illusion of reality which enables us to be moved by the thoughts and feelings of an imagined character. All the novels and memoirs that follow in Coetzee's career possess this power, the power that the young John dreams of as he reads Burchell in the British Library in *Youth*. Magda, the spinster on an isolated farm in what appears to be the Great Karoo, is capable of vivid expression of her emotions, and we share, as the bare narrative unfolds, the modulations and eruptions in her anger, her bitterness, her self-pity, her hatred of her father, her attraction toward the servants Hendrik and Anna. When her father takes Anna to his bed, she kills him by firing through the window with his rifle. In the aftermath of that event, drawn out by the father's slow death, she tries to achieve some intimacy with Hendrik and Anna, for both of whom she feels physical desire. The passage I want to focus on—for again I can best make the points I want to make in relation to a short segment of the work—occurs when Hendrik arrives back at the house from a two days' journey to the post office in a vain attempt to withdraw some money. (The passage is written in the "impossible" first-person present narration we first encountered in "The Vietnam Project," though unlike Eugene Dawn, Magda does not break off to comment on the convention that allows her to write in this way.)

In paragraph 205, Hendrik, furious at his wasted journey, grabs Magda's arm as she tries to leave the kitchen. She stabs pathetically at his shoulder with a fork, and he throws her down and beats her. She crawls toward the door, he kicks her in the buttocks, and she rolls over onto her back and lifts her knees. "This is how a bitch must look; but as for what happens next, I do not even know how it is done. He goes on kicking at my thighs" (105). The paragraph ends here, with Magda half terrified of Hendrik, half inviting him to have sex with her. The moment is one of powerful narrative expectation, but the reader's involvement is suddenly ruptured. Paragraph 206 does not begin where 205 left off, but reverts instead to the moment where Magda turns to walk out of the kitchen. The feeble stabbing is described again, in similar words, but in this telling Hendrik throws Magda against the wall and rapes her. The violation is described with painful vividness, and it's unlikely that any reader remains conscious for long that the event is, like Klawer's second death, a narrative impossibility. It's as if the capacity of mimetic writing to overcome the metafictional apparatus is being demonstrated, though we aren't aware of it at the time of reading.

The paragraph ends with Hendrik's semen seeping out of Magda as she sobs in despair. The following paragraph, 207, once more reverses time, beginning at a moment that had been registered soon after the beginning of the previous paragraph. Hendrik again throws Magda against the wall and thrusts himself against her, but what follows this time is not the rape on the kitchen floor. Instead, we have a bitter monologue from Magda, ending, "Please not like this on the floor! Let me go, Hendrik!" The following paragraphs return to a normal temporal sequence, and describe a different sexual act from the one depicted in paragraph 206. Paragraph 208 begins with the couple in the bedroom: Hendrik has presumably taken Magda there after her plea that they not have sex on the kitchen floor. Magda undresses, accepting her "woman's fate"; in 209 she finds that in spite of that acceptance she "cannot help him" and he forces himself on her; in 210–12 he sleeps and, with something of a change of heart, she begins to caress his detumescent penis.

Twice in this sequence, then, the narrative backtracks to an earlier point and develops in a different direction; as a result, Hendrik's rape of Magda is described twice, or rather, two rapes are described, since there are significant differences between the two events (to which I shall turn in a moment).[38] The effect of these narrative anomalies is clearly related to that of Klawer's double death: we are made aware of the construct-edness of the events and the craftedness of the descriptions, as well as of the author's sovereign power to do whatever he pleases with the narra-tive. The alterity which Hendrik, as coloured, as servant, represents for Magda, could have been compellingly conveyed without the distortions, but these distortions produce a fuller sense of an unknowable other, un-knowable to such a degree that the conventions of narrative accounting break down. We might compare this passage with the enigmatic final sec-tion of *Foe,* in which Friday's alterity, already powerfully suggested in the novel, is given even greater force when an unnamed first-person narrator ascends Foe's, or Defoe's, staircase and comes upon the black servant in

38. The rape sequence is not repeated "several times," as Attwell states (*J. M. Coetzee,* 67), nor are there four "versions" of it, as Kossew has it (*Pen and Power,* 65), nor is it "described five times in consecutive sections," as Head claims (*J. M. Coetzee,* 58). It was members of my graduate class on Coetzee at Rutgers University in 2001–2 that made me aware of the exaggeration in these assertions.

mysterious circumstances—and then the account is repeated, with a quite different outcome.[39] It is as if in its dealings with otherness the main part of the story, for all its subversion of realist narrative, has been too conventional.

The realist narrative can be saved, however, if we assume that the two rapes are another example of Magda's fantasizing. She has, after all, already imagined, in some detail, being raped by Hendrik. Paragraph 167 presents Magda's fantasy of a monologue uttered by Hendrik to Anna as the two servants lie in bed—and it is notable that in conjuring up Hendrik's words, Magda at first converts what would be third-person references to herself in Hendrik's speech to first-person pronouns: "Someone should make a woman of me, he tells her, someone should make a hole in me to let the old juices run out." But then the pronouns switch to the third person, perhaps to achieve a safer mental distance, as she imagines Hendrik's speculations about sex with her and thus imagines the act itself (the "I" now is, of course, Hendrik): "Would she pretend it was a dream and let it happen, or would it be necessary to force her? Would I be able to fight my way in between those scraggy knees?" There is, therefore, some plausibility in interpreting the narrative inconsistencies in paragraphs 205–7 as the outcome of Magda's indulgence in two separate fantasies of rape.[40]

The differences between the two rapes certainly suggest two alternative ways of imagining the event. The first is presented as wholly undesired, with the emphasis on Magda's pain, disgust, and distress: "Something is going limp inside me, something is dying. . . . I am nauseous with fear, my limbs have turned to water. If this is my fate it sickens me. . . . I sob and sob in despair" (para. 206). The second, though Magda is again violated and feels humiliated and revolted, is more ambiguous: they have apparently walked to the bedroom, Magda undresses herself, she mentions her "fate" but this time not that it "sickens" her, she "sobs and sobs" but this time not "in despair." Whereas in the first rape her thoughts are dedicated to getting Hendrik to stop, in the second they range more widely: she realizes with some mortification that she has forgotten to take her shoes off, she reflects that Hendrik's ripping of her pants means "more woman-work" for her, she revolves in her mind his words "Everyone likes it" (para. 209).

---

39. See below, p. 83.

40. Attwell, for example, believes that the repetition denies the rape "the status of an 'event'" and establishes it as "a colonial fantasy on Magda's part" (*J. M. Coetzee*, 67).

Yet, as we have seen, there is nothing in the entire narrative from start to finish that, in the final analysis, could escape the possibility of being read as fantasy. A responsible reading procedure will keep the appeal to psychological explanations (like unbridled fantasizing) to a minimum. A different way of responding to these paragraphs is to read the first rape as a product of Magda's fears, and the second, with its moments of ambivalence and its unexpected details (the shoes, the thought of "woman-work"), as real. Supporting this reading is the fact that the narrative flows on in a coherent sequence after the second rape: Hendrik sleeps, Magda ruminates, she begins to feel some tenderness toward him, he leaves, and then in paragraph 213 she visits the servants' cottage and thinks to herself as Anna greets her, "So she knows nothing."

Hendrik is soon visiting Magda regularly during the night, and she is doing her best to learn the ways of physical love. We have already encountered this pattern of a corrective sequence—first a fantasized version that comes to an abrupt halt, then a more grounded one that carries the narrative on to the next stage. The account of the arrival of Magda's father and his new bride at the opening of the book (which is followed by Magda's murderous attack on them) is corrected, as we have seen, when we learn that he is alone; and the fantastic sequence in which Magda and Hendrik seal up the room containing the corpse and watch it float into the night air (paras. 153–56) is corrected by the relatively more realistic sequence (realism here is distinctly a relative matter) in which the corpse is pushed into a porcupine hole in the graveyard (paras. 173–85). A short sequence with a similar corrective rhythm occurs in paragraphs 197 and 198, in the first of which Magda shoots Hendrik and in the second of which she shoots and misses—and the story goes on from there.[41]

But such a recuperation of these problematic sequences can never be secure enough to restore our faith in the realism of the narrative. The consistency of style, the lack of any overtly signaled transitions between what might be fantasy and what might be reality, the improbabilities that remain in the latter (culminating in the impossible final pages, in which Magda's father is once more alive—unless he has been alive the whole time): all these make clear distinctions highly problematic. As a result,

---

41. In the film *Dust*, the few short fantasy sequences—the arrival of the father's bride, the double murder, the reappearance of the father at the end—are clearly distinguished as such. There is only one version of the disposal of the corpse, the shooting at Hendrik, and the rape, and no Spanish voices or passing aircraft.

Hendrik and Anna remain enigmatic presences, never wholly grasped by the machinery of the text, never securely "in their place." Although Magda's language for describing or speaking to them is relatively free of the conventional formulae that we noted in Jacobus Coetzee's discourse (a conventionality that is more evident in Magda's father's language, or what she imagines as his language, in addressing Hendrik, especially in the Afrikaans version), she cannot be said to achieve *knowledge* of them.

The pressure of Hendrik's unknowable otherness finally prompts an extraordinary outburst of questions from Magda:

> What more do you want? Must I weep? Must I kneel? Are you waiting for the white woman to kneel to you? Are you waiting for me to become your white slave? *Tell me! Speak!* Why do you never *say* anything? . . . How can I humiliate myself any further? Must the white woman lick your backside before you will give her a single smile? Do you know that you have never kissed me, never, never, never? Don't you people ever kiss? (para. 228)

But if we find ourselves responding to this tirade (and I have quoted only a small part of it) as the climax in the (non)relationship between Magda and Hendrik, the moment when the concealed truth is shaken out by sheer emotional violence, we are soon disabused. The ironic self-undercutting characteristic of Magda's narrative begins again in the following paragraph: "Where was it in this torrent of pleas and accusations that he walked out? Did he stay to the end?" We may be reminded of Klawer's apparent noncomprehension of Jacobus's philosophical speculations, and think ahead to the painfully self-reinventing speech made by Mrs. Curren to Vercueil in *Age of Iron* during which he appears to be asleep. There are no communicative breakthroughs in Coetzee's fiction; just moments at which a character talks himself or herself into a new mental position, a new constellation of thought and feeling, with no guarantee that the addressee will take the slightest notice—with the likelihood, in fact, that the alterity of the addressee will be underscored all the more. (Soon after Magda's tirade Hendrik and Anna flee the farm by night.)

For the otherness which makes demands on us as we read Coetzee's novels is not an otherness that exists *outside* language or discourse; it is an otherness brought into being by language, it is what two thousand years of continuously evolving discourse has excluded—and thus constituted—as other. Not simply *its* other, which would, as an opposite, still be part of its system; but heterogeneous, inassimilable, and unacknowledged unless it imposes itself upon the prevailing discourse, or unless a fissure is created in that discourse through which it makes itself felt, as happens at some of the most telling moments in Coetzee's writing. Modernism's foregrounding of language and other discursive and generic codes through its formal strategies is not merely a self-reflexive diversion but a recognition (whatever its writers may have thought they were doing) that literature's distinctive power and potential ethical force reside in a testing and unsettling of deeply held assumptions of transparency, instrumentality, and direct referentiality, in part because this taking to the limits opens a space for the apprehension of the otherness which those assumptions had silently excluded.[42] Since it is language that has played a major role in producing (and simultaneously occluding) the other, it is in language—language aware of its ideological effects, alert to its own capacity to impose silence as it speaks—that the force of the other can be most strongly represented. The effect is one that I would want to describe as textual otherness, or *textualterity:* a verbal artifact that estranges as it entices, that foregrounds the Symbolic as it exploits the Imaginary, that speaks of that about which it has to remain silent.

The importance of *Dusklands* and *In the Heart of the Country* does not lie in their critique of colonialism and its various avatars; there needs no Coetzee to tell us that the white world's subjection of other races has been brutal and dehumanizing, for both its victims and for itself. These novels—unlike some that are classified under the rubric "postcolonial"—provide no new and illuminating details of the painful history of Western domination. All this brutality and exploitation is certainly there in the novels to be felt and condemned, but it is not what makes them singular, and singularly powerful. It is what they do, how they happen, that matters: how otherness is engaged, staged, distanced, embraced, how it is manifested in the rupturing of narrative discourse, in the lasting uncertainties of reference, in the simultaneous exhibiting and doubting of the

---

42. This is not to say that modernist disruptive practices are, and will be, effective in this way in all circumstances and for all time: inventive literature is a response to the cultural givens of its time, and these undergo constant change. Coetzee has noted that "anti-illusionism" may only be "a marking of time, a phase of recuperation, in the history of the novel" (*Doubling the Point,* 27)—although we might also note that his character Elizabeth Costello, in a text that plays self-consciously with the tenets of realism, argues that what she calls the "word-mirror" of realist representation is broken, "irreparably, it seems" (*Elizabeth Costello,* 19), and elsewhere in *Doubling the Point,* Coetzee talks of a "massive and virtually determining effect on consciousness" that has undermined our faith in access to an unmediated reality (63).

novelist's authority. Whether we call this modernism or postmodernism is, finally, inconsequential; what is important is the registering of the event of meaning that constitutes the work of literature—the event that used to be called "form," and that was given new potential by modernist writers. In Coetzee's hands the literary event is the working out of a complex and freighted responsibility to and for the other, a responsibility denied for so long in South Africa's history. The reader does not simply observe this responsibility at work in the fiction, but, thanks to its inventive re-creation of the forms and conventions of the literary, experiences, in a manner at once pleasurable and disturbing, its inescapable demands.

CHAPTER TWO

Against Allegory

Waiting for the Barbarians and *Life & Times of Michael K*

All is allegory, says my Philip. Each creature is key to all other creatures. A dog sitting in a patch of sun licking itself, says he, is at one moment a dog and at the next a vessel of revelation.

"Postscript," *Elizabeth Costello*

: I :

It's hardly surprising that one of the terms in the critical lexicon most frequently applied to Coetzee's novels and novellas is *allegory*. Their distance—with the exception of *Age of Iron* and *Disgrace*—from the time and place in which they were written, the often enigmatic characters (the barbarian girl, Michael K, Friday, Vercueil, and many others), the scrupulous avoidance of any sense of an authorial presence, the frequently exiguous plots: all these encourage the reader to look for meanings beyond the literal, in a realm of significance which the novel may be said to imply without ever directly naming.

These proposed allegorical meanings vary in their specificity. At one extreme, manifested in many journalistic reviews, the novels are said to represent the truths—often the dark truths—of the human condition.[1]

---

1. Clive Barnett writes interestingly about the appeal to allegory as a way to displace potential political readings by universal readings. He cites Bernard Levin's review of *Waiting for the Barbarians* in the London *Sunday Times* of 23 November 1980: "Mr. Coetzee sees the heart of darkness in all societies, and gradually it becomes clear that he is not dealing in politics at all, but inquiring into the nature of the beast that lurks within each of us" ("Constructions of Apartheid," 290–91).

Somewhat more narrowly, they may be taken to allegorize the conflicts and abuses that characterize the modern world, or that have been fully acknowledged only in modern times. (We can find both these types of allegorical reading in abundance in the criticism of several other modernist writers, such as the two I have already mentioned as Coetzee's most important precursors, Kafka and Beckett.) But there is a different and more specific type of allegorization that Coetzee's fiction invites, deriving from the widespread assumption that any responsible and principled South African writer, especially during the apartheid years, will have had as a primary concern the historical situation of the country and the suffering of the majority of its people.[2] The consequence of this assumption is the impulse to translate apparently distant locales and periods into the South Africa of the time of writing, and to treat fictional characters as representatives of South African types or even particular individuals.[3] This kind of reading is, of course, often dismissive of the first mode of allegory but is deserving of the label all the same, though it is not in conformity with common usage. Even the two novels set entirely in the time and place of their composition solicit allegorical readings of this historicist kind, *Age of Iron* as an exemplification of the condition of South Africa during the township wars and States of Emergency of the mid-1980s, and *Disgrace* as a schematic portrait of the country in the early years of democracy after the official end of apartheid.

My purpose is not to deny the valuable insights that this mode of reading has produced and no doubt will continue to produce.[4] But we are

2. Although the national backgrounds of Beckett and Kafka have played a part in some readings of their work, they are less subject to the preconception that their writing is "really" about Ireland or about the Austro-Hungarian Empire. (Kazuo Ishiguro hits the nail on the head when, irritated by the frequent suggestion that *The Remains of the Day* is "really" about Japan, he observes that if he had written *The Trial* he would have to put up with comments like "What a strange judicial system the Japanese have" ["Between Two Worlds," 44].)

3. Examination of the records of the South African government censors points to the fascinating possibility that enlightened academic advisors may have used the distance in space and time that characterizes many Coetzee novels as a way of preventing them from being banned—by resisting, that is, a localized allegorical reading. See Peter D. McDonald, "'Not Undesirable'" and "The Writer, the Critic, and the Censor."

4. Dominic Head's *J. M. Coetzee* does full justice to allegorical readings of the fiction, and Head refers in the course of his book to many other such readings. Sue Kossew also discusses the frequent appeal to allegory among Coetzee's commentators in her introduction to *Critical Essays on J. M. Coetzee*, 5, 9–11. A different kind of allegory is proposed by Teresa Dovey in her book on Coetzee, as its title indicates: *The Novels of J. M. Coetzee: Lacanian Allegories.*

dealing here with novels which, to a greater degree than most, concern themselves with the acts of writing and reading, including allegorical writing and reading. Before relying too heavily on allegorization as a primary mode of interpretation, therefore, we need to ask how allegory is thematized in the fiction, and whether this staging of allegory as an *issue* provides any guidance in talking about Coetzee's *use* of allegory (and about allegory more generally).[5]

Although there is, to my knowledge, no generic rule that prohibits allegories from referring to allegory, these moments in the texts inevitably have the effect of puncturing any consistent experience of extraliteral correspondences, just as those moments when Shakespeare's characters talk about acting in a play suspend for an instant our suspension of disbelief. One well-known example occurs in *Life & Times of Michael K* when the medical officer imagines calling after K as he runs away: "Your stay in the camp was merely an allegory, if you know that word. It was an allegory—speaking at the highest level—of how scandalously, how outrageously a meaning can take up residence in a system without becoming a term in it" (166). This interpretation of K's mode of existence in the Kenilworth camp has frequently been extended by commentators to embrace the whole novel;[6] yet the fact that it is advanced by the well-meaning but uncomprehending medical officer must throw some doubt on it, and on allegorical readings of the work more generally.

Similarly, interpretations of Vercueil in *Age of Iron* that allegorize him as the angel of death must take account of Mrs. Curren's own tendency to do just that throughout the novel. She terms his arrival an "annunciation" (5), refers to him as a "messenger" (48), and imagines that he and his dog are "fulfilling their charge, waiting for the soul to emerge" (186). Toward the end, she relates how she asked herself (jokingly? seriously?) as he carried her in his arms, "When would the time come when the jacket fell away and great wings sprouted from his shoulders?" (160–61). What is even more significant is that such interpretations must take

---

5. Coetzee's character Elizabeth Costello, facing a panel of judges who are weighing up her beliefs, nominates a particular Australian frog as what she believes in, adding by way of clarification, "The life cycle of a frog may sound allegorical, but to the frogs themselves it is no allegory, it is the thing itself, the only thing" (*Elizabeth Costello*, 217).

6. One instance is David Attwell, who quotes the medical officer's allegorical interpretation to Coetzee (*Doubling the Point*, 204). Coetzee, instead of endorsing or rejecting this proposed interpretation, speaks of his reluctance to comment on his own novels. (Attwell, I should add, is fully aware of the novel's undermining of the medical officer's attempts to interpret K.)

account of Mrs. Curren's *rejection* in many places of this allegory. "Not an angel, certainly," she thinks. "An insect, rather, emerging from behind the baseboards when the house is in darkness to forage for crumbs"; after this thought, she reads Tolstoy's "story of the angel who takes up residence with the shoemaker" and decides that the suburbs are "deserted by angels" and that "when a ragged stranger comes knocking at the door he is never anything but a derelict, an alcoholic, a lost soul" (14). Later, he is "No Odysseus, no Hermes, perhaps not even a messenger" (140). Soon after this she admits to Vercueil that when he first arrived she wondered if he were "an angel come to show me the way," and continues, "Of course you were not, are not, cannot be—I see that. But that is only half the story, isn't it? We half-perceive but we also half-create" (168). At the very least, we have to say that an allegorical reading of Vercueil's part in the novel cannot be straightforward.[7]

Other instances of this self-reflexive gesture—and there are many— would include Magda's "If I am an emblem then I am an emblem," in *In the Heart of the Country* (9), and the Magistrate's assertion in *Waiting for the Barbarians* that the wooden slips found in the ruins "form an allegory" (112)—or his passionate self-accusation, "*No! No! No!* . . . It is I who am seducing myself, out of vanity, into these meanings and correspondences" (44). Allegory, or the impulse to allegorize, is thus clearly a theme in Coetzee's fiction; as Dominic Head says of the presence of allegory in *In the Heart of the Country,* there is a "coinciding use and interrogation of its procedures" (50).[8]

With this encouragement from the fiction itself, I want to ask what happens if we *resist* the allegorical reading that the novels seem half to solicit, half to problematize, and take them, as it were, at their word. Is it possible to read or discuss them without looking for allegorical meanings, and if one were to succeed in this enterprise would one have emptied them of whatever political or ethical significance they might possess?[9] This is

7. Coetzee himself proffers two alternative views in referring in an interview to Vercueil as someone Mrs. Curren "recognizes as, or makes into, a herald of death" (*Doubling the Point,* 340).

8. Attwell, too, notes that *Waiting for the Barbarians* "continually frustrates the allegorizing impulse" (132), though he ends his chapter with an allegorical touch, suggesting that the children at the close of the novel may "represent a future community" (87).

9. This is not an enterprise without precedents. For example, Brian Macaskill forcefully rejects allegorical readings of *In the Heart of the Country,* arguing that a poetics of the "middle voice" "calls such baneful readings into question by denying the facile transitivity under which allegorical exegetics marshals its master code into battle against idiolect, the

not an easy project, not least because, as Northrop Frye has observed, all commentary of a traditional kind is, in a sense, allegorical, in that it attaches ideas to the images and events it encounters in the text (*Anatomy of Criticism*, 89). For Fredric Jameson, too, "Interpretation is . . . an essentially allegorical act" (*Political Unconscious*, 10). To say what a fictional work is "about," or to find any kind of moral or political injunction in it, is to proceed, in an extended sense of the word, allegorically. If a wholly nonallegorical reading of a literary work were possible, it would refrain from any interpretation whatsoever, and would seek rather to do justice to the work's singularity and inventiveness by the creation of a text of equal singularity and inventiveness.[10] An example of such a nonallegorical reading of a literary work, in this case Defoe's *Robinson Crusoe*, might be Coetzee's *Foe*.

My interest, however, is in the protocols and practices of literary commentary—whether those of informal conversation, the newspaper review, the classroom lecture, or the academic essay or book—and therefore in the kinds of speaking and writing about the novels that *do* make claims, in discursive rather than literary language, about their importance and the pleasure and insight to be gained from them. What I mean by a "nonallegorical reading" in this context will, I hope, emerge from what follows, but I want to make it clear at the outset that I don't mean the avoidance of any interpretation whatsoever, but rather the avoidance of certain *kinds* of interpretation.[11] What Coetzee himself has said about storytelling is not far from my own project:

> No matter what it may appear to be doing, the story may not really be playing the game you call Class Conflict or the game called Male Domination or any of the other games in the games handbook. While it may certainly be possible to read the book as playing one of those games, in reading it in that way you may have missed something. You

---

notion of doing-writing" ("Charting J. M. Coetzee's Middle Voice," 79). Chiara Briganti also questions allegorical readings of *In the Heart of the Country* (" 'A Bored Spinster,' " 93). Peter D. McDonald proposes a reading of *Disgrace* that resists allegorical interpretation ("*Disgrace* Effects").

10. I have argued for this position at greater length in *The Singularity of Literature*.

11. Of course, there would be something misguided about attempting a wholly nonallegorical reading of some works—*Pilgrim's Progress* or *Animal Farm*, for instance—since they clearly have continuous allegorical interpretation as their raison d'être (though even in these cases I would argue that making such an attempt might produce some interesting and important insights). Coetzee's novels can hardly be said to fall into this category, however.

may have missed not just something, you may have missed everything. Because (I parody the position somewhat) a story is not a message with a covering, a rhetorical or aesthetic covering. ("The Novel Today," 4)

Some of the impetus for my undertaking comes from two well-known essays which I first read a long time ago, and which have lingered in my memory with the sense that their implications were somehow more far-reaching than I had allowed. The earlier is Susan Sontag's 1964 essay "Against Interpretation"[12] (the title of this chapter is, of course, an echo of Sontag's). This famous piece is a protest against all commentary implying that the point of an art-work is to *say* something. As Sontag puts it, "The interpreter says, Look, don't you see that X is really—or, really means—A? That Y is really B? That Z is really C?" (654). Fourteen years later, Donald Davidson, in "What Metaphors Mean,"[13] issued an equally forthright challenge, this time to the idea that metaphors convey a special meaning over and above their literal meaning: for Davidson, "metaphors mean what their words, in their most literal interpretation, mean, and nothing more" (30). I have never seen a connection made between these two essays, but it seems to me that—leaving aside the details of their arguments—they are motivated by the same impulse: for Sontag what is important about art-works, and for Davidson what is important about metaphors, is not what they *mean* but what they *do*.[14]

: II :

Over the centuries, the fortunes of allegory have had something of a roller-coaster ride. Preeminent as a medieval Christian technique of reading

12. After its initial publication in the *Evergreen Review* in 1964, the essay was included in, and gave its title to, a 1966 collection of Sontag's essays.

13. First published in *Critical Inquiry* in 1978, and included in Davidson's *Inquiries into Truth and Interpretation*.

14. Sontag notes that we cannot "retrieve that innocence before all theory when art knew no need to justify itself, when one did not ask of a work of art what it *said* because one knew (or thought one knew) what it *did*" (4–5). Davidson claims that "metaphor belongs exclusively to the domain of use" (31)—though in a later essay, "Locating Literary Language," he muddies the distinction, renaming "literal meaning" "first meaning" and allowing what he had insisted was entirely a matter of use to be given the title "meaning." The claims of these essays have been much debated, but my purpose in citing them is only to provide a starting point. A related argument is Louise Rosenblatt's critique of what she calls "efferent" reading—reading that seeks to carry something away from the encounter with the text (see, in particular, *The Reader, the Text, the Poem*).

(originally developed as a method for extracting New Testament meanings from the Old Testament, and Christian meanings from Classical literature), allegory was downgraded by the Romantics—notably the Schlegels and Coleridge—as the bad mechanical, disjunctive twin of the organic, unifying symbol. Walter Benjamin's mid-1920s thesis on German baroque drama started the process of allegory's rehabilitation, though it did not have a considerable effect until the mid-1950s, when it became easily available for the first time. In the English-speaking world allegory was championed most influentially, though rather differently, by Paul de Man and Fredric Jameson.[15] More recently, some studies of post-colonial literatures have argued for a significant role for allegory, albeit allegory redefined in the light of both this recent theoretical revaluation and the literary practices of post-colonial writers themselves. Thus Jameson has somewhat notoriously proposed the "sweeping hypothesis" that all "third-world" works of literature are "national allegories," since in these cultures the private and the public are not opposed ("Third-World Literature"). Stephen Slemon, too, has argued that, whereas imperialism relies on old-fashioned allegory, many post-colonial novels use a revitalized version of the trope to reveal the discursive and revisable nature of colonial history ("Post-Colonial Allegory").

It is certainly possible, and frequently rewarding, to read Coetzee's fiction through the lens of one of these modern or postmodern theories of allegory (*Waiting for the Barbarians*, in fact, is one of Slemon's examples).[16] But what the novels seem most powerfully to solicit from the bulk

15. See Walter Benjamin, *The Origin of German Tragic Drama*; Paul de Man, *Allegories of Reading* and "The Rhetoric of Temporality"; and Fredric Jameson, *The Political Unconscious*. Jameson summarizes the postmodern revaluation and reinterpretation of allegory in *Postmodernism*, 167–68. A somewhat more traditional account of allegory is the subject of Angus Fletcher's wide-ranging book, *Allegory*, while a proposed reconceptualization of allegory as self-reflexively language-oriented is detailed in Maureen Quilligan's *The Language of Allegory*. Although de Man did a great deal to rehabilitate allegory, he sometimes writes interestingly of literal readings, as when he objects to the notion that the landscapes that begin many of Hölderlin's poems represent spiritual truths: "To state this would be to misjudge the literality of these passages, to ignore that they derive their considerable poetic authority from the fact that they are not synecdoches designating a totality of which they are a part, but are themselves already this totality" ("The Rhetoric of Temporality," 190).

16. See, for instance, Teresa Dovey, "Allegory vs. Allegory" and "*Waiting for the Barbarians*: Allegory of Allegories"; Jean-Philippe Wade, "The Allegorical Text and History"; Bill Ashcroft, "Irony, Allegory and Empire"; and Kwaku Larbi Korang, "An Allegory of Re-reading."

of their readers, and what I wish to focus on, is a relatively straightforward process of allegorization, whereby characters and the events that befall them are taken to represent either wider (in some cases, as I've said, universal) or more specific meanings. (Most gatherings of undergraduate essays or newspaper reviews about a work of Coetzee's are likely to substantiate this claim.) The urge to allegorize Coetzee—and I am including here the urge to treat elements in the text as symbols or metaphors for broader ideas or entities—is, I believe, rooted in the formidable power of this traditional trope to make sense of texts that, for one reason or another, are puzzling when taken at face value.[17] It is one form of the reading for meaning from which both Sontag and Davidson, in the essays mentioned above, try to escape.

The simplest term for the kind of reading I am opposing to the allegorical is *literal*.[18] It is important to note, however, that the opposition literal/allegorical does not map directly onto the opposition realist/antirealist or mimetic/nonmimetic: it is just as possible to give an antirealist or nonmimetic work a literal reading as it is to give an apparently realistic or mimetic text an allegorical reading. What I am calling a literal reading is one that is grounded the experience of reading as an *event*.[19] That is to say, in literary reading (which I perform at the same time as I perform many other kinds of reading) I do not treat the text as an object whose significance has to be divined; I treat it as something that comes into being only in the process of understanding and responding that I, as an individual reader in a specific time and place, conditioned by a specific history, go through. And this is to say that I do not treat it as

17. My reservations about allegory should not be construed as echoing Lukács's attack in "The Ideology of Modernism," in *The Meaning of Contemporary Realism*, 17–46, on what he sees as the allegorical method of modernism: Lukács's own approach to realistic fiction, which seeks to translate particular detail into historical and social types, and subjects the alterity and singularity of the works it reads to an existing master-narrative, is, in the sense in which I am using the term, highly allegorical.

18. A term which might signal something closer than allegory to the kind of reading I am exploring is "parable": as J. Hillis Miller argues, parables do not point to a content elsewhere but work performatively on the reader's grasp on meaning ("Parable and Performative"). There are different kinds of parable, however: Coetzee's fictions are closer to Kafka's parabolic narratives, with their reliance on a kind of literalism, than to the oblique suggestiveness of some other South African fictions—of Breyten Breytenbach's *Mouroir* or the magic realism of Mike Nicol's *The Powers that Be*, for example. (Coetzee comments interestingly on *Mouroir* in *Doubling the Point*, 380.)

19. See above, pp. xii and 9, and for full discussion, Attridge, *The Singularity of Literature*.

"something" at all; rather, I have an *experience* that I call *Waiting for the Barbarians* or *Life & Times of Michael K*. It is an experience I can repeat, though each repetition turns out to be a different experience and therefore a non-repetition, a new singularity, as well.

In every event of reading a fictional text, the meanings of the words solidify into the customary ingredients of such writing—characters, places, relationships, plot complications and resolutions—which are derived from my familiarity with the genre, my participation in the shared meanings of my culture, and from my own personal history. At the same time, I respond emotionally to these meanings as they engage with my own stores of knowledge and memory. In some reading experiences, however, there seems to be more to what happens: I register a strangeness, a newness, a singularity, an inventiveness, an alterity in what I read. When this happens, I have two choices (putting a complicated matter very crudely): I can deploy reading techniques that will lessen or annul the experience of singularity and alterity—and this will usually involve turning the event into an object of some kind (such as a structure of signification)—or I can seek to preserve the event as an event, to sustain and prolong the experience of otherness, to resist the temptation to close down the uncertain meanings and feelings that are being evoked. In both cases, I am concerned with "meaning," but in the first case I understand it as a noun, in the second as a verb.[20] I can, one might say, *live* the text that I read.[21] This is what I mean by a literal reading. By the end of this chapter, in fact, I will be arguing that an equally apt term for literal reading, in this sense, is *literary* reading.

: III :

We've noted that allegorical interpretation is frequently spurred by a lack of specificity or some other peculiarity in a work's temporal and geographical locatedness, rendering the literal interpretation problematic and encouraging the reader to look for other kinds of meaning. (The examples of Kafka and Beckett, already mentioned—and cited also by Sontag—are

20. A related distinction is Levinas's contrast between the "Said" and the "Saying"; see, in particular, his discussion of these terms in many places in *Otherwise than Being*.

21. Coetzee's essay on Kafka's *The Burrow* is a superb analysis of how syntax can be used to involve the reader in the narrative as an event, and to challenge conventional notions of time (*Doubling the Point*, 210–32).

clear cases in point.) The first novella of *Dusklands* is set in the time and place of writing—the United States during its war with North Vietnam in the late 1960s—but then shifts its focus to the eighteenth-century exploration of South Africa by white colonists, and the juxtaposition itself seems to call for some kind of allegorical account relating the two "colonial" projects. Coetzee's next novel, *In the Heart of the Country,* although it conveys powerfully the Karoo locale, is characterized by historical shifts and ambiguities: what seems like a nineteenth-century setting at the start (travel by horse-drawn dog-cart, the use of a fire for domestic hot water) has become by the end the late twentieth century (regular traversals of the sky by airplanes). *Waiting for the Barbarians* is locatable neither in time nor place, and *Life & Times of Michael K,* though very precisely situated in the Western Cape, takes place in an undetermined future. The novels that follow, by contrast with the previous three works, are all set in specific times and places: early eighteenth-century London for *Foe,* Cape Town in the mid-1980s for *Age of Iron,* nineteenth-century St. Petersburg for *The Master of Petersburg,* and Cape Town and the Eastern Province in the late 1990s for *Disgrace.*[22] (The two autobiographical works, *Boyhood* and *Youth,* although they are written in the third person and thus have a pseudo-fictional quality, are of course the closest to a historical accounting and thus give the least encouragement to the allegorizing reader.) This is not to say that the later novels do not invite allegorization (we've already noted the way in which the representation of Vercueil both invites and resists allegorical readings), but the greater specificity of time and place in the later works means that there is more for a nonallegorical reading to get its teeth into.[23] Because of the particular temptations they offer for allegorical reading, I shall concentrate in this chapter on *Waiting for the Barbarians* and *Michael K,* though I hope my comments will be seen to be relevant to all Coetzee's fiction (and beyond it).

The paradigm case of Coetzee's temporally and spatially unspecific fiction is *Waiting for the Barbarians.* This was the work which, on its

22. The novels of Nadine Gordimer, so often contrasted with Coetzee's, are much more specific in their historical and fictional locations (even when they are set in the future, like *A Guest of Honour* or *A Sport of Nature*), and this is one reason why they are less prone to be allegorized. Probably the most often allegorized novels are *The Conservationist* and *July's People,* which offer less of the historical detail than usually characterizes Gordimer's work.

23. Michiel Heyns, in "Houseless Poverty," contrasts the fictional modes of *Michael K* and *Age of Iron,* finding it most profitable to treat the former as allegory and the latter as realism.

publication in 1980, brought Coetzee to the world's attention, and it remains his best-known novel (though *Disgrace* may now be challenging that preeminence). Charting an undetermined year in the life of an unnamed outpost of an unidentified Empire, and centered on an act of torture, the novel was published at a time when memories of Steve Biko's murder in detention by the South African security police—and the subsequent cover-up—were still fresh in many minds.[24] In a sense, the novel was able to have its cake and eat it: a powerful posing of the question of torture and of the responsibilities of those in power in the places where it is allowed to happen, it could be read both as an indictment of the atrocities that were keeping apartheid in place at the time of its publication and as a universally relevant, time- and place-transcending narrative of human suffering and moral choice. The first type of reading stresses, for instance, that Colonel Joll's report on the death of a prisoner being interrogated (6) echoes the official accounts of Biko's death, while the second is perhaps best summed up by the King Penguin blurb: "J. M. Coetzee's second prize-winning novel is an allegory of oppressor and oppressed. Not simply a man living through a crisis of conscience in an obscure place and remote times, the Magistrate is an analogue of all men living in complicity with regimes that ignore justice and decency."[25]

Both of these readings (which are not mutually exclusive) do justice to significant aspects of the novel: the sense of helpless anger which the reader shares with the Magistrate is both strengthened and given a real-world focus when the connection with South Africa in the late 1970s is made, and the painful dilemma of the liberal conscience gains added resonance from the awareness that it has been, and will be, played out, if perhaps not on a universal scale, then at many times and in many places. In their different ways, these readings are both allegories: the events traced in the novel are understood as standing for other events, either historically specific events or generalized and endlessly repeated events.[26] The danger

24. For an account of these events in relation to Coetzee's novel, see Susan VanZanten Gallagher, *A Story of South Africa,* 112–18. The novel that at the time of publication was read as an allegory of the South Africa of its time—as an intervention, in other words—now offers itself as an allegory of a historical moment, as, that is, an elucidation.

25. It is this type of reading that leads Abdul JanMohamed to class the novel among colonialist works which promote what he calls "Manichean allegory," in which racial difference is mapped on to a series of other differences ("The Economy of Manichean Allegory").

26. In their books on Coetzee, Dovey, Gallagher, and Head all refer to the allegorical aspects of *Waiting for the Barbarians,* and in doing so contribute valuably to our understanding of the novel's procedures.

they both court is of moving too quickly beyond the novel to find its significance elsewhere, of treating it not as an inventive literary work drawing us into unfamiliar emotional and cognitive territory but as a reminder of what we already know only too well.

The most economical way to give some sense of a nonallegorical response is to describe a few moments in the continuous experience of reading, and, for the duration of the reading, living, this novel. Here is a characteristic passage, which occurs after the barbarian girl, partially blinded by her torturers, has been left behind in the town as a beggar, and the Magistrate has brought her into his apartment:

> The fire is lit. I draw the curtains, light the lamp. She refuses the stool, but yields up her sticks and kneels in the centre of the carpet.
>
> "This is not what you think it is," I say. The words come reluctantly. Can I really be about to excuse myself? Her lips are clenched shut, her ears too no doubt, she wants nothing of old men and their bleating consciences. I prowl around her, talking about our vagrancy ordinances, sick at myself. Her skin begins to glow in the warmth of the closed room. She tugs at her coat, opens her throat to the fire. The distance between myself and her torturers, I realize, is negligible; I shudder.
>
> "Show me your feet," I say in the new thick voice that seems to be mine. "Show me what they have done to your feet." (27–28)

A standard commentary on this passage, unhampered by the qualms about allegory I have been voicing, would probably focus on the fact that this is one of many passages that signal the novel's insistence on the self-deceptions of the liberal conscience, in the thinness of the dividing line between overt repression achieved by violent methods and the subtler forms of oppression produced by laissez-faire attitudes, the pursuit of personal gratifications, and an unwillingness to rock the boat. The fascination with the body that characterizes erotic attachment cannot, the novel tells us, be separated from the fascination of the body evident in the torture chamber.[27] The Magistrate's acknowledgment of this connection, however, is a moment of insight from which he appears not to profit.

The soundness of this analysis can't be doubted, and these are indeed important claims powerfully made and deserving of our attention. But how thin it is compared with the experience of reading the passage, especially in the context of the novel! How much it has to leave out! There

---

27. For a full discussion of this and related issues, see Rosemary Jane Jolly's account of the novel in *Colonization, Violence, and Narration*, 122–35.

exists no critical vocabulary that will do full justice to the multiple, simultaneous, constantly changing effects of a passage like this; all I can do here is present in somewhat prosaic terms a few of the events—intellectual, affective, and physical—that may occur in an engaged reading.

Encouraged by the present tense and first person, we undergo, along with the Magistrate, the complex unfolding of feelings and associations. (The "impossibility" of this mode of narration, which we have already noted in Coetzee's earlier work, is never signaled, and is no barrier to the experience of immediacy.) We sense his own awareness that he is playing out the standard rituals of seduction—the fire, the drawn curtains, the lamp; the disappointment embodied in "refuses" followed by the promise of satisfaction in "yields" and "kneels." We are conscious—as he is—of a history of sexual exploitation (of women, of servants, of subordinate races) tending to make the scene little more than the repetition of a host of previous such scenes. But the denial that follows ("This is not what you think it is"): is this the standard seducer's lie? Yes and no, it appears: the reluctance with which the words come shows that it is not a straightforwardly transparent statement. It is the beginning of an excuse—but an excuse for what exactly? Neither the Magistrate nor the reader knows. Awareness that there is some deception involved leads to a moment of self-revulsion as the Magistrate imagines himself from the woman's point of view, an old man with a bleating conscience. Better to do what he wants to do, whatever it may be, than agonize about it and apologize for it, a ridiculous figure skulking around her, talking but not touching. Yet there is of course also a sense of the ethical rightness of this hesitation, this self-doubt: he is sick at himself both for his making of excuses and for his obscure and unnamed desires.

And all the while we are aware that the girl remains closed to him (and therefore to us), that his "This is not what you think it is" is premised upon an access to her thoughts which he does not in fact have, and knows he does not have. How she reads this scene, with its lamplight and its circling, prattling old man, remains wholly inaccessible. Her clenched lips may not be a response to the Magistrate's self-exculpations; her ears, contrary to his assumption, may be wholly alert. And although the subsequent action is perceived by the Magistrate in highly erotic terms—"Her skin begins to glow"; "opens her throat to the fire"—his own thought-processes help us to resist the temptation to ascribe erotic motives to the girl.

Nothing obvious leads to the Magistrate's grim realization that follows this action, and at one level it is an absurd statement: the distance between him and the girl's torturers is anything but negligible. The association is felt, not thought, however: the sudden vulnerability of the exposed throat, the surge of erotic attraction, the obscurity of the impulses that make themselves known—these are elements in the reader's experience as well as the Magistrate's. And that complex of feelings, that momentary complicity with something dark and destructive, as something that happens to the reader, is more significant testimony to the power and distinctiveness of literature, and to the brilliance of Coetzee's art, than any extracted moral about the errors of liberal humanism. The Magistrate is, to be sure, not some kind of floating, self-determining subject; he is the precipitate of a familiar history of oppression and exploitation, but that history is experienced as an individual composite of assumptions, proclivities, and fears. By the time we reach the "new thick voice that seems to be mine" we have ourselves tasted a little of that sensation of being taken over, of something foreign to us uttering itself through us.

What I have just presented is a description of part of my own experience of these sentences; the use of "we" is of course a rhetorical gesture rather than a genuine plural. There is no guarantee that it coincides with the way anyone else experiences the passage (and of course the next time I read it I will be a different reader—if only in minor ways—and perhaps will want to say different things about it). But after many conversations about Coetzee's fiction, after reading many responses to it, I know there's a good chance that others have experienced something like this—and, most important for my present argument, that they have valued the experience for itself, not because it pointed to some truths about the world in general or South Africa in the 1970s in particular.

If the highlighting of those truths is an important function of the novel—and it's certainly the case that we can never be reminded too often of them—this fact has to be qualified by an awareness that the experience of such passages complicates any process of allegorical transfer by questioning the rational procedures on which this type of interpretation itself depends. Once we attend to the details of our encounter with the novel, these seem far in excess of the allegorizations we are tempted to produce—and more explanatory of our enjoying and prizing of the novel than the political, historical, or moral truths that we can apprehend perfectly well without Coetzee's aid. This kind of reading is not a matter of coming to the text naked, as if such a thing were possible: any individual's response is informed by what he or she has read up to this point of the novel—or by the memory of the whole if this is a re-reading—and by his or her knowledge of Coetzee's other fiction, of other South African novels, of the tradition of Western literature and art, as well as by relevant historical, geographical, and other types of knowledge. It is also, inevitably, colored by the reader's personal situation and history. Doing justice to a work of literature involves doing justice at the same time to who, where, and when we are.

Of course, the passage I have discussed is thematically a pivotal one, and not in that sense typical. But it is not only such narratively significant passages that work powerfully without needing to be placed in an allegorical scheme. Take the short paragraph that occurs a little before it:

> A day passes. I stare out over the square where the wind chases flurries of dust. Two little boys are playing with a hoop. They bowl it into the wind. It rolls forward, slows, teeters, rides back, falls. The boys lift their faces and run after it, the hair whipped back from their clean brows. (27)

This is not just expendable matter between significant moments, filling out the novel to a slightly more respectable length. The passage separates the first encounter with the barbarian girl from the second, and although it is more orthodox in the way it engages the reader it still possesses a haunting suggestiveness. This is the period during which the Magistrate's urge to find, and in some way become intimate with, the tortured girl—we might even say with her torturedness—grows to the point of uncontrollability; the next paragraph begins "I find the girl . . ." The boys with the hoop operate for the Magistrate as one of those objects onto which the eye locks while the mind is focused elsewhere—and they function somewhat in this manner for the reader as well as for the narrative consciousness, precisely because of the exact, almost over-exact, description: we follow the words one by one as the Magistrate follows with his eyes the changing movements of the hoop, rolling forward, slowing, teetering, riding back, falling. We sense, too, the passing of time not just as a fact enunciated but an experience lived through: both the emptiness of a day without further contact with the girl, about whom we and our alter ego in the fiction have many more questions to ask, and the feeling of seasonal change so important in the novel, as the wind grows stronger and begins to interfere with the perennial pastimes of summer. The passage of time is thus registered through a timeless image: two boys with a hoop, children at play, the Empire and all its problems apparently an irrelevance.

This experience of temporality is another feature of narrative that allegorical interpretation ignores. To allegorize is to translate the temporal and the sequential into the schematic: a set of truths, a familiar historical scene. Even if the narrative is mapped onto another narrative—say, the story of pigs taking over the running of a farm onto the history of the

Russian Revolution—the *experience* of events in time is displaced by the acknowledgment of a series of well-known occurrences.[28]

And what of the many moments in the novel when the Magistrate finds interpretation simultaneously invited and baffled? The wooden slips and the ruins among which they are found, the marks of torture on the barbarian girl, the words of the old barbarian man to whom he returns the girl, the moment in front of the waterbuck when "events are not themselves but stand for other things" (40), the many dreams? Apart, as we've seen, from problematizing the very idea of allegorical interpretation, they contribute to the novel a sense of realms of meaning inaccessible to the Magistrate's rational powers, yet perhaps all the more strongly effective because they cannot be translated into words. Take the dreams: there are several in the novel, including a series of related dreams set in the town square, usually seen as snow-covered and always involving a figure that the Magistrate refers to as "the girl."[29] (Although the first such dream predates the arrival of the barbarian girl in the Magistrate's life, a connection is soon established between her and the girl in the dream, who, after initially revealing a blank face, on two later occasions has black eyes like the barbarian girl and once has the heavy plait typical of the barbarian women [53, 109].) The reader is, of course, invited to interpret them, and to relate them to aspects of the Magistrate's waking life (such as his frequent vision of the barbarian girl's face as blank), but part of their haunting power derives from their refusal to succumb completely to the interpretive drive. When, at the very end of the novel, the Magistrate sees some children playing in the snowy square, the reader's immediate recall of the repeated dream is balked by his "This is not the scene I dreamed of" (156). The absence of the girl is clearly crucial to the disavowal; but the inability to draw any more specific conclusion is experienced both by the Magistrate, who feels "stupid, like a man who lost his way long ago," and by the reader.

28. It may seem paradoxical that for de Man it is precisely temporality—the reliance of all signification on temporal sequentiality—that is signaled by allegory; but we must remember that allegory is being contrasted with the symbol, with, that is, the mystification of the temporal relations of meaning. I am here not distinguishing between allegorical and symbolic modes, both of which reduce temporal experience to static meanings. My concern is with the fictional evocation of temporality as an element in the event of reading, not the exposure of the underpinnings of language.

29. Versions of the "child in the square" dream are described on pp. 9–10, 37, 52–53, 86–87, 109, and 136. Other dreams or visions occur on pp. 13, 120, 148.

The point I wish to make is that allegorical reading of the traditional kind has no place for this uncertainty and open-endedness, this sense that the failure to interpret can be as important, and quite as emotionally powerful, as success would be. (To say that these moments are allegories of the incertitude of human experience would not get us very far in registering their singularity.) The dreams in the novel evoke a yearning for the normality of life in which children play in the snow (like the boys with their hoop), a normality which seems achieved in the final, waking, encounter; yet their very elusiveness suggests the fragility of that hoped-for state. And it is through responsive reading, an immersion in the text, that we participate in, and perhaps are changed by, this complex understanding of hope and fear, illusion and disillusionment.

These, then, are some of the qualities of the novel that are unaccounted for by an allegorical reading. In order to move to parallels outside the world of the book, many of the rich and sometimes apparently quite contingent details of the text have to be ignored, as do narrative temporality and succession (and this includes the extensive use made of gaps in the narrative sequence).[30] The powerful physical depictions, the intimate experience of an individual's inner states, the unsuccessful attempts at interpretation, the posing (but not resolving) of delicate ethical dilemmas: all these have to be played down if we are to seek meanings in worlds elsewhere. Yet these are surely what give the work its uniqueness and its appeal, these are what engross and move readers (though most of us would be hard put to name the complex affective responses that are aroused). And all of these attributes, which reach us as events of reading, are brought into being by the shaping of language, the phrasing of syntax, the resonating of syllables, the allusions and suggestions—historical, cultural, even physical—that play continually through the text: a manifestation of linguistic power that is central to our enjoyment of the novel.

: IV :

Life & Times of Michael K invites a different sort of allegorical reading. Since it, too, occurs in a setting that is outside actual history (though in this case not outside real geography), there is an immediate obstacle to taking

---

30. Coetzee both discusses and enacts the skipping of narrative material in chapter 1 of *Elizabeth Costello*.

it on its own terms. South Africa in an imaginary future (since 1994 we have had to read it as a future that fortunately did not happen) is therefore understood as an extension of South Africa at the time of writing, that is, the early 1980s. Once again, this allegorical interpretation responds to important features of the novel: the portrayal of a country ruled by means of military and police coercion, in which there are no unpatrolled spaces for the misfit, the opter-out, the maverick, and in which the liberal conscience—personified now by the medical officer—struggles (largely unsuccessfully) to find a way of palliating the violence of the state. And once again, I want to ask what else there is to the novel's power and singularity, and in particular what it is that grips and compels us as we read, producing an experience, disturbing and pleasurable at the same time, of new possibilities at the very limits of our habitual thoughts and feelings.

As in all Coetzee's fiction, the work is full of detail far in excess of any allegorical reading. Vivid physical particularity, complex emotions, evocations of the passage of time, moments where interpretation is thwarted, narrative gaps—these and many more features have their own effectiveness, and resist integration into an account of the novel as a description of the apartheid state or a warning about its likely future. Equally, details of this kind play little part in a more universal allegorizing reading, such as the one proposed by the medical officer and mentioned above: Michael K as the signifier that escapes systematization, the force of *différance,* if you like, that both subverts and makes possible the articulation of meaning. But I shall focus briefly on another aspect of what I see as the novel's unallegorizability: its invitation to the reader to apprehend, and follow in its twists and turns, a consciousness unaffected by many of the main currents of modernity, including modernity's emphasis on generalized moral norms, its preoccupation with the measuring and exploitation of time, and its sense of the importance of profit and progeny.[31] (These aren't, of course, peculiar to modernity, but take on a particular modern intensity.)

At first sight, it may seem paradoxical that Coetzee extends this invitation through a narrative style that not only avoids the first person—except for the section in the voice of the medical officer—but that makes only intermittent use of free indirect discourse, the technical device apparently

---

31. For a discussion of this aspect of the novel in terms provided by Deleuze and Guattari (K is untouched by the desiring-machines of culture) see Sarah Dove Heider, "The Timeless Ecstasy of Michael K."

most suited to conveying an individual's inner world while remaining in the third person (and one which Coetzee uses abundantly in other novels). Even rarer in *Michael K* is the mimicking of thought itself by syntactical elisions and interruptions, Joycean "interior monologue." The consequence is that phrases like "He thought" are frequently resorted to, continually reminding us that we are outside Michael K's consciousness.[32] Yet this stylistic choice—together with the use of the past tense—allows Coetzee to sustain throughout the fiction the otherness of K's responses: although we learn in moving detail of his thought-processes and emotions, we never feel that we have assimilated them to our own.

The language in these accounts is not necessarily that which K would use in articulating his thoughts—indeed, we often suspect that what are represented as "thoughts" scarcely exist in an articulated form. We frequently encounter sentences that begin as statements about K's mental world but which carry on in language that hardly seems his. Here is one example:

> When he heard the rumble of an approaching convoy he would creep away into the bushes, though he wondered whether by now, with his filthy clothes and his air of gaunt exhaustion, he would not be passed over as a mere footloose vagrant from the depths of the country, too benighted to know that one needed papers to be on the road, too sunk in apathy to be of harm. (39)

Rewriting this in the first person—"I wonder whether by now, with my filthy clothes and my air of gaunt exhaustion..."—makes it instantly clear that this is not word-for-word representation of K's thought. An even more striking example is the following, which shifts into a mode reminiscent of George Eliot:

> He thought of himself not as something heavy that left tracks behind it, but if anything as a speck upon the surface of an earth too deeply asleep to notice the scratch of ant-feet, the rasp of butterfly teeth, the tumbling of dust. (97)

Such uncertainties as to the source of the sentences we read are in strong contrast to the Magistrate in *Waiting for the Barbarians,* who speaks in

---

32. Benita Parry has criticized the repeated use of "he thought," "he found," "he said" as involving a "speaking for" the character ("Speech and Silence," 154). My argument is that they signal just the opposite: the authorial voice's inability or reluctance to speak for the character by means of free indirect discourse.

the first person and the present tense, and is an altogether far more familiar and knowable character; in his case, it is what happens to him—his encounter with otherness—that produces the novel's powerful singularity.

Another distancing device is the use of the letter "K." On encountering it in the novel's opening—"The first thing the midwife noticed about Michael K when she helped him out of his mother into the world was that he had a hare lip" (3)—we are likely to be highly conscious of its distancing effect, as it renders an otherwise exemplary realist sentence, redolent of Thackeray or Dickens, slightly puzzling, and that oddness is continued in the next paragraph when Michael's mother is named Anna K. It seems unlikely, even at this stage of the novel, that the reason for the abbreviation is that the surname is too famous to be spelled out in full, as sometimes happens in nineteenth-century novels; the name is more likely, as Nadine Gordimer remarks in "The Idea of Gardening," to be quite ordinary—Gordimer mentions Kotze (a version of Coetzee) or Koekemoer, familiar Afrikaans surnames, and plausible names for a member of the Cape coloured community. However, there's no escaping the allusion to another antihero in modernist literature, Kafka's Josef K.[33] (Gordimer's assertion that the initial "has no reference, nor need it have, to Kafka" seems to contradict itself in the act of making the connection.) The tension between the naturalistic narrative and this antirealist, high-cultural, self-conscious contrivance, of which we're reminded on nearly every page (except in the medical officer's narrative, in which K is called "Michaels"), contributes to our sense that this is a character whom we can't easily pretend that we know. It also constantly distances the narrative voice from the inner consciousness of the character, who presumably doesn't think of himself as "K." (It must be said, however, that the noticeability of the use of the initial letter fades as we read, and the power of fictional discourse soon persuades us that it is a perfectly normal way to refer to a man.)

---

33. One reviewer, at least, complained about the intrusiveness of the allusions to Kafka: Christopher Lehmann-Haupt, in the *New York Times*, noted the novel's "heavy debt to Franz Kafka," including the use of "K," the reference to the central military headquarters as "the Castle" (though anyone who has visited Cape Town knows that this is a real enough building, with just this significance), the frequent comparison of K to insects, and K's role as a hunger-artist. He comments: "These are doubtless meant to be tributes to a master as much as borrowings from him, but they are overdone and call an unnecessary amount of attention to themselves" (C22). On this self-conscious claim to canonic forebears, see the following chapter.

Let us look at a few of many possible passages as examples of the representation of K's inner world. K is hiding in a cave above the Visagie farm, no longer able to water the pumpkin seeds he has planted there:

> He thought of the pumpkin leaves pushing through the earth. Tomorrow will be their last day, he thought: the day after that they will wilt, and the day after that they will die, while I am out here in the mountains. Perhaps if I started at sunrise and ran all day I would not be too late to save them, them and the other seeds that are going to die underground, though they do not know it, that are never going to see the light of day. There was a cord of tenderness that stretched from him to the patch of earth beside the dam and must be cut. It seemed to him that one could cut a cord like that only so many times before it would not grow again. (65–66)

The sentences of this paragraph lead from a simple thought about the distant pumpkin plants into an extraordinary conceptual and emotional realm, a realm that—at least for the duration of the sentences—we share, yet one that retains its foreignness. In their vocabulary, the two first-person sentences offered as a direct quotation of K's thoughts are plausible representations, although their rhythm of successive, paratactically ordered phrases is recognizably Coetzean. The thoughts and associated feelings they convey are those of a remarkable consciousness, however: the spring of hope in the idea of running all day to save the seeds, the pang of pity in the notion of seeds unaware of their fate.

The following sentence, with its startlingly material conceit of the "cord of tenderness," seems more likely to be an external rendition of a complex of thought and feeling not articulated in words: it is presented in the third person, readable as a narrator's statement *about* K's state of mind. One has only to rewrite it in the first person to sense that it belongs to a different mental and verbal domain from the previous two sentences: one cannot easily imagine K thinking, or Coetzee writing, "There is a cord of tenderness that stretches from me to the patch of earth..." Yet by the end of the sentence we seem to have swerved back to K's consciousness by means of free indirect discourse: the imperative of "must be cut" sounds more like an echo of K's thought than a comment by the narrator. And the final sentence, with its explicit "It seemed to him...," encourages us to think that the cord *is* K's imaginative creation, now less an umbilical cord than the stem of a plant (like a pumpkin) that has to be carefully nurtured—although the continuing use of the third person means that we still can't be sure.[34]

It would be crudely reductive to say that Coetzee here (and in the many related passages in the novel) celebrates or advocates an ecological sensitivity, though what he does do is convey as few other writers have done the intensity which the bond between human and plant life can acquire. He does this through a writing that demands the closest engagement, the living-through by means of language of a singular experience, moving undecidably between two consciousnesses.

Just as K's relation to the earth and to cultivation (and one could find many more instances of this tenderness) implies a resistance to modernity's drive to exploit natural resources—though a resistance that never becomes an alternative moral norm—so his behavior toward other people obeys no codes given in advance. Here's a characteristic meditation by K, prompted by the comment "People must help each other, that's what I believe," spoken by a stranger who has, unasked, given him food and lodging:

> K allowed this utterance to sink into his mind. Do I believe in helping people? he wondered. He might help people, he might not help them, he did not know beforehand, anything was possible. He did not seem to have a belief, or did not seem to have a belief regarding help. Perhaps I am the stony ground, he thought. (48)

Once again, we are on terrain outside the familiar moral world; for K, the fundamental injunction of neighborliness (from which he has just benefited) is something of a conundrum, a riddle which he cannot solve.[35] And again, Coetzee uses directly represented thought and something that hovers between free indirect discourse and narratorial reporting to engage us with K's mental process while registering the strangeness of this

---

34. The image returns when K finds he does not wish to announce his presence to the guerrilla fighters who visit the farm: "There must be men to stay behind and keep gardening alive, or at least the idea of gardening; because once that cord was broken, the earth would grow hard and forget her children" (109). Again it is difficult to imagine K using these words, yet we register them as an accurate representation of his thought.

35. An echo of K's dilemma, in a more sophisticated register, can be heard in David Lurie's puzzlement in *Disgrace*: "Bill Shaw believes that, because he and David Lurie once had a cup of tea together, David Lurie is his friend, and the two of them have obligations towards each other. Is Bill Shaw wrong or right? ... Does the drinking of tea seal a love-bond, in the eyes of Bill Shaw? Yet but for Bill and Bev Shaw, but for old Ettinger, but for bonds of some kind, where would he be now?" (102).

attitude. The rhythm of the clauses, the quasi-philosophical speculation ("a belief regarding help" sounds as though it has come from a philosophy textbook), are not K's, but they convey all the more powerfully the challenge to conventional morality he embodies. Finally, the echo of the parable no doubt heard long ago in Huis Norenius, the institution in which he was raised, brings us back to reported thought and a sentence K can be imagined articulating.

What are we to make of this challenge? That K is some kind of amoral being, more animal than human, or that he is perhaps still an infant at heart? Certainly not; the very fact of his open-minded speculation on this matter indicates a profound ethical awareness. Rather, I would argue, passages like this provide a taste of what it might mean to resist the urge to apply preexisting norms and to make fixed moral judgments—which, as I've suggested, is one form of allegorizing reading—and to value instead the contingent, the processual, the provisional that keeps moral questions alive. It's not for nothing that both the passages we've looked at from the novel have sentences beginning "Perhaps." Allegory cannot handle perhapses.[36]

At other places in the novel, we find ourselves participating momentarily in an attitude toward time and toward futurity that is alien to the dominant modern mentality. For instance, this passage occurs when K is lying on his back in the sun during his first experience of, as he calls it, "living off the land":

> I could live here forever, he thought, or till I die. Nothing would happen, every day would be the same as the day before, there would be nothing to say. . . . He could understand that people should have retreated here and fenced themselves in with miles and miles of silence; he could understand that they should have wanted to bequeath the privilege of so much silence to their children and grandchildren in perpetuity (though by what right he was not sure); he wondered whether there were not forgotten corners and angles and corridors between the fences, land that belonged to no one yet. Perhaps if one flew high enough, he thought, one would be able to see. (46–47)

Again, this state of mind is not being advocated as a norm, but we are being invited to participate in it, at least for the duration of the paragraph. For K,

---

36. Derrida has written illuminatingly on the significance of "perhaps"; see *The Politics of Friendship*, 26–45, and "Perhaps or Maybe." Sue Kossew notes the frequency of "perhaps" in *In the Heart of the Country* (*Pen and Power*, 65), as does André Viola (*J. M. Coetzee*, 27).

with his hare lip and his dislike of being required to speak, the thought of limitless silence is particularly appealing, but this psychological realism is also a way of exploring mental states that have much wider significance. K's thoughts move from the inheritance of farmland (with a typically oblique appreciation of the injustices involved) to the dream of unclaimed land, no-one's inheritance, where he might live out his eventless, silent, existence. It's not difficult to feel the appeal of this prospect as we read.

Later, after his return to the farm, K finds himself luxuriating even more fully in the sensation of endless time, freed—now that he has fulfilled his responsibility toward his mother by burying her ashes on the farm where he believes she was born—from any obligation to use time fruitfully:

> Since time was poured out upon him in such an unending stream, there were whole mornings he could spend lying on his belly over an ant-nest picking out the larvae one by one with a grass-stalk and putting them in his mouth. (102)

The fullest expression of this luxuriance is an extraordinary passage worth quoting in full. As so often in the novel, the words and phrases shape themselves into memorable sequences and resonate across the English literary tradition in a manner that is hardly likely to mirror K's mental world, but that enables us to share in the experience more completely than an attempt at a literal rendition would do (even the final "he thought" sentence has a Coetzean ring, though we can accept that its content is K's):

> But most of all, as summer slanted to an end, he was learning to love idleness, idleness no longer as stretches of freedom reclaimed by stealth here and there from involuntary labour, surreptitious thefts to be enjoyed sitting on his heels before a flower-bed with a fork dangling from his fingers, but as a yielding up of himself to time, to a time flowing slowly like oil from horizon to horizon over the face of the world, washing over his body, circulating in his armpits and his groin, stirring his eyelids. He was neither pleased nor displeased when there was work to do; it was all the same. He could lie all afternoon with his eyes open, staring at the corrugations in the roof-iron and the tracings of rust, all that was moving was time, bearing him onward in its flow. Once or twice the other time in which the war had its existence reminded itself to him as the jet fighters whistled high overhead. But for the rest he was living beyond the reach of calendar and clock in a blessedly neglected corner, half awake, half asleep. Like a parasite dozing in the gut, he thought; like a lizard under a stone. (115–16)

K's relishing of time without divisions and duties is linked to an understanding of the future: in complete contrast to the drive to make one's mark before one dies, K longs to leave no trace:

> The worst mistake, he told himself, would be to try to found a new house, a rival line, on his small beginnings out at the dam. Even his tools should be of wood and leather and gut, materials the insects would eat when one day he no longer needed them.... (104)

> There will be not a grain left bearing my marks, just as my mother has now, after her season in the earth, been washed clean, blown about, and drawn up into the leaves of grass. (124)[37]

And this desire to disappear without bequeathing anything to the future is related to K's sense of total lack of responsibility:

> How fortunate that I have no children, he thought: how fortunate that I have no desire to father. I would not know what to do with a child out here in the heart of the country, who would need milk and clothes and friends and schooling. I would fail in my duties, I would be the worst of fathers. Whereas it is not hard to live a life that consists merely of passing time. I am one of the fortunate ones who escape being called. (104)[38]

When one thinks of the centrality in so many religious, ethical, and philosophical traditions of the notion of "calling," the remarkableness of this celebration of an absence of responsibility is evident. We can derive no ethical lesson from K's condition, but we can return from living through it in a reading to the world of obligation, to that "other time" which is ours, with a changed sense of its status. (K's body cannot, however, endure this existence, and he falls ill. We do not hold out much hope of his survival at the end of the novel, which closes with his fantasy of living, back on the farm, on teaspoonfuls of water.)

There is, however, something positive in K's temporal experience as embodied in these passages. It lies in the very fact of his ability to give himself

---

37. The allusion to Whitman is typical of the oscillation between K's mental world and that of the culturally informed author and presumed reader. We may note also the reference to an earlier novel of Coetzee's in the quotation that follows.

38. The medical officer understands something of K's relation to time, to productivity, to the future, to decision-making: "You... have managed to live in the old way, drifting through time, observing the seasons, no more trying to change the course of history than a grain of sand does" (151–52).

up to the endlessness of time, to empty days and a profitless existence. There is a kind of openness to the future here, a kind of trust in events that has no relation to the calculations by which most of us live. This way of experiencing time is evident in the curious modality to K's life when he lingers near the hospital where his mother has died:

> It appeared that he had to stay in Stellenbosch for a certain length of time. There was no shortening the time. He stumbled through the days, losing his way often. (34)

The end of this period comes suddenly, with the same sense that his movements are subject to something outside himself:

> K, hesitating for a moment, peering down the long avenue of mist, found that there was after all nothing any more to keep him. (35)

We are never made privy to K's decision-making; it is almost as if he acts without going through the process of deciding what to do next. (Thus we don't hear of any preliminary thoughts about the construction of a barrow to make the journey to Prince Albert; we simply read: "Early one Sunday morning he visited De Waal Park and broke the lock on the shed..." [10].) This is, of course, only one example of many mental processes we're not allowed to share, and it can't be construed as evidence of a mind so peculiar that it acts completely on instinct; but this particular exercising of the novelist's prerogative to withhold has the effect, as we read, of allowing us to try out, as it were, a mode of existence in which decision-making is reduced to a minimum. We've already noted that K feels unable to predict whether he will help other people—"he did not know beforehand, anything was possible" (48). A similar tonality colors his days in the cave above the farm:

> He did not know what was going to happen. The story of his life had never been an interesting one; there had usually been someone to tell him what to do next; now there was no one, and the best thing seemed to be to wait. (67)

There is a kind of trustingness in K's attitude to the future and the events that it will bring, and although he occasionally acts out of duty—most notably in seeking to honor his mother's wishes, both before and after her death—or in avoidance of some perceived evil—as when he leaves the farm or escapes from the camps—he often appears to do the absolute minimum to stay alive. Even his capacity to survive is something that takes him unawares: "He had not eaten for two days; however, there seemed no limit to his endurance" (35). And he can be surprised by his own thought-processes: "curiously he watched the thought begin to unfold itself in his head, like a plant growing" (94). Yet K, no less than the Magistrate, is the product of a specific history, for all his abnormality: a history that is embedded in the discourses he employs and encounters, in the events of his life, in the social, economic, and political arrangements he resists.

When K reflects on his experiences at the end of the novel (and probably of his life, though the novel is deliberately inconclusive), not only does he sum up the remarkable relation to time that we have already sensed in earlier passages, but he notes with some surprise that this summing-up has come from nowhere:

> Because if there was one thing I discovered in the country, it was that there is time enough for everything.
>
> (Is that the moral of it all, he thought, the moral of the whole story: that there is time enough for everything? Is that how morals come, unbidden, in the course of events, when you least expect them?) (183)

K's thoughts are often in the form of questions like this; they reflect his somewhat bemused attitude to the events that befall him, the natural consequence of his naive outlook. (Given Coetzee's choice of style, they are often in the form of reported thought: a particularly cherishable example is "He wondered if he were living in what was known as bliss" [68].) Meditative questions are a particularly effective way of drawing the reader into a character's experience—they invite us to share a moment of uncertainty or curiosity without arriving at any conclusion—and they characterize all Coetzee's primary consciousnesses to a greater or lesser degree. Eugene Dawn and Jacobus Coetzee tend to turn to questions only when their certainties crumble, but both Magda and the Magistrate interrogate themselves and their surroundings repeatedly. Susan Barton asks herself as many questions as she does Cruso and Foe, while the experiences of Mrs. Curren, Dostoevsky, and David Lurie lead to a great deal of self-questioning. John in *Boyhood* and *Youth* is perhaps the closest to K in the kinds of question he asks, often in extreme bemusement, as he tries to make sense of an enigmatic and often hostile world. *Youth* may well have a higher count of questions per page than any of Coetzee's works to date.

What, though, of the features of these novels that seem to invite the allegorical reading that I am resisting? Why is one novel set in an indeterminate time and place, and the other in the future, for instance? Rather than accepting the carping answer that was common when these works appeared—that Coetzee wished to avoid having the novels read as pertaining closely to the South Africa of his time (an answer rendered less plausible by *Age of Iron* and *Disgrace*)—I would argue that his aim is to put his characters, and therefore his readers, in situations of peculiar intensity, stripped of the often distracting detail of historical reference. These situations are nevertheless entirely relevant to the South Africa of the time of writing, though not only to that time and place. The liberal administrator faced with consequences of political extremism, the innocent consciousness finding a way to live outside the driving impulses of modernity: these are not presented to us as figures to contemplate and assess, but are the air we breathe while we are absorbing the words by means of which they are created. K's hare lip is less an allegorical indicator of the handicaps suffered by certain sectors of the South African population[39] than an important part of the causal chain that has produced the particular individual he is revealed to be during the events of the novel.

I have been focusing on particular passages in these novels, but it is important to stress that the reading experience that I am trying to describe is one of continuous engagement, of the texture of a singular consciousness sustained with remarkable consistency. (This is why the medical officer's

---

39. Questions of race are strikingly absent from the novel—one reason for the unspecific "K" and the namelessness of the medical officer who narrates part of the novel. True, Michael is identified as CM (Coloured Male) on a charge sheet (70), but this categorization, like the guess at his age—forty—and the garbled name ("Michael Visagie"), is the product only of official perception. (Another indication for readers familiar with the socio-economic conditions of apartheid South Africa is K's mother's position: the domestic servant of a white family is unlikely to be white.) Although most readers assume that the civil war is between black insurgents and white guardians of the status quo, this is never stated in so many words. Up to a point, the omission of overt references to race might be recuperable within realism by reading it as a sign of its irrelevance (for differing reasons) to the consciousnesses which dominate the novel, those of K and the medical officer; but the lack of even incidental references from which racial types might be deduced testifies to a willed exclusion from the writing. Coetzee's "realism" can leave out details just as purposefully as it can include them. Race is thus revealed as the cultural/political construct that it is by the pressure it exerts, as an absence, upon the reader. (Viola states that the "CM" was deleted after the first editions of *Michael K* [*J. M. Coetzee*, 65], but it is still present in all the later editions I have consulted.)

As we shall see, the absence or uncertainty of racial references is typical of Coetzee's novels: both Vercueil in *Age of Iron* and the Isaacs family in *Disgrace* can be said to be "probably" coloured, but to discern this the reader has to be familiar with the niceties of South African racial groupings under apartheid. This uncertainty of categorization exposes, of course, the groundlessness of the racial discriminations which determined all South African lives during the era of state racism, and which, regrettably, have not disappeared.

section of *Michael K* hits us with such a shock when we reach it—though it too quickly engages us with a contrasting consciousness.) Sentences that grip, tantalize, or explode occur on every page, not as exercises in fine writing but as invitations to apprehend ways of being outside, but highly relevant to, the comfortable patterns of our daily lives.

: V :

The argument I am making has two levels. First, I want to suggest that *all* engagements with literary works—insofar as they are engagements with *literary* works—benefit from what I have been calling a literal reading: a reading that defers the many interpretive moves that we are accustomed to making in our dealings with literature, whether historical, biographical, psychological, moral, or political. Still speaking rather generally, I would label all these modes of interpretation—they are evident in virtually any published introduction to an author, and in many more sophisticated commentaries—allegorical, in that they take the literal meaning of the text to be a pathway to some other, more important, meaning. When carried out with subtlety and responsibility, such accounts can inform and enrich the experience of the text, but if they displace the literal reading they do damage to the work as a work of literature. (In pure allegory, of course, this displacement is essential—which is why I prefer to think of allegory as a nonliterary mode.) It's important to add that I am not speaking here of all the estimable effort that has gone into enriching the reading of literary works by illuminating relevant historical and cultural contexts: indeed, literal reading *fails* if the reader is not possessed of the necessary contextual information. Literal reading needs all the history— literary history, social history, political history, cultural history, intellectual history—it can get.

And by a literal reading, let me repeat, I mean a reading that occurs as an event, a living-through or performing of the text that responds simultaneously to what is said, the way in which it is said, and the inventiveness and singularity (if there is any) of the saying. There is nothing new about this kind of reading; it is the most basic, perhaps the most naive, way of interacting with a literary work. But this does not mean that it is the easiest way to talk or write about literature; on the contrary, there exists a significant gap between, on the one hand, what we do and what we enjoy and even what we learn when we read works of literature with the fullest engagement, and, on the other, what we feel is appropriate to say as commentators (casual or academic), or even what we are *able* to say in the vocabulary we have available to us. Allegorizing readings arise less, I would suggest, from the actual experience of works of literature than from the imperatives that drive literary commentary. We feel the pull of allegory whenever we introduce a novel to a class, or write an essay (for a teacher or for a literary journal) in which we have to summarize a poem, or engage in conversation with a friend about a work we have both just read. The more sophisticated and complex our critical tools become, and the more varieties of commentary the academic community endorses, the less attention is given to the primary engagement with the literary work. Approaches that examine the process of reading and interpretation itself—using the techniques of stylistics, psychology, or cognitive science—also tend to operate at a remove from this experience, whatever their analytic value may be.

There is, however, a very important qualification to be made to this account. If reading a work as literature means making the most of the event of reading, an event by which our habits and assumptions are tested and shifted (if only momentarily), then part of the literary experience may be *the event of the allegorizing reading*. In a similar way, the event of the historicizing or psychologizing reading may be an element in that experience, although the historical or the psychological facts arrived at are only secondary, elements in a different type of reading. In other words, one may be doing justice to the singularity and inventiveness of a literary work by responding to its invitation to allegorize, to its quality of what we might call "allegoricity," because in so doing we are working through the operations of its meaning—irrespective of whether we arrive at some stable allegorical scheme. Allegory may thus be *staged* in literature, along with so many other aspects of the way we make sense of the world.[40] The reader may become conscious of the power and allure of allegory, of the temptation to generalize or codify meaning, and at the same time gain a heightened awareness of the specificity and contingency of language and human experience as these resist such generalizations and codifications.[41] In fact, a responsive reading of a literary work will always

40. The list of what can be staged or performed in literature—all the various ways in which language works in our ears, on our bodies, and in the world—is potentially endless, including truth, knowledge, goodness, beauty, representation, objectivity, and meaning. For further discussion, see Attridge, *The Singularity of Literature*, chap. 8.

41. The temptation of allegory is something that is staged in "He and His Man," Coetzee's Nobel lecture, in which the returned Robinson Crusoe rather wildly interprets a variety of incidents as allegories of his past life as a castaway. Even wilder is the state of frenzied allegorizing described by Elizabeth, Lady Chandos, in the "Postscript" to *Elizabeth Costello*, and cited in the epigraph to this chapter.

be alert to the possibility of allegorical meaning, to the constant leaking of meaning away from the literal. Given the extensive suffering caused in South Africa by dehumanizing codifications, it is perhaps not surprising that many of its writers, including Coetzee, have staged the allegorizing process in their works.[42]

The history of literary criticism contains many examples of literal reading, and many literary critics have advocated an approach to the text that does justice to the event of its performance. (The present moment, however, is one in which the focus, in teaching and discussing literature in academic contexts, seems to be elsewhere.) My comments on the passages I have selected could, for the most part, have come from critical works written forty or fifty years ago. Yet this is not a call to turn the clock back. Although a revisiting of some of the literary commentary of Richards, Leavis, Empson, Wimsatt, Brooks, Burke, Rosenblatt, and many others is overdue, there are limitations and omissions in this earlier work that have become visible as a result of subsequent developments in both criticism and literary production. The various chapters of this book are intended to suggest some of the constituents of a close reading that takes account of these developments, including an openness to alterity, an acknowledgment of the historical and cultural situatedness of both writing and reading, a responsiveness to the work as invention, a sensitivity to the mediations through which we experience the world, and a registering of the event of the text in a performance of its own stagings of language's multiple powers.

The second level of my argument has to do more specifically with Coetzee's writing, and with *Waiting for the Barbarians* and *Life & Times of Michael K* more particularly. If all literary works demand a literal reading, in the sense in which I am using the term, Coetzee's works yield more richly to this kind of reading than most. Many contrasts with other works would be possible (including all those works, like Spenser's *Faerie Queene,* Mann's *Doktor Faustus,* or Solzhenitsyn's *The First Circle,* where reading for the allegory, as well as for the experience of allegoricity, is crucial), but let me just mention one of the few novels by a South African novelist that can match Coetzee's in brilliance and importance: Zoë Wicomb's *David's Story.* This is a novel that involves us, through supple and focused writing, in a moving sequence of felt events taking us into unfamiliar

---

42. Another South African writer who stages the process of allegorizing in memorable fiction is Ivan Vladislavic, in his novels *The Folly* and, in the post-apartheid era, *The Restless Supermarket.*

territory—moments in the experience of a woman participating in a male-dominated liberation struggle, for example, or of a man re-living the endeavors of his forebears to found a nation. But its importance also lies in the contribution it makes to our understanding of South African history, not just by rehearsing some little-known facts but by conveying their significance through the immediacy of the writing and characterization. We are not only informed about but given a way of engaging with and emotionally relating to the nomadic existence of the Griqua people as they strive to forge an identity and a viable home, or to the sometimes brutal treatment of women in the ANC during the fight for freedom. Although the novel achieves what it achieves as literature, its importance is finally not only literary.

I'm not sure one could say the same of Coetzee's work, though such claims have often been made. The significance of *Age of Iron*, for instance, seems to me much less as a portrayal of the 1980s in South Africa than as an invitation to participate in, and be moved by, a very specific narrative: if we learn from it, what we learn is not about South Africa (or, to take the opposite kind of allegorical interpretation, about death and love and commitment), it's not a "what" at all, it's a how: how a person with a particular background might experience terminal illness, violent political oppression, the embrace of someone who is entirely other. *Disgrace*, to take another case, was immediately read as a depiction of, and bleak comment on, post-apartheid South Africa; but this, to me, is an allegorical reading that must remain secondary to the singular evocation of the peculiar mental and emotional world of an individual undergoing a traumatic episode in his life, challenging us to loosen our own habitual frameworks and ways of reading and judging.[43] This is not to claim that the historical and political dimensions of these novels are somehow irrelevant; on the contrary, the intensely particularized representation of South Africa (or rather the Cape) in several of the novels, and in the memoirs, is a major ingredient in a literal reading, which involves a constant testing of, and by, the ethical dilemmas that arise from those particulars.

I am not against allegory, then, in spite of this chapter's title; allegorical readings of many kinds have been and will continue to be of the greatest

43. See McDonald's discussion of the novel in "*Disgrace* Effects," and chapter 7 below. Gareth Cornwell, though he contends that all Coetzee's fictions "are essentially allegorical rather than mimetic plots," speaks of these two modes as operating in *Disgrace* "in a relationship of negotiation or mutual interrogation" ("Realism, Rape, and J. M. Coetzee's *Disgrace*," 320). I would argue that this holds true of all of Coetzee's novels.

significance, ranging from allegories of actual history (where a novel is read as if it were about real people, places, and events) to universal allegories (where the novel is read as if were about abstractions). But I am *for* reading as an event, for restraining the urge to leave the text, or rather the experience of the text, behind (an urge that becomes especially powerful when we have to produce words about it), for opening oneself to the text's forays beyond the doxa. If Coetzee's novels and memoirs exemplify anything, it is the value (but also the risk) of openness to the moment and to the future, of the perhaps and the wherever. Allegory, one might say, deals with the *already known,* whereas literature opens a space for the other. Allegory announces a moral code, literature invites an ethical response.

Notice, however, that I am not saying that in order to understand a work as allegory, we have first to experience it as literary, as if allegorical reading were a secondary mode entirely dependent on the primary, literal, mode. This claim is often made about literary allegory in an attempt to save it for literature, but cultural history shows that it's perfectly possible to apprehend allegorical meanings without paying any attention to the aesthetic subtlety or emotional force of a work of art. Reading allegory as such is a quite different activity from reading literature, even though both can be appropriate for a single work.

In presenting this argument, I take my lead from Coetzee's writing: not only from the rewards to be gained from reading his work in this way, but from the experiences of allegorizing that it invites us to participate in but also to judge—whether it be the mythography of Eugene Dawn, the interpretations sought by the Magistrate and the medical officer, the grand allegory of apartheid whose effects are depicted so bleakly in *Age of Iron,* or the accountability demanded by the university authorities in *Disgrace.* Coetzee ended his inaugural lecture as a professor at the University of Cape Town by asking by what privilege criticism claims to tell the truth of literature, the truth which literature cannot tell itself. Perhaps literary criticism, he suggested, cannot afford to say "why it wants the literary text to stand there in all its ignorance, side by side with the radiant truth of the text supplied by criticism, without the latter supplanting the former."[44] His novels demand, and deserve, responses that do not claim to tell their truths, but ones that participate in their inventive openings.

44. "Truth in Autobiography," 6.

CHAPTER THREE

The Silence of the Canon

Foe

> In the last corner, under the transoms, half buried in sand, his knees drawn up, his hands between his thighs, I come to Friday.
>
> I tug his woolly hair, finger the chain about his throat. "Friday," I say, I try to say, kneeling over him, sinking hands and knees into the ooze, "what is this ship?"
>
> But this is not a place of words. Each syllable, as it comes out, is caught and filled with water and diffused. This is a place where bodies are their own signs. It is the home of Friday.
>
> He turns and turns till he lies at full length, his face to my face. The skin is tight across his bones, his lips are drawn back. I pass a fingernail across his teeth, trying to find a way in.
>
> His mouth opens. From inside him comes a slow stream, without breath, without interruption. It flows up through his body and out upon me; it passes through the cabin, through the wreck; washing the cliffs and shores of the island, it runs northward and southward to the ends of the earth. Soft and cold, dark and unending, it beats against my eyelids, against the skin of my face. (157)

The final paragraphs of *Foe* achieve their power in large measure as a result of their relation to what has gone before, though even out of context they convey something of the resonating quality of Coetzee's distinctive style in this novel. Precise, vividly physical, but seldom contained within the conventions of realistic description as developed through the eighteenth and nineteenth centuries, this style achieves its distinctive effects partly by means of the half-heard echoing of the literary tradition it thereby claims association with. Here, for example, the first two scenes of *The Tempest,* with their memorable blending of loss and salvation, though never quite quoted, shimmer through the writing. The passage contains a number of words that occur, some of them several times, in these two Shakespearean scenes, all of them in speeches having to do with shipwreck: "sink," "ooze," "ship," "water," "cabin," "wreck," "washing," "shore," "island," "earth." But the allusiveness remains uncertain because these *are* single words. How can a single word be a quotation? One or two longer verbal fragments from these scenes may drift into the back of the reader's mind as well: "What, must our mouths be cold?," "Would thou mightst lie drowning / The washing of ten tides!," " 'Tis beating in my mind," "Full fathom five thy father lies, / Of his bones are coral made."[1] Echoes other than Shakespearean ones play about the passage too, such as the Book of Common Prayer's version of Psalm 45, which also concerns fears of shipwreck and the hope of safety: "Thou that art the hope of all the ends of the earth, and of them that remain in the broad sea." That note of hope will also be evoked for any reader who recalls the "gentle breeze" which, in the opening of Wordsworth's *Prelude,* "beats against my cheek / And seems half-conscious of the joy it gives."

There is also in this closing passage a continuation of the delicate play between a contemporary and an earlier literary style that characterizes all of *Foe.* An older rhetorical mode can be heard in the rhythmic and syntactic repetitions, many of them involving a successive phrasal lengthening— "I say, I try to say"; "without breath, without interruption"; "through the cabin, through the wreck"; "it flows . . . ; it passes . . . ; . . . it runs"; "against my eyelids, against the skin of my face"—and in the slight archaisms, like the prepositions "about" and "upon." The five qualifying phrases

---

1. One could extend the verbal similarities to other parts of these two scenes, such as Miranda's reference to the "words" which Caliban has learned, Ariel's promise to obey Prospero "to th' syllable," or even—by implication—Prospero's phrase "the fringed curtains of thine eye"; but this would probably be more a product of conscious critical labor than an intertextual effect to which readers may respond without even being aware of it. As will emerge in the course of this chapter, *The Tempest*'s status as one of the founding literary texts of English colonialist attitudes is also highly relevant to Coetzee's novel.

with which the passage begins—before the main clause of the sentence is reached—are also part of this highly deliberate and carefully paced rhetoric. But it is only when the passage is read as the conclusion of the novel that the force of this image and of these stylistic nuances can be fully felt; the narrator of the closing section (what name do we use?—Susan Barton, Daniel Foe, Daniel Defoe, J. M. Coetzee, our own?) has made the last of many attempts to get Friday to speak, and the hauntingly allusive description of the soundless stream issuing from his body is a culmination of the book's concern with the powerful silence which is the price of our cultural achievements.

I begin at the end because what I wish to do is to read back, back from this representation of a speechless speech endlessly covering the world to the ways in which Coetzee's words—and silences—are and are not heard by the institutions of our literary culture. The question I wish to address is that of access to the canon: what does it mean for novels like Coetzee's to claim canonic status, or for critics to make such a claim on their behalf? (That the phrase "novels like Coetzee's" is problematic is indicative of one dimension of the question itself.) What does it mean, culturally and politically, for this claim to succeed or fail?

If we characterize canonization in a fairly straightforward way, as widespread recognition within the institutions of publication and education that a body of texts by a single author constitutes an "important," "serious," "lasting" contribution to "literature" (a characterization I shall considerably complicate in due course), there can be no doubt that Co-etzee has been canonized. His eight novels and two memoirs are widely available in prestigious paperback editions, and among them they have won numerous literary awards. He was the first writer to win the Booker Prize twice (for *Michael K* and for *Disgrace*), and he was more and more frequently mentioned as a possible Nobel Prize winner until 2003, when he finally received the award. The present study is the eighth book to appear on his work (a number of others are in the offing), and there have been several special issues of journals on his novels.[2] Critical articles and

2. Teresa Dovey, *The Novels of J. M. Coetzee* (1988); Dick Penner, *Countries of the Mind* (1989); Marianne de Jong, ed., "J. M. Coetzee's *Foe,*" special issue of *Journal of Literary Studies* (1989); Susan VanZanten Gallagher, *A Story of South Africa* (1991); David Attwell, *J. M. Coetzee* (1993); Michael Moses, ed., "The Writings of J. M. Coetzee," special issue of *South Atlantic Quarterly* (1994); Graham Huggan and Stephen Watson, eds., *Critical Perspectives on J. M. Coetzee* (1996); Dominic Head, *J. M. Coetzee* (1997); Sue Kossew, ed., *Critical Essays on J. M. Coetzee* (1998); André Viola, *J. M. Coetzee* (1999); Derek Attridge and Peter D. McDonald, eds., "J. M. Coetzee's *Disgrace,*" special issue of *Interventions*

parts of books on his fiction abound, and his novels appear regularly on high school, college, and university syllabi. There is no sign that the critical flood will abate any time soon.

In South Africa itself, where Coetzee lived until 2002, the standing of the novels during the apartheid era was affected by the degree to which they were perceived as hostile to the policies and practices of apartheid—and by the significance of this perception to different groups within the country. On the one hand they were subject to official scrutiny and delays, and ignored by the state-controlled media, but were not, like some more obviously antigovernment works, banned;[3] on the other hand they were championed by some of those opposed to government policies, but attacked by others for failing to engage directly in the political struggle. Since the advent of democratic rule in South Africa, negative reactions to Coetzee's work have been less in evidence (although *Disgrace* did provoke a flurry of disquiet).[4] I shall return later to this complex array of responses.

What is it about these novels that has propelled them so rapidly into the English literary canon? The answers to this question are no doubt many and diverse; since canonization depends on the convergence of a multitude of separate decisions and actions, it is bound to be overdetermined. But one answer we have already glimpsed would be that through their allusiveness the novels offer themselves not as challenges to the canon, but as canonic—as already canonized, one might say. They appear to locate themselves within an established literary culture, rather than presenting themselves as an assault on that culture. Moreover, that literary culture is predominantly European, and clearly "high." Sometimes the allusions are more overt than those in the last paragraph of *Foe,* and run the risk

---

(2002); Symposium on *Disgrace* in *scrutiny2* (2002). Viola mentions two French special issues on Coetzee of the journals *Commonwealth* (Dijon, 1992) and *Les Cahiers FORELL* (Poitiers, 1994). Forthcoming volumes include studies by Kai Easton and Kim Worthington and a collection of essays edited by Jane Poyner.

3. In a 1985 interview with Claude Wauthier in *Le Nouvel Observateur,* Coetzee comments on the fact that *Waiting for the Barbarians* and *Michael K* were not subject to the banning which the works of black writers in particular suffered, but were held up by customs delays. He goes on to observe that there are more subtle modes of pressure, such as the total overlooking by South African radio and television of writers hostile to apartheid. In two revealing articles, Peter D. McDonald has examined the newly available censors' reports on Coetzee's novels; see "Not Undesirable" and "The Writer, the Critic, and the Censor."

4. See David Attwell, "Race in *Disgrace*" and McDonald, "*Disgrace* Effects" for discussions of the repercussions of the novel in South Africa.

of appearing as intrusive attempts to claim membership of the existing tradition.

I have mentioned Jacobus Coetzee's citation of Blake, and discussed the way the narrator of *In the Heart of the Country* weaves into her text the words of canonic writers, and hears, or believes she hears, fragments of the Western cultural encyclopedia descending to her from passing aircraft. *Waiting for the Barbarians* takes its title, and one aspect of its sociopolitical dynamic, from a poem by Cavafy,[5] and alludes as well to Beckett's best-known play; while the name of the central character in *Life & Times of Michael K,* often referred to just as "K," cannot, as we noted in chapter 2, fail to recall Kafka. However, it was in *Foe* that Coetzee made canonic intertextuality a fundamental principle: its manner of proceeding is to rewrite, and fuse together, the biography of Daniel Defoe and those of several of Defoe's fictional characters. The perpetuation of any canon is dependent in part on the references made to its earlier members by its later members (or would-be members); and in this respect Coetzee's novels could be said to presuppose and to reproduce the canonic status of their predecessors while claiming to join them.[6]

It might be argued that a further claim to belong to an existing canonic tradition is exerted by the *style* of Coetzee's novels; as the closing passage of *Foe* also demonstrates, the deliberate, chiseled prose has little to do with the exorbitance or casualness (however studied) by which texts we might characterize as "postmodern" frequently affront the traditional valorization of literary form. If Joyce is one of Coetzee's stylistic forebears, it is the Joyce who created the "scrupulous meanness" of *Dubliners;* more obvious are the stylistic affinities with Beckett, especially the meticulous prose, the present tense, the isolated figures, of the Trilogy. Here, for instance, is a sentence from *In the Heart of the Country* that, apart from its South African references, could easily have come from one of Beckett's first-person prose narratives: "I would have no qualm, I am sure, if it came to the pinch, though how it could come to this pinch I do not know, about living in a mud hut, or indeed under a lean-to of branches, out in the veld, eating chickenfeed, talking to the insects" (6).

---

5. Cavafy, *Collected Poems,* 30–33.

6. In the later novels, some motivation for the allusive style is provided by the occupations of the central characters whose thoughts are being reflected—teachers of literature (Mrs. Curren in *Age of Iron,* David Lurie in *Disgrace*) and a writer of canonical literary works (Dostoevsky in *The Master of Petersburg*). This shift is in keeping with the greater reliance on realist techniques in these novels.

Coetzee's is writing which invites the reader to savor it, sentence by sentence, word by word, for its economy and efficiency; and although the style of each novel has its own unmistakable character, the reader receives the consistent impression in all of them that words have been chosen with extraordinary care. In fact, as with the use of allusions and citations, the very deliberateness of this highly literary language may for some tastes smack too obviously of canonic pretensions.

Also interpretable as consistent with the traditional humanist concerns of the canon is the novels' *thematic* focus: for instance, they return again and again to the solitary individual in a hostile human and physical environment to raise crucial questions about the foundations of civilization and humanity. The American military propagandist pushed into madness and the hunter-explorer clinging to life in the inhospitable interior; the self-tormenting farmer's daughter alone with her father's corpse on the isolated farm; the well-meaning state official enduring himself the barbarism on which his "civilization" depends; the nomadic victim of a violent society surviving on the margins of death; the elderly, dying woman driven out of her house by the thugs of the apartheid state; the debt-ridden writer driven to the limits of sanity by personal and political demands; the disgraced academic devoting his life to the putting down and burning of dogs: these figures may appear as so many versions of Lear's experience on the heath, one poor, bare, forked animal after another. Or one might emphasize, as I did in chapter 1, the repeated motif of masters (or mistresses) and servants—also important in *King Lear,* of course, and, in its yoking of a moral discourse of human bonds and rights with an actual relationship that combines economic exploitation and personal intimacy, a recurrent source of tension in the bourgeois conscience and the novels which represent it. Once again, it is *Foe* which foregrounds this relation to the tradition: not only is *The Tempest,* with its questioning of the place and obligations of the human in the nonhuman or partly human world, present in the background (Caliban is clearly one of the ancestors of Friday), but the novel of which *Foe* is a rewriting, *Robinson Crusoe,* is probably Western culture's most potent crystallization of its concern with the survival of the individual, the fundamentals of civilized life, and the dialectic of master and servant.

This account of the canonic claim made by the novels themselves, and by *Foe* in particular, needs to be complemented by factors external to the writing which also bear on the question of canonization. As a white male (like Daniel Defoe), Coetzee has a degree of privileged access to most canons, and as a South African, especially one who chose during the apartheid years to remain in South Africa, he possesses a certain

mystique: that country, for all its geographical marginality to the canonization processes of Western culture, has a notorious centrality in the
contemporary political and ethical imagination that gives its writers a special claim on the world's attention. There is, of course, another side to this
advantage. It brings with it the danger that writing emanating from South
Africa will be read *only* as a reflection of or a resistance to a particular
political situation,[7] whereas the high literary canon, in its most traditional
form, is premised upon an assumption of universal moral and aesthetic
values. But Coetzee's works seem expressly designed to escape that danger: of his eight novels, only four-and-a-half are set in South Africa, and
in all but two of these cases it is a South Africa distanced, by temporal
or geographical displacement, from the one we read about in the newspapers. An apologist for the traditional canon might argue that Coetzee's
novels are not about the South African situation per se, which would render them contingent and propagandist, but about the permanent human
truths exemplified in that situation.[8]

Within South Africa, however, this departicularization has often rendered Coetzee subject to the argument that he has abused his privileges
as a member of the white elite in addressing not the immediate needs of
his time but a mystified human totality. If the account I have given of his
work's amenability to canonization is accurate and complete, this critique
must stand as valid. The unproblematized notion of a canon is complicit
with a mode of literature—and of criticism—which dehistoricizes and
dematerializes the acts of writing and reading while promoting a myth
of transcendent human truths and values. By the same token, however,
a mode of fiction which exposed the ideological basis of canonization,
which drew attention to its own relation to the existing canon, which
thematized the role of race, class, and gender in the processes of cultural
acceptance and exclusion, and which, while speaking from a marginal

---

7. Asked during an interview by Tony Morphet, apropos of *Michael K*, "Did you conceive
of the novel as in any way a task presented to you by history—the history of South Africa
specifically?" Coetzee replied: "Perhaps that is my fate. On the other hand, I sometimes
wonder whether it isn't simply that vast and wholly ideological superstructure constituted
by publishing, reviewing and criticism that is forcing on me the fate of being a 'South African
novelist'" ("Two Interviews," 460). An interesting light is shone on this question in *Elizabeth
Costello*, when the Australian novelist is asked her opinion about the extermination of
the Tasmanian aborigines, and she answers that she writes only in response to the voices
who summon her—whether these be of the murdered and violated or their murderers and
violators (202–4).

8. As I noted in chapter 2, the appeal to allegory has frequently been used to universalize
the themes of the novels.

location, addressed the question of marginality—such a mode of fiction would have to be seen as participating in the struggle to achieve a voice for those who have been silenced, even if it did so by literary means that have traditionally been celebrated as characterizing canonic art. A more careful reading of Coetzee's novels, I would argue, shows just these qualities.

: II :

Foe came as something of a disappointment to many readers and reviewers.[9] Coetzee's previous novel, *Life & Times of Michael K,* allowed itself to be read as, to quote the Penguin paperback's blurb, a "life-affirming novel" that "goes to the center of human experience," seeming to confirm those elements in *Waiting for the Barbarians* which could be taken as expressions of a spiritual and moral truth beyond politics or culturally determined structures of signification. Moreover, *Michael K* satisfied those who wanted Coetzee to deal more directly with the struggle against racist oppression in South Africa, while avoiding the adoption of a narrowly based political position.[10] But *Foe* is not only temporally and geographically further removed from the South Africa of its time of writing than its predecessor; it has no character whose interior life is depicted in such a way as to evoke the reader's moral sympathy (as the Magistrate's and K's do in the previous novels), and it seems to lack evidence of what one reviewer called, in discussing *Michael K,* Coetzee's "tender and unwavering faith in the individual."[11]

Instead of taking *Foe* as a swerve away from a clear and established mode of fiction and set of values, however, it is worth asking whether it

9. Thus George Parker asserted in *The Nation* that *Foe* was a "wrong, if interesting step" in a novel-writing career concerned with "the fate of conscience in the face of its own oppressive power," while Nina Auerbach, writing in *The New Republic,* complained that the new novel "never quite comes to life." In South Africa, the hostility was, if anything, more marked: Neil Darke of the *Argus* (Cape Town) found the novel "often pointless, incomprehensible and tiresome," and one G. H., in the *Natal Mercury,* called it "a literary indulgence likely to prove too oblique for any but the converted to contend with, and to estrange even some of these."

10. The role of South African politics in the novel is far from simple: as we have seen, the opposing forces in the war are never identified, and there are no overt mentions of racial conflict.

11. Alan Ryan, in the *Cleveland Plain Dealer;* cited on the jacket of the 1987 Viking Edition of *Foe.*

can provide a perspective from which to reexamine Coetzee's novels and their pertinence to the canon and to contemporary political and cultural life. We may do this by returning to the three qualities of Coetzee's writing that I mentioned earlier, and by scrutinizing more carefully the argument that they constitute a straightforward, if dangerously self-conscious, claim to canonic status.

Although the overt intertextuality in Coetzee's novels can, as I have suggested, be read as an implicit claim to a place in the established canon, it is also possible to regard it as drawing attention to the way the text, like any text, is *manufactured* from the resources of a particular culture in order to gain acceptance within that culture, an operation that canonic works, and those who uphold the canon as an unproblematic reflection of inherent values, cannot fully acknowledge. (The most powerful upholders of the canon are, of course, those who do not acknowledge such a concept at all.) In *Foe* this process becomes inescapably evident, as the larger part of the novel consists of a memoir and several letters written by the newly returned castaway Susan Barton to the well-known author Daniel Foe, quotation marks before each of her paragraphs reminding us constantly that this is not the mysterious immaterial language most fiction uses as its medium, nor even a representation of speech, but a representation *in* writing *of* writing. And it is presented not as a simple day-to-day record of experience, as in a novel of letters or diary-entries, but for the explicit purpose of proffering a narrative—the story of Barton's year on an island with another, earlier, castaway named Robinson Cruso—for insertion into the canon of published English texts.

When, toward the end of the novel, the quotation marks disappear, the reader is forced to ask questions which fiction seldom invites: on what occasion and by what means are *these* words now being produced, and to what audience are they being directed? Moreover, the intertextuality of *Foe* works to unsettle any simple relation between historical report and fictional invention. The Cruso we encounter in this novel appears as the historical original of the fictional Crusoe we already know from our access to the canon,[12] yet even within the novel he is part of Susan Barton's narrative, which is clearly to some extent—but how much, and

---

12. The spelling "Cruso" is that used by the Norwich family in the hosiery business which was Defoe's most likely source for his hero's name (see Bastian, *Defoe's Early Life*, 90). Alexander Selkirk—the acknowledged model for *Robinson Crusoe*—has no place in Coetzee's narrative, though Barton does speculate on Foe's possession of "a multitude of castaway narratives, most of them, I would guess, riddled with lies" (50).

how deliberately?—a work of fiction on her part. At the same time, Barton herself is troubled by the repeated appearance of a girl claiming to be her daughter, whose reality, within the fictional world, is thrown into question by the reader's awareness that her story, and that of her maid Amy who often accompanies her, is told in another of Defoe's novels, *Roxana*.[13] From this perspective, the quotations in *In the Heart of the Country* and the name "Michael K" seem less like somewhat intrusive claims to belong to a tradition of great writing than determined reminders—working against the skillfully contrived immediacy of the narrators' thoughts—that all cultural work is a reworking, that all representations achieve vividness by exploiting culturally specific conventions and contexts.

Turning to the second claim to canonicity proposed above, Coetzee's chiseled style can be seen not as a bid for admission to the pantheon of great writers but as drawing attention to itself in a way that undermines the illusion of pure expression; the slight self-consciousness of its shaped sentences—what one critic has aptly described as "that style forever on its guard against itself"[14]—goes hand-in-hand with the intertextual allusiveness to reinforce the awareness that all representation is mediated through the discourses that culture provides. Certainly by the time we reach *Foe* in a traversal of Coetzee's oeuvre it is no longer possible to regard this quality of the writing as an inadvertent one, an inability to achieve total unselfconscious limpidity. Whereas in the earlier novels a reader might decide that the echoes of Beckett's style are an excusable failure to evade a powerful precursor rather than a calculated effect, the tinges of eighteenth-century diction that characterize the language of *Foe* cannot be anything other than a distancing device rendering us conscious of the artifact we have before us—a device which, remarkably, does not diminish the writing's capacity to produce for the reader a powerful experience of reality. Reading is usually a more complex process than we allow for in our theories of it, and one of the pleasures of reading Coetzee is realizing this—and realizing that this realization need not spoil our more traditional literary pleasures. (The alternative versions of Klawer's death in "The Narrative of Jacobus Coetzee" and of Magda's rape in *In the Heart of the Country* discussed in chapter 1 may seem guaranteed

13. The hero of Defoe's *Colonel Jack* also makes an appearance in Coetzee's novel as the young pickpocket employed by Foe. Clearly, "the reader" alluded to here is one well versed in Defoe's fiction: Coetzee exploits the canon's lack of definite boundaries by using allusions that range from the familiar to the scholarly. The novel does not depend upon the recognition of all its allusions by a single reader, however.

14. Peter Strauss, "Coetzee's Idylls," 128.

to shatter any sense of immediacy in the first-person accounts that they claim to be; yet many readers have testified that there is no loss of the traditional power of storytelling in these works.)

Lastly, with regard to the thematic concerns of Coetzee's fictions, one finds that whatever accommodation was possible between the earlier novels and the humanist tradition, the isolated individuals in *Foe* function—as I hope to demonstrate—not as representatives of the motif of naked humanity granted universal insight on the stormy heath, but as compelling subversions of this motif. They demonstrate that what we call "insights" are produced and conveyed by the narrativizing agencies of culture; experience in itself is insufficient to gain credit as knowledge or truth. Even if the transmutation of experience into knowledge occurs in the privacy of the individual consciousness, it does so by virtue of internalized cultural norms, of which each of us is a repository; but without external validation, such "knowledge" must remain uncertain and insubstantial.

: III :

Every writer who desires to be read (and that is perhaps part of what it means to write) has to seek admittance to the canon—or, more precisely, *a* canon, since any group approval of a text is an instance of canonization. Like languages, canons are not monolithic entities but complex, interrelated, and constantly changing systems which can be subdivided all the way down to individual preferences (idiocanons, we might call them). Awareness of this necessity, conscious or not, governs the act of writing quite as much as the need for self-expression or the wish to communicate. What *Foe* suggests is that the same imperative drives our self-presentations and representations; unless we are read, we are nothing. And taking together the features of this and Coetzee's other novels that I have discussed, it would seem that it is not possible to separate the processes of canonization that operate within the domain of high, or for that matter popular, culture from the very similar processes that operate in our everyday experience; constructing and sustaining an identity, making sense of one's own past, establishing an intelligible relationship with one's fellows, are all in part a matter of telling one's story (the story of who one is, was, and aspires to be) in such a way as to have it accepted and valorized within the body of recognized narratives—with their conventions of plot, character, symbolization, moralization, etc.—that are part of the cultural fabric, and therefore part of our individual systems of judgment and interpretation.

Acceptance into the canon is not merely a matter of success in the marketplace: it confers *value,* although the value it confers is necessarily understood as not conferred and contingent but inherent and permanent. What is unusual about *Foe* is the way that it simultaneously seeks admittance to the literary canon on these terms *and* draws attention to the canon's cultural and historical contingency, just as Barton, in seeking cultural acceptance for her story and through it an assertion of her unique subjectivity, shows an increasing awareness of the double bind which this implies.

If we extend the meaning of "canonization" to include these wider processes of legitimation, it might be said that the novel dramatizes the procedures and problems of canonization four times over. Cruso, who shows none of the practical ingenuity or the spiritual intensity we expect from the figure of bourgeois resourcefulness we are familiar with, has, by his isolation from culture, lost touch with its founding narratives and need for narrative: not only has he rescued very little from the wreck and made only minimal attempts to improve the quality of his life, he has kept no journal (he doesn't even mark the days on a notched stick as they pass) and has no desire to leave the island. He spends most of his time leveling the island's hill into terraces—a parodic version of the canonic castaway's taming of nature, since he has nothing with which to plant them. Most interesting for my present argument is that he appears to have lost any firm sense of the distinction between truth and fiction. Barton writes to Foe (I keep the quotation marks, since they play an important part in our experience of the text):

> "I would gladly now recount to you the history of this singular Cruso, as I heard it from his own lips. But the stories he told me were so various, and so hard to reconcile one with another, that I was more and more driven to conclude age and isolation had taken their toll on his memory, and he no longer knew for sure what was truth, what fancy." (11–12)

To her exhortation to Cruso to write a narrative of his experiences he makes two replies: "Nothing is forgotten" and "Nothing I have forgotten is worth the remembering" (17).

Barton herself, by contrast, feels that she lacks substance as an individual until the story of her year on the island with Cruso (who dies on the return journey) is written as a legitimated narrative, yet is barred from the domain of authorship by her gender, her social status, her economic dependence, and her unfamiliarity with the requirements of the canon of published narratives. It is not merely that publication of her story will bring fame and money; she has an obscure sense that her experience will remain lacking in reality until it is told as a publicly validated narrative:

> "Return to me the substance I have lost, Mr Foe: that is my entreaty. For though my story gives the truth, it does not give the substance of the truth (I see that clearly, we need not pretend it is otherwise). To tell the truth in all its substance you must have quiet, and a comfortable chair away from all distraction, and a window to stare through; and then the knack of seeing waves when there are fields before your eyes, and of feeling the tropic sun when it is cold; and at your fingertips the words with which to capture the vision before it fades. I have none of these, while you have all." (51–52)

When Foe goes into hiding from his creditors, she waits for his return, reminding him that her life is "drearily suspended till your writing is done" (63), and later takes up residence in his empty house. But the longer she waits, the more conscious she becomes that to depend for her identity on a process of writing is to cast doubt on that identity: "In the beginning I thought I would tell you the story of the island and, being done with that, return to my former life. But now all my life grows to be story and there is nothing of my own left to me" (133). (One curious, but relevant, effect of Coetzee's strategy is that, for all the vivid first-person writing, Susan Barton does have an aura of insubstantiality, precisely because of the canonic success and consequent power of Defoe's novel.)

Our third dramatization of the processes of canonization occurs with Foe, the professional author, who makes little progress with Barton's story of her experiences on the island; he thinks of including it as one episode in the longer story of a woman in search of her daughter, or spicing it with additional material about cannibals and battles. She insists that he should concentrate exclusively on the story of the island, although she becomes increasingly aware of its unsuitability for the established canon:

> "I am growing to understand why you wanted Cruso to have a musket and be besieged by cannibals. I thought it was a sign you had no regard for the truth. I forgot you are a writer who knows above all how many words can be sucked from a cannibal feast, how few from a woman cowering from the wind. It is all a matter of words and the number of words, is it not?" (94)

To assess how much rewriting Barton's story of the island requires in order to render it fit for the developing bourgeois canon of the early eighteenth century we need only turn from Coetzee's novel to the novel published in 1719 as *The Life and Strange Surprising Adventures of Robinson Crusoe* by Daniel Defoe, the more aristocratic name adopted by plain Daniel Foe in 1695 as part of *his* campaign to be admitted to the British canon.[15] One of the striking absences from Defoe's highly successful novel, of course, is that of any female voice: the gender requirements of acceptable narrative forms allow for women heroines in certain roles (the entrepreneur in larceny and marriage exemplified by *Moll Flanders,* for instance), but these appear not to include stories of the mastering of natural forces and the colonizing of primitive cultures.[16] Within Coetzee's novel, Foe's decision to exclude Susan Barton from his published narrative altogether is not represented; but we do witness how the professional author is much more attracted to Barton's own story before and after the period on the island, involving her lost daughter, and, we are encouraged to suspect from several hints thrown out, the colorful life of a courtesan. In other words, Susan Barton's story—the one she does not want told—becomes Defoe's novel *Roxana.*[17]

15. The events of *Foe* are not securely located at an identifiable moment in Defoe's life. It is likely that he went into hiding from his creditors for a period in 1692, but Susan Barton has read *A True Relation of the Apparition of One Mrs. Veal* (written, she says, "long ago" [134]), Defoe's vivid report of the appearance of a ghost to a Canterbury woman in September 1705, which he published soon after the event. He was still trying to satisfy his creditors in 1706, and when he left for Scotland on a secret mission for Harley's ministry in that year he allowed a story to circulate that he was fleeing because of debts (see John Robert Moore, *Daniel Defoe,* 97). However, *Robinson Crusoe* (his first substantial work of fiction, received by many as a factual report) was not published until 1719. Moreover, in imagining the papers which lie in Foe's chest, Barton describes materials on which a number of Defoe's works *after Robinson Crusoe* were based (50), and she mentions on more than one occasion the tales of thieves, courtesans, and grenadiers he has worked on, characters in his flourishing career as a writer of fiction. Another inconsistency is that Defoe's wife outlived him, whereas Foe is said to be widowed (62). One effect of this chronological uncertainty, germane to the novel's concerns, is that it remains unclear whether Foe's reputation is as a reporter of fact or, as was the case only later in Defoe's career, a creator of fiction.

16. I do not mean to suggest that the properties of texts accepted by the canon are wholly determined in advance. Defoe is a good example of a writer whose work, while it clearly answered to a growing need arising from changing economic and social conditions, played its own part, once it was admitted, in transforming the literary canon. Some degree of resistance to canonic demands can itself be a canonic requirement: I have already suggested that a possible disability of Coetzee's novels is that they may appear to conform too obviously to the requirements of the canon.

17. Roxana's real name is mentioned once in that novel: it is Susan, as is that of the daughter who haunts her and who is murdered by her maid Amy (205). (No surname is given for either of the Susans.) The daughter in *Foe* says that her name is also Susan Barton, and her account of her mother's desertion by a husband who was a brewer (76) tallies with the events of *Roxana.*

It would be misleading to suggest that the novel uses a range of characters to lay out neatly a number of different attitudes to canonic narrative; it is itself a narrative that offers strong resistance to the masterful reader or critic, frequently becoming opaque just when a systematic or allegorical meaning seems to be emerging. But it may be possible to think of Cruso and Foe as opposites, one who no longer has any use for narrative, and the other who lives for, and through, narrative. Susan Barton, who, for all we are allowed to know, might be the author of the narratives of both Cruso and Foe, is aware of the constituting capacities of narrative and the emptiness of existence outside her culture's canonic stories, yet irresistibly (and understandably) attached to the notion of a subjectivity and substantiality which does not have to be grounded in the conventions of narrative. She explains to Foe why she pursues him, instead of finding employment:

> "I could return in every respect to the life of a substantial body, the life you recommend. But such a life is abject. It is the life of a thing. A whore used by men is used as a substantial body. The waves picked me up and cast me ashore on an island, and a year later the same waves brought a ship to rescue me, and of the true story of that year, the story as it should be seen in God's great scheme of things, I remain as ignorant as a newborn babe. That is why I cannot rest, that is why I follow you to your hiding-place like a bad penny." (125–26)

Yet she attempts to resist, as she must, what is implied by this self-perception: that her story is determined not by herself but by the culture within which she seeks an identity. Thus in refusing to tell Foe of her life before the shipwreck, she insists:

> "I choose not to tell it because to no one, not even to you, do I owe proof that I am a substantial being with a substantial history in the world. I choose rather to tell of the island, of myself and Cruso and Friday and what we three did there: for I am a free woman who asserts her freedom by telling her story according to her own desire." (131)

At the end of her long debate with Foe, however, she appears to move toward his position: that there are no distinctions to be made between characters invented by an author and individuals with an independent reality. In answer to Foe's question about the substantiality of the girl claiming to be her daughter, the girl from the pages of *Roxana*, she concedes: "No, she is substantial, as my daughter is substantial, and I am substantial; and you too are substantial, no less and no more than any of us. We are all alive, we are all substantial, we are all in the same world" (152). (For us, of course, that world is the world created by Coetzee's novel.)

Foe might be read, then, as an exploration of a fact that is central to the processes of canonization, in the narrower as much as in the wider sense that I am giving it: human experience seems lacking in substance and significance if it is not represented (to oneself and to others) in culturally validated narrative forms, but those narrative forms constantly threaten, by their exteriority and conventionality, the specificity of that experience. A similar concern could be traced in the other novels—in the different written versions of Jacobus Coetzee's journey beyond the Great River, in the alternative stories Magda tells herself in *In The Heart of the Country,* in the difficulty Michael K has in telling his story, or in Mrs Curren's struggle to articulate the truth of her life. One could thus base these novels' claim to canonic literary status in part on their critique of the traditional unproblematized notion of the canon, showing it to be the reflection of a transcendental humanism oblivious to the role of cultural production and historical materiality. This would suggest one of the ways in which these novels challenge the structures of apartheid, a political and social system whose founding narratives claim to reflect a prior and "natural" truth of racial superiority.

: IV :

But Barton's reluctant conclusion that "we are all substantial, we are all in the same world" may be too hasty; and it is perhaps significant that it is Foe, the author, who raises the possibility of an exception to this generalization: "You have omitted Friday." The presence of this fourth major figure in the novel adds to, and considerably complicates, the portrayal of Coetzee's fiction I have just given; it also constitutes the greatest risk which Coetzee takes in the artistic and ethical project in which he is engaged. It is in the representation of Friday that the novel engages most powerfully with otherness, and resists—or more accurately, invites only to resist—the kind of allegorical reading I discussed in the previous chapter.

One could say that the inner significance of Susan Barton's experience on the island, that she senses but cannot write down and that she hopes (fruitlessly) will emerge when Foe's retelling achieves canonization, is embodied not in her story nor in Cruso's, but in Friday's. Throughout the novel, Friday is presented not in his own terms—we have no sense of what they might be—but as he exists in relation to Susan Barton. Her memoir opens with his appearance to her on the shore of the island, and his carrying her to Cruso's encampment in a "strange backwards embrace" (6), and the narrative of her letters ends with a comparison of her importance to him with that of an unwanted child to a mother who has nevertheless reared it: "I do not love him, but he is mine. That is why he remains in England. That is why he is here" (111).

Friday is a being wholly unfamiliar to her, in terms of race, class, gender, culture. He may be a cannibal. But Friday's story will never be known: he has had his tongue cut out, and cannot even tell the story of the mutilation.[18] His silence, his absolute otherness to her and to her words, is at the heart of Barton's story, both motivating and circumscribing it:

> "On the island I accepted that I should never learn how Friday lost his tongue.... But what we can accept in life we cannot accept in history. To tell my story and be silent on Friday's tongue is no better than offering a book for sale with pages in it quietly left empty. Yet the only tongue that can tell Friday's secret is the tongue he has lost!" (67)

Later she tells Foe, "If the story seems stupid, that is only because it so doggedly holds its silence. The shadow whose lack you feel is there: it is the loss of Friday's tongue" (117).

To put this experience of absolute otherness into words—at least any of the words Barton has been granted by her cultural experience—would be to reappropriate it within the familiar, and to lose exactly that which makes it other, and therefore of the greatest possible significance, to her. She herself articulates this process of appropriation in her debate with Foe:

> "Friday has no command of words and therefore no defence against being re-shaped day by day in conformity with the desires of others. I say he is a cannibal and he becomes a cannibal; I say he is a laundryman and he becomes a laundryman. What is the truth of Friday? You will respond: he is neither cannibal nor laundryman, these are mere names, they do not touch his essence, he is a substantial body, he is himself, Friday is Friday. But that is not so. No matter what he is to himself (is he anything to himself?—how can he tell us?), what he is to the world is what I make him." (121–22)

She has, by this stage in the novel, made strenuous but unsuccessful attempts to teach Friday a language in which he might tell something at

---

18. To be strictly accurate, our only reason for believing that Friday has been mutilated is Barton's report of Cruso's statement to this effect; she herself has no evidence of the cause of Friday's speechlessness, as she finds herself unable to look into his mouth (85).

least of his story; even music proves to be a medium in which nothing approaching communication between the two can occur. Unlike her own silence about her experiences before the island, Friday's silence, she insists in this discussion with Foe, is not a concealment. (The same could be said of her silence about Friday's silence—which is also Coetzee's silence.) Yet its powerful *effects* are everywhere. Barton tells Foe:

> "When I lived in your house I would sometimes lie awake upstairs listening to the pulse of blood in my ears and to the silence from Friday below, a silence that rose up the stairway like smoke, like a welling of black smoke. Before long I could not breathe, I would feel I was stifling in my bed. My lungs, my heart, my head were full of black smoke." (118)

In Foe's view, Friday's silence is simply a riddle that must be solved: "In every story there is a silence, some sight concealed, some word unspoken, I believe. Till we have spoken the unspoken we have not come to the heart of the story" (141). He allegorizes this depth to be plumbed by means of an imaginative interpretation of Friday's mysterious act of paddling out on a log and dropping petals on the surface of the sea, an allegory which Barton takes up and revises, concluding: "It is for us to descend into the mouth (since we speak in figures). It is for us to open Friday's mouth and hear what it holds: silence, perhaps, or a roar, like the roar of a seashell held to the ear" (142). For her, there can be no assurance that all silences will eventually be made to resound with the words of the dominant language, and to tell their stories in canonized narratives. This is not because there is an inviolable core of silence to which the dominant discourse can never penetrate, but because the most fundamental silence is itself produced by—at the same time as it makes possible—the dominant discourse. The wordless stream that closes the novel runs to the ends of the earth, in a moment of loss that is also salvation.

Foe's most telling challenge to the literary canon, therefore, is not its insistence upon cultural construction and validation (an insistence to which we have become accustomed in postmodern writing); it is its representation, through this most powerful of nonrepresentations, of the silence which is constitutive of canonicity itself. All canons rest on exclusion; the voice they give to some can be heard only by virtue of the silence they impose on others. But it is not just a silencing by exclusion, it is a silencing by *inclusion* as well: any voice we can hear is by that very fact purged of its uniqueness and alterity. Who is Friday's foe, who has cut out his tongue and made it impossible for his story to be heard? Is it perhaps Foe, the writer, the one who tells people's stories, whatever their race, gender, class, and who in writing, rewrites, driving into deeper and deeper silence that which his discourse necessarily excludes? Barton speculates near the end of the novel about Foe's efforts as an author:

> But might the truth not be instead that he had laboured all these months to move a rock so heavy no man alive could budge it; that the pages I saw issuing from his pen were not idle tales of courtesans and grenadiers, as I supposed, but the same story over and over, in version after version, stillborn every time: the story of the island, as lifeless from his hand as from mine? (151)

Yet it is important to remember that it is only from the point of view of his oppressors (however well meaning) that Friday figures as an absolute absence. Included among those oppressors are Coetzee and the reader, and hence it is only by indirection that the substantiality of Friday's own world (in which he is not, of course, "Friday"—perhaps not even "he") can be suggested. One example is the uninterpretable (though repeatedly interpreted) act of strewing petals on the sea's surface, another is the equally uninterpretable series of marks Friday makes on the slate when Barton tries to teach him—at Foe's bidding—to write. There is also the extraordinary final section, in which an unidentified first-person narrator makes two visits to Foe's hideaway, the second in our own time (since the house bears a blue-and-white plaque inscribed *Daniel Defoe, Author*); in the house are the bodies of Foe, Barton, the girl who claimed to be her daughter, and Friday, but on both occasions it is Friday who commands attention. On the second occasion, the narrative blends into Susan Barton's own story of the island, as we have heard it more than once, but the now multiple "I" achieves what neither she nor Foe had been able to achieve: the descent into the sunken wreck, "the home of Friday" which "is not a place of words" but "a place where bodies are their own signs," and the sight of the dark mouth opening to emit its wordless, endless stream.[19]

19. The narrator(s) of this final section is/are not invested with any greater authority than earlier speakers in the novel; if anything, the uncertainties of interpretation are increased by the sense of historical distance. We have already noted that the final passage functions as a palimpsest of major documents of Western culture, and we might add to this the affinities between the account of the "home of Friday" and Montaigne's treatment of the body and language of the savage in "Des Cannibales." See also the discussion of Montaigne's essay by Michel de Certeau—which focuses on the place of the other in travel writing—in "Montaigne's 'Of Cannibals.'"

This moment answers to the moment when Jacobus Coetzee speculates on the unknowability of the South African people he has moved among:

> I am an explorer. My essence is to open what is closed, to bring light to what is dark. If the Hottentots comprise an immense world of delight, it is an impenetrable world, impenetrable to men like me, who must either skirt it, which is to evade our mission, or clear it out of the way. (106)[20]

It answers (without answering) Magda's repeated questions in *In the Heart of the Country* about the others she cannot know, her father and her servants (and the other that is herself), and the questions the magistrate in *Waiting for the Barbarians* constantly asks the barbarian girl ("'What do I have to do to move you?'... 'Does no one move you?'" [44]). It provides a reply of a kind to the despairing insistence of the medical officer in *Michael K* as he tries, unsuccessfully, to get K to open his mouth, both to eat, and to tell his story:

> You are going to die, and your story is going to die too, for ever and ever, unless you come to your senses and listen to me.... No one is going to remember you but I, unless you yield and at last open your mouth. I appeal to you, Michaels: *yield*! (207–8)

We might note that K, however, comes to think of himself as a mole "that does not tell stories because it lives in silence" (248).

: V :

It is a necessary property of any canon that it depends on what it excludes, and since culture as we understand it could not exist without canonic processes at all levels of its functioning—including, as we have seen, the constitution of individual subjectivity—there is no question of eradicating this source of exclusion. To be made aware of it, however, is to be reminded of the violence always implied in canonization, in the construction of cultural narratives, in the granting of a voice to one individual or one group,

---

20. Jacobus Coetzee is not just an explorer, but a writer too, and much of his writing is as destructive of the other as his gun; it evinces the characteristically self-contradictory claim of the colonizer, both to know everything that needs to be known about the other, and to find the other a wholly mysterious and inassimilable entity. (On both counts the other—upon whom the colonizer in fact depends—is regarded as dispensable.) See Homi K. Bhabha, *The Location of Culture*, 70–71.

necessary and productive as that process is. In enforcing this awareness, Coetzee's fictions have engaged directly with the changing political conditions in South Africa, doing so not primarily as political argument, vivid reportage, or—this was the argument of my previous chapter—point-by-point allegory, but as an exploitation of the traditions and potencies of the novel understood as a central form in Western culture, offered to the reader as an experience to be lived through.

Foe, in particular, focuses on what might be considered the most fundamental narrative of bourgeois culture not only to examine the processes of canonization and legitimation implicit in it and in its popular success, but also to bring forcefully to its readers' attention the silences which those processes generate and upon which they depend: in particular, a gender silence and a race silence.[21] At the same time, the novel refuses to endorse any simple call for the granting of a voice within the socio-cultural discourses that are already in place; such a gesture would leave the silencing mechanisms, and their repressive human effects, untouched.[22] In 1986, Njabulo Ndebele spoke for black South Africans in these terms:

> There have been diverse cultural interests to whom the challenge of the future has involved the need to open up cultural and educational centers to all races. Missing in these admirable acts of goodwill is an accompanying need to alter fundamentally the nature of cultural practice itself. It is almost always assumed that, upon being admitted, the oppressed will certainly like what they find. ("The English Language," 223–24)

21. Since my particular interest here is in Coetzee as a South African novelist, I am focusing on the question of race rather than the question of gender, but I am conscious that this is to do less than justice to the novel's richness and importance. A longer discussion would consider the differences between the treatments of the two exclusions in *Foe*, as well as the connections that link them. (One would want to consider, for instance, the relationship between Friday's mutilation and that of female victims such as Philomela and Lavinia.) And this discussion could lead to other exclusions, such as those of class, religion, nationality. See also Gayatri Spivak's suggestive engagement with *Foe* in *A Critique of Postcolonial Reason*, 174–97.

22. See Derrida's demanding scrutiny of the question of the other (of philosophy, of politics, of literature) in "Psyche" (55–56, 59–62). For Derrida, to avoid programming the other into a version of the same, "one does not make the other come, one lets it come by preparing for its coming" (60); and this means preparing for its arrival by opening up and destabilizing the existing structures of foreclosure. The relevance of Derrida's discussion to Coetzee's fictional project would be clear even without the footnote which observes: "Racism is also an invention of the other, but in order to exclude it and tighten the circle of the same" (63).

Coetzee's fiction, as I read it, brings out both the necessity and the difficulty of the process of genuine structural change in a society like South Africa's. Just as canonization inevitably involves, as a condition of the audibility of the canon, a continuous act of silencing, so political, cultural, and material domination of a social group produces, as far as the ears of the dominant class can determine, an impenetrable silence which is at the same time a necessary condition of the latter's power (and therefore a constant threat to it). Friday's tonguelessness is the sign of his oppression; it is also the sign of the silence, the absolute otherness, by which he appears to his oppressors, and by which their dominance is sustained. Foe observes to Barton: "We deplore the barbarism of whoever maimed him, yet have we, his later masters, not reason to be secretly grateful? For as long as he is dumb we can tell ourselves his desires are dark to us, and continue to use him as we wish" (148). What Foe is less conscious of is the cost of this inheritance of mastery, a cost which Barton—herself subject to the logic of exclusion and silencing—is acutely aware of.

But for those who find themselves unwillingly in the dominant group— and during the apartheid period Coetzee, like most of his readers, found himself determined in advance as a member—there is no simple remedy to be understood in terms of investing Friday with speech. If he could have his tongue restored to him, he would melt into a class which is already constituted and socially placed by a pervasive discourse (Foe suggests that, even without the faculty of speech, he might join one of London's strolling Negro bands); for insofar as the oppressed *are* heard, it is as a marginalized dialect within the dominant language. Even those who speak against oppression from the position of the oppressed have to conform to the dominant language in order to be heard in the places where power is concentrated, as Susan Barton discovers.

Effective social and political change, then, is not merely the granting or the seizing of a voice (and the power that goes with it) by one or other predetermined group; it also entails work on the part of members of both oppressed and oppressing groups to create breaks in the totalizing discourses that produce and reify that grouping itself. The burden of this work necessarily falls on the oppressed, who will themselves produce the discursive transformation that will allow themselves to be heard (as part of the process of effecting the material shift of power that any lasting discursive shift is tied to). But the members of the oppressing group who seek to secure change have a role, too; not Foe's project of teaching Friday to write the master discourse with which the main part of the novel ends (though there are indications—which could never, for us, be wholly legible—that Friday is in fact *subverting* the master discourse with his multiply interpretable graphics), but Coetzee's project of representing the processes of authorship, empowerment, validation, and silencing in a narrative that is constantly aware of the problems inherent in its own acts of representation (an issue that we have already considered in relation to Coetzee's earlier novels), and makes this awareness part of the reader's experience.

I observed earlier that the settings of Coetzee's novels render them less likely to be read as concerned exclusively with the South African struggle, and that they may run the opposite risk of being taken as having little specifically to do with that struggle. There is clearly some significance in the fact that Friday is a black African in *Foe*, unlike Defoe's tawny-skinned creation, just as there is in the fact that the people who remain outside Jacobus Coetzee's or Magda's or the medical officer's or Mrs. Curren's or David Lurie's comprehension are, for the most part, South Africans excluded from white privileges. On the other hand, the barbarians in *Waiting for the Barbarians* cannot be identified so clearly; they function as a less specifically historicized representation of otherness, upon whose necessary exclusion from its narratives, and occasionally from its physical spaces and economic resources, the civilization of the Empire depends. Furthermore, the least comprehensible figure in *Age of Iron,* Vercueil, is not racially identified, while racial difference is not an issue in the Russian setting of *The Master of Petersburg.*

This occasional absence of precise empirical grounding is a necessary feature of Coetzee's fiction, I would argue, since the novels are addressed as much to those outside South Africa as to those within it. (Indeed, to be white and to write oppositional fiction in English during the apartheid years was to restrict your readership inside the country, making access to an international canon of peculiar importance.)[23] There are two relatively easy responses by outsiders to the issue of racial conflict in South Africa that Coetzee's writing inhibits, however: first, that what is at stake is a battle of universal human principles, a version of similar battles in every

---

23. To write "modernist" fiction is to limit your audience further, of course. Neil Lazarus, writing in 1986, argues interestingly that, since the modernist text resists reductive appropriation by the dominant discourse, "the relative underestimation, within South Africa itself, of the work of Gordimer and Coetzee ought to be taken as an index of the oppositional cogency of this work, and not, as it is usually taken, as an index of its irrelevance" ("Modernism and Modernity," 136).

society and every period, another manifestation of the tragic complexity of the human condition;[24] and second, that the conflict is entirely a local matter of a particular history and a particular set of problems in need of urgent resolution by those on the spot. What these novels work to suggest instead—and again, this is a task that falls peculiarly on the shoulders of the white South African writer in English—is that the South African struggle for justice and equality is *part* of a wider, and entirely concrete, struggle, that it has a particular history which is continuous with the particular histories of all other countries participating in the rise of Western capitalism and the liberal ideology on which it depends, and that one requirement in moving toward a just future (one of many, but one in which works of art might have a special role) is an understanding—as much affective as rational—of the ways in which the cultural formations that we have inherited through those histories are, for all their indisputable value, complicit with many barbarities being committed all around us today.

: VI :

Turning back to the question of Coetzee's novels and the literary canon, the question that presses itself is this: is the cost of these works' admittance to the canon their being re-read (and thus rewritten) as stories— as the same story—of essential humanity and transcendent values, their textuality disguised, their otherness expunged, their ethical power annulled? The novels themselves might appear to give a pessimistic answer, for the work of art is clearly in the same powerless situation as characters like the barbarian girl, K, or Friday. It is the subject of stories (both before and after it appears), and only through stories—commentaries, criticism, discussion, internal reflection—does it acquire meaning and value

---

24. This might be a significant difference between Coetzee and his precursors Kafka and Beckett: Coetzee's fiction is so directly concerned with the economic and political fabric of cultural existence that it is more difficult to derive from it general statements about the human predicament. There are moments, however, when the inadequacy of representation being dramatized appears to be not so much the inadequacy of a particular set of available discourses but that of language itself; notably when the body feels or acts in ways that exceed or escape any possible conceptualization—as, for instance, in the magistrate's obscure physical desires in *Waiting for the Barbarians* or K's body's refusal to eat the food of the camps in *Michael K*. But this does not diminish the importance of the more specific questions relating to the cultural validation of certain discourses at the expense of others, and of the price to be paid for cultural acceptance.

for us.[25] But anything like a "full" understanding of it would require an apprehension of what remains uncaptured in the critical and interpretive discourse by means of which we represent the work of art to ourselves and others, that discourse which tends, as I have argued, toward the allegorical substitution of structure for event, meaning as a noun for meaning as a verb. It is important to recognize, however, that this is in no sense a mystical or Romantic notion; Coetzee's novels do not represent a yearning for some realm of richness and plenitude beyond language, a meaningfulness behind the emptiness of our conscious lives. They attempt strenuously to avoid both terms of the colonizer's contradiction I mentioned earlier (see note 20): that the other is wholly knowable, and that the other is wholly mysterious; that the other has no boundaries, and that the boundaries of the other are impenetrable.[26]

As Coetzee's novels enter the canon, then, it becomes increasingly difficult to read them *against* the canon, as their uniqueness is dissolved by the legitimized voice which the canon grants; yet if they were to fail in their bid for canonicity, it would become increasingly difficult to read them at all, since the only voice available to them is the voice granted by one canon or another. This, we have seen, is the double bind dramatized in *Foe* at the level of the individual, and inherent in any attempt to combat political and cultural repression. If I may end with a utopian

25. The most compelling (and therefore most occulting) of these stories are often those told by the authors themselves. It is notable that Coetzee observes a scrupulous reserve in relation to his texts, as is evidenced in many interviews. For instance, here he is in conversation with Morphet: "Q: Friday has no tongue. Why? COETZEE: Nobody seems to have sufficient authority to say for sure how it is that Friday has no tongue" (462). And later Coetzee remarks: "Your questions again and again drive me into a position I do not want to occupy. (But what legitimacy has that 'want'?) By accepting your implication, I would produce a master narrative for a set of texts that claim to deny all master narratives" (464). See also *Doubling the Point*, 205–6. In *Foe*, Susan Barton discovers the simultaneous impossibility and necessity of metanarrative commentary: "Alas, my stories seem always to have more applications than I intend, so that I must go back and laboriously extract the right application and apologize for the wrong ones and efface them" (81).

26. Michel Tournier's *Vendredi*, another modern rewriting of Defoe's novel which is in productive triangulation with Coetzee's work, offers a very different view of the other of colonialism: although in both reworkings the black servant represents a consciousness radically alien to the Western mind he serves, this otherness in Tournier's work is more easily assimilated to a Eurocentric primitivistic myth. Tournier's novel surfaces elsewhere—and is perhaps gently mocked—in Coetzee's oeuvre: Jacobus Coetzee, alone in the veld, tries to imitate the earth-fecundation of Tournier's Crusoe: "I bored a sheath in the earth and would have performed the ur-act had joy and laughter not reduced me to a four-inch dangle and helpless urination" (95).

thought, however, it would be that the canonization of Coetzee's novels, along with other texts (fictional and otherwise) that question the very processes of canonicity itself, could slowly transform the ideology and the institutions from which the canon derives its power, so that new and presently unimaginable ways of finding a voice, and new ways of hearing such voices, come into being. Instead of canons premised upon a notion of transcendental and inscrutable value, we can hope for cultural practices and formations that encourage an awareness of the historical production of value, of the part played by ideological systems in political domination and exclusion, of the necessarily provisional and historically contestable nature of any arrangement which allows some to speak and in that gesture renders others—and a part of themselves—silent. This project is a small component of a much greater struggle, which took (and is still taking) a violent form in South Africa, to fashion cultural and political structures and procedures that will allow us not just to hear each other's stories, as the liberal humanist dream would have it, but to hear—and this will entail a different kind of hearing—each other's silences.

CHAPTER FOUR

Trusting the Other

Age of Iron

: I :

To read *Age of Iron* is to read, or overread, a strange kind of letter, written in 1986 by a dying woman in Cape Town to her married daughter in the United States. This, at least, is the fictional contract we enter into, though we are given little in the way of realistic reinforcement that might enable us to imagine the words issuing from a pen onto a sheet of paper. Even the highly implausible epistolary activity of a Clarissa Harlowe or a Saint-Preux is conducted with occasional nods to the mechanical requirements of letter-writing, but here the novelist places no constraints on the verbal creativity of his character. Yet in one sense Mrs. Curren's words are more fully imbued with what might be regarded as the spirit of epistolarity than most fictional letters (or, for that matter, nonfictional ones): that is, in their utter dependence on and directedness toward a single, absent, other, an other whose absence is the force which brings the words into being while rendering their task—of communication, above all the communication of love (whatever that might mean)—impossible. Mrs. Curren's daughter is the living being she is closest to, the one she most easily trusts, the one she turns to as soon as she hears the news—which sets in progress the letter and therefore the novel—that the cancer she is suffering from is terminal.

The intensification of love brought about by the news is expressed without embarrassment (one of the habitual human reactions the novel seeks to move beyond) in an early passage describing Mrs. Curren's feelings when she enters the empty house on her return from the doctor, one of many passages that could be quoted to show the powerful other-directedness of the writing:

> So: how I longed for you! How I longed to be able to go upstairs to you, to sit on your bed, run my fingers through your hair, whisper in your ear as I did on school mornings, "Time to get up!" And then, when you turned over, your body blood-warm, your breath milky, to take you in my arms in what we called "giving Mommy a big hug," the secret meaning of which, the meaning never spoken, was that Mommy should not be sad, for she would not die but live on in you. (5–6)

Living on in her daughter is, for Mrs. Curren as she approaches death, a matter of bequeathing her what she has learned, not as a body of doctrine or information, but by way of sharing the learning experience itself—an experience in which unlearning is as important as learning. Hence the long letter, which moves between recountings of the extraordinary events of these last weeks and difficult reassessments of values and habits built up over a lifetime, all produced as a loving gift for a daughter who will not receive it until the donor is dead—except that, if the gift is truly received, the mother will live on in the daughter. As she puts it later in the letter: "These words, as you read them, if you read them, enter you and draw breath again. They are, if you like, my way of living on. Once upon a time you lived in me as once upon a time I lived in my mother; as she still lives in me, as I grow toward her, may I live in you" (131).

It is hard to know what to call the gift, the message; words like "insight," "knowledge," "wisdom," and "understanding" all belong too irredeemably to the discourse from which Mrs. Curren is achieving a difficult escape, the discourse of knowledge as content and inheritable property rather than an always contextualized responsiveness, activity, and self-questioning. ("I may seem to understand what I say, but, believe me, I do not," she admits at one point [131]; and just before the end, she calls hers "a death without illumination" [195].) The gift is, of course, the text of the whole novel, or rather the opportunity to read, to live through, that text; it is John Coetzee's as well as Mrs. Curren's gift (even though we must keep distinct the operations of posthumous letter and published fiction), and there is no possibility of summing up its moral or political "lesson." It's not even clear that something positive is being bequeathed, and I therefore prefer the term "understanding" over other alternatives in that it may be taken in a verbal sense, in the sense, that is, of an activity that need not correspond to a noun. The gift that the letter represents can be offered and received only as an act that is at the same time an event.

To describe *Age of Iron* in this manner is to emphasize its staging of a personal struggle, but it is also significant that this struggle is born out of and conducted within a highly specific historical situation, which produces a radical reinterpretation, and in some ways a critique, of the age-old motif of wisdom achieved in the shadow of death. Indeed, it is the history of South Africa, and more specifically the policies of Afrikaner nationalism, which have determined that the gift of mother's love will take the form of a letter, since they are the direct cause of the daughter's decision to leave the country. (She has vowed not to return until the people responsible for these policies are "hanging by their heels from the lampposts," when she will "throw stones at their bodies and dance in the streets" [75].) This is not to say that the daughter's presence would have made the giving, and the living on that is its potential outcome, easier. The longing for unmediated communication, for a physical bond to seal and perfect what is thought of as merely verbal transmission, is driven by a fantasy of total union that cannot, in reality, exist between individuals;[1] and there is even a sense in which the distance and the necessity of written correspondence make possible for Mrs. Curren an exceptional fullness of giving, and hence of love and of living on, in that it enables the gift to be posthumous, without thought of return.[2]

---

1. Mrs. Curren contemplates this image of union, half-blaming her historical location for its impossibility, but half recognizing it as a fantasy: "In another world I would not need words. I would appear on your doorstep. 'I have come for a visit,' I would say, and that would be the end of words: I would embrace you and be embraced. But in this world, in this time, I must reach out to you in words" (9). Mrs. Curren's refusal to use the telephone to communicate the news of her condition to her daughter can be understood as a rejection of a medium which offers neither presence nor the possibility of a posthumous verbal gift. We learn of one unsatisfactory phone call some time after the event—"Not words, not living breath passing between us, but the ideas of words, the idea of breath"—which may have conveyed "love but not truth"; in this letter, however, are "truth and love together" (129). (The novel suggests that it is finally only in conveying truth—not a transcendent content, not "the" truth, but a historical, contingent experience, what Mrs. Curren calls "my truth: how I lived in these times, in this place" [130]—that love is transmitted.)

2. As this paragraph will have begun to indicate, my engagement with *Age of Iron* has been informed by a number of theoretical writings. (It is likely that Coetzee is familiar with many of these, though this is not part of my argument.) Most important are several texts by Jacques Derrida, including *Given Time*, "Living On/Borderlines," "Force of Law," and

But the gift, the love, the narrated experience, must be received; this, as far as Mrs. Curren is concerned, is their raison d'être. What arises, therefore, is the crucial question of the agent or messenger: Mrs. Curren must trust someone to get the letter to her daughter after her death. It is not just a matter of engaging someone to carry out a commission which can be checked on and then, if it turns out that the trust was misplaced, rectified; Mrs. Curren has to rely on another person to perform a task which, by its very nature, is unverifiable and unrectifiable. The recipient of her trust will never be called to account; the daughter will never know of the letter's existence if it does not arrive. Hence there is something absolute about the trust that is called for, as there is about the gift of understanding that it makes possible (and, as I shall argue, that makes it possible).

The person to whom Mrs. Curren entrusts the letter is someone who has entered her life as if in response to the intense longing I have already described, a homeless man who chooses, for no satisfactorily explained reason, to take up residence in her backyard on the very day she receives the fateful medical prognosis. Through this coincidence, he takes the place of the absent daughter, although one could hardly imagine a less likely individual for this office. Mr. Vercueil, as Mrs. Curren comes to call him (without being sure of the spelling or indeed the pronunciation—"'His name is Mr. Vercueil,' I said. 'Vercueil, Verkuil, Verskuil'" [37]),[3] is a

---

"Psyche." Some aspects of Emmanuel Levinas's many discussions of the Other have also been helpful, most obviously *Totality and Infinity,* as has the work of Jean-François Lyotard (*The Differend*) and Maurice Blanchot (*The Writing of the Disaster*).

3. The subject of names in Coetzee's work is worth an essay in itself, which would point out the repeated undermining of their supposed simple referentiality, and the making evident of the power relations within which they function. It might begin with Coetzee's decision to withhold from his readers his own forenames, which has given rise to an uncertainty rather like Mrs. Curren's over "Vercueil": thus while Ian Ousby's *Cambridge Guide to Literature in English* and D. L. Kirkpatrick's *Contemporary Novelists* both confidently give his name as "John Michael Coetzee," Dick Penner, in *Countries of the Mind,* 1, and Kevin Goddard and John Read, in *J. M. Coetzee: A Bibliography,* 15, with equal assurance give "John Maxwell Coetzee," and it is under this name that he received the Nobel Prize for Literature in 2003. *Le Nouvel Observateur* presents him to its readers as "Jean-Marie Coetzee" (interview with Claude Wauthier, 69); and Linda Hutcheon calls him just "Michael Coetzee" (*A Poetics of Postmodernism,* 77, 107, 198). The entry in *Contemporary Literary Criticism* (vol. 66), contrary to its usual practice but perhaps wisely, settles for "John M. Coetzee" as his "full name."

An analogous ambiguity plays around the name of the letter-writer in *Age of Iron.* She is unnamed at first, but we eventually learn that her married name is "Curren" and that her initials are "E. C." However, both Coetzee himself, in the interviews in *Doubling the Point* (250, 340), and some critics—presumably following the author's extra-textual

survivor on the fringes of South African society, living on the streets, alcohol-dependent, unaffected by the obligations of human relationship or community; a man so removed from the structures of social and political life that he even appears to have escaped the grid of racial classification on which apartheid rests. (His race, at least, seems to be an issue of no significance to the other characters, whereas their own lives, as the novel graphically demonstrates, are largely determined by the position in which their racial categorizations place them.)[4] He has shown himself to be outside any of the normal codes which govern interpersonal relations (which is also to say outside the dominant codes of the realist novel); his unpredictability and unreadability, his imperviousness to the logic of an economy of labor and reward, service and indebtedness, often exasperating to Mrs. Curren, would seem to render him the least appropriate repository for anyone's trust.[5] But it has been clear from the very opening of the novel that Vercueil will play a central role in Mrs. Curren's revision of her selfhood and her values: it is with his arrival that the letter begins, and he is from the start associated both with the daughter and with Mrs. Curren herself ("Why do I give this man food? ... For the same reason I gave you my breast" [7]; "When I write about him I write about myself" [9]).

It is worth following closely the way the text presents the act of entrusting, since this moment goes to the heart of the strange relationship between the old lady and the derelict, and, as I've suggested, the entire project of the letter depends on it. Mrs. Curren has had very little experience of Vercueil when she comes to her decision to lay on him the responsibility of posting the letter, a decision which seems to be unusually

---

comments–refer to her as "Elizabeth Curren." This is even shortened to "Elizabeth" (out of the same unconscious sexism that makes critics speak of "Susan"—but not "Robinson" or "Daniel"—in *Foe*), a familiarity at which we can imagine Mrs. Curren—who always addresses and usually speaks of Vercueil as "Mr. Vercueil"—wincing sharply. (The name "Elizabeth" and the initials "E. C." will, however, make it into print in *Elizabeth Costello* some years later.)

Coetzee's fiction also repeatedly presents us with nameless characters—the barbarian girl, the medical officer—or characters whose names are in one way or another problematic—Michael K, Friday, and the two Sorayas in *Disgrace*. The question of naming is, of course, central to any question of the relation to, and the resistance of, the other.

4. A possible exception to this lack of concern with Vercueil's race is the anger with which the two black boys react to his drinking, for them a capitulation to white domination: "They are making you into a dog!" (45). This response implies that they identify him as a potential ally in the struggle and hence probably coloured; a white derelict would be more likely to arouse simple scorn.

5. Tony Morphet, in his appreciative review of the novel, "The Inside Story," gives an excellent description of Vercueil's imperviousness to comprehension.

pure: that is to say, it appears not to be the product of a calculation, and is not explicable in terms of any rational scheme.[6] The process whereby she reaches a decision is not articulated; the request she has made to Vercueil is cited in the letter without preparation or explanation:

> "There is something I would like you to do for me if I die. There are some papers I want to send to my daughter. But after the event. That is the important part. That is why I cannot send them myself." (31)

There is a startling lucidity about Mrs. Curren's insistence that she can convey what she wants to convey only after her death; her daughter must read this letter in the knowledge that its writer is not there to be questioned or negotiated with, that its claimed authority—from the vantage of approaching death—has been justified, and that it is not, for all its expression of longing and love, a plea for sympathy and comfort. ("I tell you this story not so that you will feel for me but so that you will learn how things are" [103]). The letter will thus function more like literature than most letters, since the work of literature, too, casts itself off from its author and renders interrogation problematic—something that Coetzee, when questioned about his fiction, frequently insists upon.[7]

Mrs. Curren emphasizes that the task is, as an action, about as undemanding as any task could be:

> "All you will have to do will be to hand the parcel over the counter at the post office. Will you do that for me?"
> He shifted uncomfortably.
> "It is not a favor I would ask if I could help it, but there is no other way. I will not be here."
> "Can't you ask someone else?" he said. (31)

6. Carl Schmitt's discussion of what he calls "the decision in absolute purity," constituted by a moment which is not derivable from any preexisting norms, is relevant here (*Political Theology*, 13), and in part underlies Derrida's exploration of the issue of deciding in such texts as "Afterword" and "Force of Law." The question of the decision is related to the questions of justice, of the gift (see Derrida's *Given Time*), and, as in this novel, of trust. We have already noted that some of Michael K's decisions–to leave Stellenbosch, for instance–are made without calculation (see p. 57 above).

7. One of many instances is the following in *Doubling the Point:* "I am immensely uncomfortable with questions—like this one—that call on me to answer for (in two senses) my novels, and my responses are often taken as evasive.... What I say is marginal to the book, not because I as author and authority so proclaim, but on the contrary because it would be said from a position peripheral, posterior to the forever unreclaimable position from which the book was written" (205–6). See also chap. 3, n. 25.

To make a promise, to accept someone's trust, is something Vercueil cannot or will not do; he lives his life without commitments, without reference to the future (and with references to the past that hardly have the
ring of truth).[8] We should not be too quick to assume, however, that
he is some sort of innocent primitive or noble savage, ignorant of the
basic ties of human community; seeing him through Mrs. Curren's eyes
alone, we have no way of knowing what ingredients of calculation or
cynicism are at work in him (just as we cannot fathom what complexities
underlie the silence of the barbarian girl in *Waiting for the Barbarians*
or of Friday in *Foe*). It is important that we, like Mrs. Curren, remain
in the dark about his inner world, since this is what makes her trust so
remarkable.[9]

Vercueil's attempt to shift the burden (a negligible burden in itself,
but one whose weightiness simply as a promise he seems accurately to
perceive) is typical of his behavior. But Mrs. Curren is convinced, against
all logic, that he is the man for the job:

> "Yes, I can. But I am asking you. These are private papers, private letters.
> They are my daughter's inheritance. They are all I can give her, all she will
> accept, coming from this country." (31–32)

And Vercueil continues to be evasive and ill at ease:

> "I don't know," said the man, the messenger, playing with his
> spoon.
> He will make no promise. And even if he promises, he will do, finally,
> what he likes. (32)

"Never mind," says Mrs. Curren, and a little later, as if in response to
being let off the hook, Vercueil makes his unreliable commitment: "'I'll
post your parcel for you,' he said." Mrs. Curren or Coetzee (does it
make sense to ask which?) ends the first section of the text on this sentence.

---

8. Nietzsche's account in *The Genealogy of Morals* of humanity's reaching the stage of
being able to promise is helpful in understanding Vercueil's reluctance; as Nietzsche puts it,
"Man himself must first of all have become calculable, regular, necessary, even in his own
image of himself, if he is to be able to stand security for his own future, which is what one
who promises does!" (58).

9. Benita Parry's assertion that Vercueil "means more than he says" ("Speech and Silence," 153)—part of her complaint about the "plenitude of perception and gifts" she feels
is implied by the silences of Coetzee's figures of alterity—is unverifiable; he may in fact mean
exactly what he says and no more.

Much later in her letter, Mrs. Curren returns to this future act upon which her project depends:

> If Vercueil does not send these writings on, you will never read them. You will never even know they existed. A certain body of truth will never take on flesh: my truth: how I lived in these times, in this place.
>
> What is the wager, then, that I am making with Vercueil, on Vercueil?
>
> It is a wager on trust. So little to ask, to take a package to the post office and pass it over the counter. So little that it is almost nothing. Between taking the package and not taking it the difference is as light as a feather. If there is the slightest breath of trust, obligation, piety left behind when I am gone, he will surely take it.
>
> And if not?
>
> If not, there is no trust and we deserve no better, all of us, than to fall into a hole and vanish.
>
> Because I cannot trust Vercueil I must trust him. (130)

Trust is a relation to the future that is based on no rational grounds; to entrust a task to someone in the certainty that it will be done is not to trust but merely to act on the basis of advance knowledge; trust, like a pure decision, is born of uncertainty and uncertainty alone. It emerges fully only in the case of someone, like Vercueil, who cannot be trusted, even to carry out the most trivial of tasks. The very triviality of the task thus makes this a supreme act of trust, the kind of trust upon which all hopes for the future rest—the future of South Africa, the future of humanity, "all of us."[10] A little further on, Mrs. Curren reiterates the magnitude and the counterlogic of her act: "I give my life to Vercueil to carry over. I trust Vercueil because I do not trust Vercueil. I love him because I do not love him. Because he is the weak reed I lean upon him" (131).

Another way of putting this is that there is only one kind of trust that truly deserves the name: trust in the other. I have discussed elsewhere Vercueil as a manifestation of otherness in Mrs. Curren's life;[11] the two points I want to stress here are that otherness is always *perspectival* and

---

10. Both Levinas and Derrida link the future indissociably to ethics, responsibility, and alterity. For Levinas, "The future is what is not grasped, what befalls us and lays hold of us. The other is the future" ("Time and the Other," 44). Derrida's thinking has always shown an acute awareness of the question of the future, emerging most obviously in, for instance, his considerations of chance, of deferral, of iterability, of the promise, of the date, and of friendship.

11. Attridge, "Literary Form and the Demands of Politics."

that it is always *produced*. In other words, there is no transcendent other (except in certain kinds of religious discourse), there is only an other that presents itself to a specific subject in a particular place and time; otherness is always otherness to someone (who inevitably, and by virtue of the existence of the other, is put in the position of the self and the same). And the other does not come from some totally other place, but is a product of the identical constituting act that has produced the self/same which perceives it as other.[12] Vercueil comes, then, as the other who challenges Mrs. Curren's daily habits of orderliness, cleanliness, and thrift just as much as he challenges her principles of moral responsibility, obligation, and charity, and his otherness arises from everything that she (or rather, her inherited culture) has rejected in developing those habits and erecting those standards.

Mrs. Curren is right to trust Vercueil; for doing so is itself a crucial part of the understanding that she is bequeathing in the act that comprises this letter. If her daughter reads the letter, she will read the words quoted above and will know that her mother's apparently imprudent choice was in fact a good one, she will experience (and not merely learn as a lesson) what trust is, the kind of trust that the future of the South Africa she left behind, in what might be regarded as a failure of trust, desperately needs. If she doesn't get the letter, of course, her mother's trust and the understanding that it implies will have been discredited, removing the very reason for reading it.

Yet there is a sense in which, for the reader, the question of whether Vercueil does or does not post the parcel is irrelevant (it remains, in any case, unknowable, entirely outside the boundaries of the novel); it is Mrs. Curren's unprogrammed and complete act of trust that saves "all of us." Trust, which is to say trust in the other and in the future, is at the moral heart of a situation such as that which prevailed in South Africa in 1986, or indeed that which prevails today.[13] This is not a political prescription, since it does not contain within itself any program indicating when, where, and how such trust should operate; nor is it a vague liberal-humanist truism, urging individuals to behave justly toward other individuals. Through its staging of an encounter (to be read neither

---

12. For an account of the other that develops these principles as they manifest themselves in literary creation, see Attridge, *The Singularity of Literature*, chap. 2.

13. Lazarus, in "Modernism and Modernity," stresses the significance and necessity of pure trust in the specific case of the white South African writer: a trust that is "sacrificial—or at least potentially sacrificial, for its outcome cannot be known in advance" (150).

as a realistic exemplar nor as a universal allegory, but as a uniquely con-figured enactment of a general truth which exists only in such unique enactments), the novel offers a precise understanding of trust, and of its relation to the vital questions of the other and the future, involving an apprehension that is no less intellectual (perhaps all the more so) for be-ing irreducible to programmatic rules. It is an understanding that can be conveyed only in such a novel, or such a letter, or such a life.[14] Whether or not it reaches the daughter is, to Coetzee, to us, immaterial (as is the question of whether the daughter understands what she has received or is disgusted or horrified by it)—and even Mrs. Curren recognizes early on that she writes, as she says to her daughter, "To you but not to you; to me; to you in me" (6). Writing is that which lives on, because its addressee is always multiple and divided; and to write is therefore to trust the other who will read, other because unknowable and unfixable in advance.

To characterize this kind of understanding, I wish to take advantage of a term already in use in many different discourses, some of which, at least, include glimpses of what I am trying to argue here: it is ethical understanding.

: II :

If I say that Mrs. Curren's relationship with Vercueil in this novel is a staging of the fundamental ethical relation, I may give the impression of a text that is highly generalized in its procedures, unless we remember that the sense in which I am using "ethics" grounds it in the specific, the singular, the historical, the contingent. ("One must love what is to hand," Mrs. Curren explains to her daughter [190].) It is in the details of the relationship, often comic, never predictable, that these sections of the novel have their force, the absurdity of the old lady's cossetings and con-versations (often one-sided), the pathos of her moments of dependence, the triumphs of collaborative actions; and it is in these details that the ethical is staged, as Mrs. Curren learns to overcome a lifetime's habits of thought and action. But hers is not the story of a saint: Mrs. Curren's

14. This is to point to the crucial importance of what has traditionally been called "form": the unique staging of human meanings that constitutes a work of literature (which need not be confined to the traditional category so named) and its reading. For further discussion, see chapter 1 above and *The Singularity of Literature*, chap. 9.

acceptance of the other has limits, as when Vercueil brings a woman into the house—when we perhaps witness unacknowledged sexual jealousy as well—or when she faces the white South Africans she detests, on her television screen or in the flesh (see, for example, the episode in the picnic-spot above Hout Bay [127]). Only in her unique relationship with Vercueil do we find a continuous generosity and openness, running under the spasms of irritation and exasperation she experiences.

Of course, the relationship as we see it is entirely constructed by Mrs. Curren; we have no access to Vercueil's motives or attitudes, and for all we know he feels no reciprocating warmth or commitment. (The contrast with another Coetzean survivor in inauspicious times, Michael K, is striking, since his thoughts are for the most part made available to us by the means discussed in chapter 2.) Quite early in the letter, Mrs. Curren describes how she played a record of the Goldberg Variations while Vercueil smoked a cigarette outside the house, and comments: "Together we listened. At this moment, I thought, I know how he feels as surely as if he and I were making love" (30). It is a moment of startling intimacy, though neither Mrs. Curren nor the reader can know if Vercueil is even listening to the music. In a different novel, Vercueil's otherness would dissolve, bit by bit, and some shared terrain would emerge where, remade by the relationship, they would achieve communication. But Coetzee is writing of an otherness that is not to be conjured away; Vercueil remains unknowable to the end, and in that end fuses—or is fused in Mrs. Curren's mind—with the equally unmodifiable otherness of death.

One of the most extraordinary qualities of Mrs. Curren's response to Vercueil is that, although it transgresses so many of her values, it is achieved without a great struggle; the code of "proper behavior" rapidly loses its relevance. The man is allowed to stay in the backyard, brought coffee the next morning (which he spits out at her feet when she begins to lecture at him), invited to sleep in the house, and eventually encouraged to join her in her bed. (It is her readers—including, one imagines, her daughter—who must struggle to comprehend and sympathize with her growing closeness to and dependence upon the dirty, foul-smelling, alcoholic at the same time that she is cutting herself off from all "normal" sources of help.) Her early condemnation of him gives way to a willingness to learn from him, and to learn from the fact of his utter difference from her.[15]

15. Mrs. Curren's response to Vercueil can be understood as a further exploration of the issues discussed in Coetzee's essay "Idleness in South Africa" in *White Writing* (12–35);

Insofar as we read this behavior "realistically," we can understand it only as a sign of the psychological effect of approaching death, which deprives conventional mores of their relevance and encourages a certain "allegorical" reading of reality. We noted in chapter 2 that at several points Mrs. Curren plays with the allegorization of Vercueil, calling him, as we saw there, "the messenger" (32), referring to his appearance as an "annunciation" (5), wondering when the time would come "when the jacket fell away and great wings sprouted from his shoulders" (161)— both believing in his other-worldliness and making fun of herself for doing so. She even raises the obvious link between her condition and that of the country as a whole (65), and at one point observes, "It was like living in an allegory" (90). The fact that the central character plays so self-consciously with allegorizations of her own experience prevents us from straightforwardly reading Coetzee's narrative as an allegory. Vercueil is readable at a perfectly literal level, a historical rather than a metaphorical sign of the breakdown of social order during the late phase of apartheid (evident also in the marauding bands of children), a scavenger seeing an opportunity in a helpless and increasingly crazy old lady, eagerly joining in her plans to commit suicide, though finally lacking the skill and sobriety to take full advantage of her—until, in one possible reading of the ending, he finally murders her.

At the same time, we cannot ignore the allegorizing cast of the story of the old woman's illness and the unaccountable visitor, especially as we read it in conjunction with, and in contrast to, the more historically plausible story of Mrs. Curren's maid and her family. Although he comes as a vagrant in need of shelter and not an annunciating angel, Vercueil's arrival and subsequent behavior, and Mrs. Curren's increasingly intimate relationship with him, do not yield wholly to the interpretive canons of the realistic novel. (Readers of Coetzee's fiction will recognize this oscillation between verisimilitude and its undermining; the figures of Jacobus Coetzee, Magda, and Michael K are earlier instances.) To take one striking example, the final sentence of *Age of Iron* fulfills the goal enunciated by Mrs. Curren near the beginning ("To embrace death as my own, mine alone" [6]) in a climactic use of the angel motif: "He took me in his arms and held me with mighty force, so that the breath went out of me

---

where the essay traces the repeated condemnation of the "Hottentots" at the Cape as "idle," the novel enacts a principled refusal to impose preexisting moral codes on those who do not acknowledge them.

in a rush. From that embrace there was no warmth to be had" (198). Yet we cannot be sure whose allegory this is, Mrs. Curren's in a letter to her daughter or Coetzee's in a sentence that abandons the conceit of the continuously written letter, nor exactly what is being allegorized in the final, hardly triumphant, coldness.[16] As I have already suggested, what makes an allegory a *literary* work is its performance of the very process of allegorizing.

So Mrs. Curren's response to the other in the form of Vercueil can be read as a kind of heightened staging of the very issue of otherness, a story that is continuous with the attempts by such "philosophical" writers as Levinas, Blanchot, and Derrida to find ways of engaging this issue. The idiosyncratic and inconsistent reality of Vercueil and the fully realized persona of Mrs. Curren do not distance the novel from these more discursive attempts; on the contrary, the philosophical argument requires concrete instances, since to apprehend the other as a general phenomenon is to take away its otherness. (At the same time, of course, no concrete instance can exhaust the issue.) As in these writers, the other is not sought, but impinges on a life without notice, without discernible reason ("I did not choose him. He chose me. Or perhaps he merely chose the one house without a dog" [12]). The other appears in the form of what Derrida calls the *arrivant* ("I didn't choose you, but you are the one who is here, and that will have to do. You arrived. It's like having a child. You can't choose the child. It just arrives" [71]).[17] We are already obligated to the other, we find ourselves responsible for it/him/her/them, and responsible in an absolute way; it is not a matter of calculating a certain degree of responsibility and then acting upon it. Of course, we can refuse this responsibility, and most often we do; but this is a story of what happens to someone who accepts it, without calculation, without forethought—or better, accepts it on the far side of calculation and forethought, at the end of a long life lived according to the rules (and as a classicist, Mrs. Curren is deeply aware of the long history of those rules). The fullest acceptance of responsibility

16. The ending has been read as a wholly positive conclusion, but this may be as much a product of the desire for positive conclusions as of attentive readings. Coetzee himself disagrees with Attwell's suggestion that it represents a final absolution for Mrs. Curren, making a comment on his own novel with his usual distance and caution: "The end of the novel seems to me more troubled (in the sense that the sea can be troubled) than you imply. But here I am stepping onto precarious ground, or precarious water; I had better stop" (*Doubling the Point*, 250).

17. For a discussion of Derrida's term *arrivant*—most simply, the one who arrives—in relation to Coetzee's writing, see chap. 5, sect. 3. below, esp. 120–21.

to and for the other may indeed be to trust the other, since this is to put the relationship to the other under the rubric of the future, and only in a willingness not to pre-program the future can the other—whose impact upon our lives remains incalculable and unforeseeable—be accepted.[18]

Crucial, too, is the way Mrs. Curren allows herself to be changed by the other. On the second day of Vercueil's residence in her backyard she chides him for wasting his life, and comments, "It is true: I do not understand it. Something in me revolts at the lassitude, the letting go, the welcoming of dissolution" (8). Much later, we find her writing to her daughter: "Letting go of myself, letting go of you, letting go of a house still alive with memories: a hard task, but I am learning" (130). With an echo, perhaps unconscious, of Heidegger's *Gelassenheit,* she charts her altering apprehension of the task that confronts her in her dying days in a convulsed society.

: III :

In the interviews with David Attwell in *Doubling the Point,* Coetzee takes it for granted that there is an opposition between the "ethical" and the "political." Although he remarks that "the last thing I want to do is to defiantly embrace the ethical as against the political" (200), his emphasis (together with the context of this comment) indicates that he does feel himself aligned with the former, albeit not in a way that, as he says, would contribute "toward marking the ethical as the pole with the lack." And later, when he comments, "I think you will find the contest of interpretations I have sketched here—the political versus the ethical—played out again and again in my novels" (338), it is evident that it is the political that is to be corrected by the ethical, and not vice versa.

My discussion of trust, otherness, and the future in *Age of Iron* will have suggested ways in which we might understand the two terms; the

---

18. The relationship between Mrs. Curren and Vercueil is clearly in many ways a rewriting of the relationship between Susan Barton and Friday in *Foe,* discussed in chapter 3. (Mrs. Curren's letter, like Barton's narrative, is an attempt to constitute a self, partly through storytelling, in a situation that could not have been predicted.) Barton, too, finds herself responsible for someone who is wholly other to her, and is baffled by the task this responsibility imposes, the task of doing justice to the other; but there is no equivalent in *Foe* of Mrs. Curren's future-directed act of entrusting.

ethical involves an always contextualized responsiveness, and responsibility, to the other (as singular) and to the future (as unknowable),[19] while the political would be the realm of generalizations, programs, and predictions. It's worth noting the reversal that this implies in the way these terms are often used: here it is the ethical, not the political, which is concerned with concrete acts and persons, and the political which deals in general rules. My argument is that in the political arena we often think we are engaging with the concrete when we are imposing generalities, and that the generalities on which philosophical ethics has usually rested are evasions of the genuinely ethical, which can only be thought through in relation to the singular and the contingent. There are, of course, many other ways of employing the terms "politics" and "ethics," but in order to understand the distinction Coetzee makes I believe we need to take them in these senses.

It would be a mistake, in any case, to think that ethics and politics are separate domains, and that Coetzee engages only with the former. A politics worth espousing is surely a politics that both incorporates the ethical and is incorporated in it, while acknowledging the inescapable tension and continual revaluation that this mutual incorporation implies. All of Coetzee's novels enact this tension, the necessary conflict of programs and persons, of a desire to know and order and a willingness to accept otherness and contingency. The story of Mrs. Curren, her absent daughter, and Mr. Vercueil has its roots, as we have seen, in the politics of modern South Africa; but in itself, it does not deal directly with the imperatives of the political. The other main narrative thread in *Age of Iron*, which weaves through and constantly impinges upon the story of the central relationship, is directly concerned with the demands and difficulties of politics—especially in its relation to ethics—in a situation of extreme oppression and courageous resistance.

Here too the question of otherness is central; Mrs. Curren again and again finds herself faced with members of the black community whose values and actions she finds it difficult to comprehend: her maid, whom she knows as "Florence," her maid's cousin or brother, Mr. Thabane, her maid's son Bheki, and above all Bheki's friend, whom we know only by his unconvincing alias, "John," and by the Afrikaans version of this

19. In *Age of Iron*, the ethical other is specifically human; in two later novels, *The Master of Petersburg* and *Disgrace*, Coetzee extends responsibility to the other to a point where the term "ethical" begins to lose its grip. See chaps. 5 and 7.

name the police have for him, "Johannes" (171).²⁰ (The policemen she
encounters at various points in the novel also affront her values, but
with the effect of reinforcing, not shaking, them.) This otherness is very
different from Vercueil's, however; indeed, the difference is itself staged as
hostility between the township people and Vercueil. Florence can see him
only as "rubbish" and as "good for nothing" (47), and the boys despise
him perhaps even more strongly.

By examining in more detail Mrs. Curren's relationship with John—let
us grant him his half-hearted *nom de guerre*—we can assess the role of the
political in the novel and its imbrication with the ethical. Bheki, Florence's
fifteen-year-old son, has come to stay with his mother and sisters in Mrs.
Curren's backyard because of the increasing violence in Guguletu, the
township where he normally lives, and his friend soon joins him. John's
first, highly characteristic, act is to take Vercueil's brandy away from him.
As this act suggests, Bheki's friend is the most strongly delineated exemplar
of the new role which the children of the township have found, leading
their elders in a revolutionary struggle which has displaced the normal
concerns of childhood and reversed traditional parent-child relationships.
("'I cannot tell these children what to do,' said Florence, 'It is all changed
today. There are no more mothers and fathers'" [39].) Mrs. Curren sees
this as a manifestation of the age of iron in which she is living, damaging
the very future that children traditionally represent: "'And when they
grow up one day,' I said softly, 'do you think the cruelty will leave them?
What kind of parents will they become who were taught that the time of
parents is over?'" (49).

Although she implicitly acknowledges an affinity between these children and her own daughter—they are "children of iron" (50), her daughter
is "like iron" (75)—she insists, at great personal cost, on preserving the
one-way passage of mother-to-daughter inheritance and love: hence her
determination that the letter will reach her daughter only after her own

---

20. Once again, the other eludes the will-to-name of the power that dominates it. Mrs.
Curren is learning that the English names by which she has known her servant's family are
not "true" names: Florence's son—"Once I knew him as Digby, now he is Bheki" (36); her
daughter: "The elder, whose name, says Florence, is Hope (she does not entrust me with
the real name)" (37); her husband: "William—not his true name but the name by which
he is known in the world of his work" (43); Florence herself: "Perhaps I alone in all the
world called her Florence. Called her by an alias. Now I was on ground where people were
revealed in their true names" (101). We might note, too, that, as so often, Coetzee weaves
one of his own names—John—into the text in an intriguing reminder of the fictionality of
this world.

death. She explains to Vercueil: "That is something one should never ask of a child, ... to enfold one, comfort one, save one. The comfort, the love should flow forward, not backward. That is a rule, another of the iron rules" (73). Of course, iron rules are just what Mrs. Curren distrusts, but her insistence is her way of living in the times; in another age, she would telephone her daughter (as Vercueil, pragmatic as ever, urges her to do), who would fly back to South Africa to comfort her dying mother. Mrs. Curren's hope, however, is that instead of taking, she can give, and in that way project her own best existence into the future; her fear, of course, is that her child will be like the township children, hardened by the circumstances of her South African upbringing and incapable of the receptivity needed to understand and, in turn, pass on the gift.

Mrs. Curren's response to the otherness of John is of a different order to that of Vercueil; we are not tempted into allegorical readings, but made to feel the acute difficulty of establishing any relations across the divide between bourgeois white liberal and committed black revolutionary. In her early encounters with the boys Mrs. Curren vents her helpless anger at their flouting of the codes of propriety, and she experiences a particular dislike for John ("The boy stopped speaking to Bheki and regarded me. I did not like that look: arrogant, combative" [47]). Then there occurs the incident in which Mrs. Curren sees a police van force the boys, who are riding together on a bicycle, to collide with a parked truck; John is badly injured, and Mrs. Curren, deserted by both Vercueil and Florence, stays with him, trying to staunch the flow of blood from his gashed forehead until an ambulance finally arrives. But this act does not establish a reciprocal bond; when they next meet, in the hospital where Mrs. Curren has eventually tracked him down, he resists her solicitude and her admonitions. "My words fell off him like dead leaves the moment they were uttered. The words of a woman, therefore negligible; of an old woman, therefore doubly negligible; but above all of a white" (79).

For Mrs. Curren, John represents absolute commitment, which, to put it in the terms I have been using, means an absolute privileging of the political over the ethical; as she sees it, his single-minded assault on white power involves sexism, agism, and racism, and deafness to any subtleties or any qualifications of his blanket classifications and prescriptions. It is an attitude that has no place whatever for a Vercueil (the only major character in the novel who is never described by means of the metaphor of iron). In the hospital she lectures him on the importance of allowing for exceptions to general rules (even while she half-acknowledges that the times do not allow for "all that close listening, all those exceptions, all that mercy" [81]), while on a later occasion she inveighs against his masculine, black-and-white, iron understanding of the world, and argues in favor of "everything indefinite, everything that gives when you press it" (146).

Mrs. Curren's opposition to John's political beliefs is not distinct from her dislike of him as a person. She portrays him as entirely unattractive, a portrayal all the more striking in that it emphasizes that he is still a child:

> I did not like him. I do not like him. I look into my heart and nowhere do I find any trace of feeling for him. As there are people to whom one spontaneously warms, so there are people to whom one is, from the first, cold. That is all. . . . A simplified person, simplified in every way: swifter, nimbler, more tireless than real people, without doubts or scruples, without humor, ruthless, innocent. While he lay in the street, while I thought he was dying, I did what I could for him. But, to be candid, I would rather I had spent myself on someone else. (78–79)

Yet she does not dismiss him; as with Vercueil, his very otherness seems to exert a strong pull on her, as if her special situation renders her exceptionally willing to allow her inherited values to be tested to the limit. She pushes her sick body into an exhausting search for him in hospital, gives up, and then returns when she learns from Florence where he is. Without making a choice, she finds herself responsible to and for him; he, too, is the other.

Later, one night, he appears in her house, a refugee, his injuries unhealed, and Mrs. Curren ministers to him. The event produces an extraordinary "confession" to her daughter, in which she struggles to find an appropriate, we might say ethical, response to the boy:

> I do not love this child, the child sleeping in Florence's bed. I love you but I do not love him. There is no ache in me toward him, not the slightest.
>
> Yes, you reply, he is not lovable. But did you not have a part in making him unlovable?
>
> I do not deny that. But at the same time I do not believe it. My heart does not accept him as mine: it is as simple as that. (136)

The recognition that the otherness to which she is struggling to open herself has been produced by the very values in whose name she claims to be acting is one that she can accept rationally but not emotionally. And this leads her to question her very capacity to love: "Not wanting to love him, how true can I say my love is for you? For love is not like hunger. Love is never sated, stilled. When one loves, one loves more. The more I love you, the more I ought to love him" (137). Her struggle is a struggle to redefine love—the love that is the origin and driving force of the entire letter—in such a way as to include that which is most resistant to it (more resistant even than Vercueil, whom she finds "hard to love" [57] for his physical repulsiveness, but to whom she does, in a strange way, warm spontaneously). It is a love that is not defined, as love usually is, in opposition to duty, but one that flows directly from duty.

When the police kill John in her backyard, Mrs. Curren—now defying all propriety for the sake of her difficult love—attempts to climb into the ambulance with the body. Prevented from doing so, she walks away from the house and into the most horrifying of her degradations, as a group of children force a stick into her mouth, prying it open in search of gold fillings, while she lies beneath an overpass, too ill to resist. Her reaction reveals how far she has traveled from the moral truisms that once nourished her: ridiculing a momentary urge to beg for mercy, she chides herself, "What nonsense. Why should there be mercy in the world?" (159). Vercueil finds her and carries her to a wooded space to sleep on a flattened cardboard box, and there she makes another "confession"—to Vercueil (who may not be awake for all of it), but also to herself and to her daughter—in which she articulates as fully as she can her new understanding of the political struggle she is caught up in. While insisting that she still detests "these calls for sacrifice that end with young men bleeding to death in the mud" (163), she nevertheless acknowledges the inadequacy, in the times she is living in, of the concepts she has hitherto been guided by—"honor," "shame," and "goodness" ("What I had not calculated on was that more might be called for than to be good" [165])— and the necessity for what she calls "heroism": a word that, having come to mean something different from what it did in her classical education, perhaps helped her to love the unlovable John, or at least to acknowledge his independence and worth as an other. This implies a new understanding of the political necessity and inevitability of the children's activism and attitudes, and therefore of a conflict—the conflict between the ethical and the political, which is also a conflict *within* both the ethical and the political—that cannot be resolved in the present by a feat of analysis that seizes the future, but that has to be worked through, stage by stage, painful detail by painful detail.[21] The understanding we glimpse here is

21. Attwell's admirable reading of the novel in *J. M. Coetzee* seems to me to underestimate the effect of Mrs. Curren's continuing attempt to revise and rearticulate her response to the political conditions of her time and place; he refers to her "direct and unsubtle" judgment of the white nationalists, and to her "condemnation of the new forms of puritanism and

not entirely new, however; it has been implicit, for instance, in her urge to record the black voices that have so implacably opposed hers, and to transfer them to her daughter as part of what she bequeaths.

It is an age of iron, the worst of times, and its particular deformations of the human spirit call for a response that is neither moralizing nor cynical. Mrs. Curren has to acknowledge that nothing she can say will detract from the heroic self-sacrifice of the township children, made vivid to her in the deaths first of Bheki and then of John; theirs is a situation in which the only possible ethic is an ethic of comradeship, single-mindedness, and blind courage.[22] For Mrs. Curren, and by implication for J. M. Coetzee and the majority of his readers, who are in a markedly different situation, the ethical appears in another guise: as the difficult task of responding with full justice to the moment, with a trust in the other and the future that is ultimately beyond measure. In understanding the nature of this task, the test posed and the example presented by Vercueil are of the utmost importance. An ethical response on the part of privileged South African whites to the violent and dehumanizing campaign of the townships would be one which is neither condemnation nor approval, neither detachment nor immersion, but a living-through (in concrete action as well as in thought and emotion) of the torsions it produces in shared value-systems.

What is enacted in this novel is the acute ethico-political trauma of the post-colonial world, where no general rule applies, where a conflict of values is endemic, and where every code of moral conduct has to be tested and justified afresh in terms of the specific context in which it is being invoked. But this is not a lesson to be learned, a conclusion to be reached.

---

militarism evident in the township youth" (122), without acknowledging that both these positions are later questioned.

22. I have not discussed the effect upon Mrs. Curren of her traumatic experience in the township and squatter camp, especially as evidenced by the long address to her daughter (109–12) and the equally long speech to Vercueil (124–26), both prompted by Bheki's death; such a discussion would have to be part of a fuller attempt to account for her ethical growth. However, this episode is reminiscent of the traditional narrative of the South African white whose eyes are opened to the horrors of the system he or she lives in and benefits from, an essentially political narrative that Coetzee is seeking to force into new territory (the territory I am calling the ethical). Mrs. Curren's meditation on her return from the township, moving and deeply felt though it is, is framed by two glimpses of a scene that reminds us of the less easily categorizable learning process she is undergoing: Vercueil sitting asleep on her toilet. It is also worth noting that, in spite of the overwhelming effect on her of Bheki's killing, she admits toward the end that John, imagined waiting with his pistol for the moment of death, is with her "more clearly, more piercingly than Bheki has ever been" (175).

Mrs. Curren's new understanding is not something she has achieved; it exists in, and cannot be separated from, the negotiations and questionings she has experienced. Although in these extreme times the political and the ethical may seem absolutely opposed, they are not. The ethical cannot be reduced to the moral injunctions about the individual and the exception enshrined in Mrs. Curren's inherited creed; it is a process of constant reappraisal and self-redefinition through which those injunctions are tested, reaffirmed, or remade. The political cannot be reduced to the need for solidarity and simplification, for fixed readings of the past and the future, which is the guise it must sometimes wear; it is always subject to the demands of the ethical.

The peculiar importance of literature as a cultural practice lies in its capacity to play out these issues, in a process that is not measured in terms of its meaning or its result. Reading a work of literature entails opening oneself to the unpredictable, the future, the other, and thereby accepting the responsibility laid upon one by the work's singularity and difference. There is also abundant evidence that *writing* a literary work is often a similar experience.[23] In a sense, the "literary" is the ethical. Literary criticism, however, can seldom make the same claim. What I have given is only a crude sketch of the rich working through of questions of trust, love, alterity, politics, and ethics, in *Age of Iron;* I have necessarily schematized and simplified where the novel remains fluid and even self-contradictory. Its power lies not in any hagiographic object-lesson—the uniqueness of Mrs. Curren's personality and predicament precludes that—but in its enactment, in charged, exploratory, sometimes consciously self-indulgent language, of a number of interrelated struggles in which the reader is invited to participate with sympathy but also with critical judgment.

It is characteristic of Coetzee that he should risk building a politically engaged novel on such overworked concepts as "trust" and "love," and one might predict that his having done so will be frequently misunderstood

---

23. Coetzee is one of those who have testified to this experience: "The feel of writing fiction is one of freedom, of irresponsibility, or better, of responsibility toward something that has not yet emerged, that lies somewhere at the end of the road. When I write criticism, on the other hand, I am always aware of a responsibility toward a goal that has been set for me not only by the argument, not only by the whole philosophical tradition into which I am implicitly inserting myself, but also by the rather tight discourse of criticism itself" (*Doubling the Point,* 246). Or again: "First you give yourself to (or throw yourself into) the writing, and go where it takes you. Then you step back and ask yourself where you are, whether you really want to be there" ("Thematizing," 289). See also Attridge, *The Singularity of Literature,* chap. 2.

(both by those who want to exclude the political and by those who want to emphasize it). Only by paying close attention to the penetrating and lucid way in which such terms are questioned in his fiction—operating always as fiction and not as disguised treatise or tract, operating, that is, in response to the contingent, the unpredictable, the other—can we do justice to Coetzee's work, which does not hesitate to engage with the dominating legacy of Western thought and culture, and to stage, with remarkable results, the transformation that it undergoes, in a curious and conflicted living-on, in our post-colonial world.

CHAPTER FIVE

Expecting the Unexpected

The Master of Petersburg

: I :

The author is familiar to me, the book is new. Not just new to me, but newly published, recently written, so that it comes to me without the filter of commentary that so quickly surrounds a work when it enters the public domain—that filter through which almost everything we read is colored and constrained. It is a work of *my time,* not yet a part of history. It might be a new novel by a writer whose previous novels I know and value, or a new set of arguments by a philosopher whose earlier writings I admire, or a report on a series of experiments by a scientific author who has been important to me in the past. What is my responsibility as a reader of such a new work? Is it different from the responsibility I have to works already received within a tradition? How am I to do justice to whatever originality the new work may possess?

As a reader my demands on such a work are contradictory. I want it to repeat what I have enjoyed in its author's earlier productions, since this is why I am reading it; at the same time, I expect it to provide something new, something unexpected, something I couldn't have predicted from all that the writer has hitherto achieved. If it doesn't surprise me in this way, I might as well have written it myself, or programmed a computer to read the earlier works and then to produce another one according to the formula it derives from them.[1] Even if one aspect of my previous enjoyment has been the experience of surprise, I want to be surprised in a new way; I want to be surprised by the kind of surprise the fresh work offers.

The result of these contradictory demands is that my response to a new work is bound to contain an element of disappointment. Either the work will traverse familiar territory, and my pleasure in revisiting a previously traveled landscape will be marred by regret that there is nothing truly new; or I will find myself in a strange, unmapped, terrain which will answer to my demand for the new but will have only an obscure relation to what I enjoy in the author's writing. There is, it is true, a possibility that the work may constitute a new departure for the author but still seem pleasantly familiar, still provide that gratifying sense of a meeting of minds: yes, that's exactly right, that's how I see it, that's a wonderful way of putting it. In this case, we can be fairly certain that what has happened is that although the author has written a work that breaks new ground for him or her, it conforms to some prevailing tendency in the culture at large—a tendency which, as a participant in my time, I inevitably share. It's this shared conformity that gives me the feeling that the writer has captured the truth in remarkably apt words. In this case, the work may constitute a new departure for the author concerned, but it cannot count as a work of originality and inventiveness with respect to its cultural milieu, and it is likely to sink quite quickly into that milieu as merely one of a number of productions typical of its time.

No doubt most works of what we call originality or inventiveness operate in both these ways. Jacques Derrida argues in his essay "Psyche: Invention of the Other" that inventiveness is impossible without programmability: the wholly new has to have the capacity to be put to work in the existing institutions even as it changes those institutions—otherwise it will have no force whatsoever (see especially 315–18). But I am interested in our responses to the new work before its programmability has been tested, before the institutions have had the opportunity to absorb, reject, or be altered by it. Of course even my initial, immediate reaction is not outside of these institutions; it is thoroughly mediated by them (and thus cannot strictly be called immediate). They include the economic institutions of publishing, advertising, and bookselling which have brought me the book, the disciplines and genres which govern the kind of reading

1. A new work by an author with whom I am *not* familiar raises somewhat different questions and expectations, since in this case the cultural context in which the work appears plays a more determining role.

I give it ("philosophy," "literature," "novel," etc.), and the educational institutions which have provided me with techniques of reading and evaluating texts. But what I want, rather artificially, to isolate here are those moments at which the new work baffles and disappoints because it refuses known pleasures and satisfactions, those moments at which it *is* new, an intervention in the discourses of its time that is unprecedented—at least within current cultural memory. (It may of course also be very old; perhaps it is inevitable that it *will* be very old. We shall consider later the question of the ghost, the revenant, that comes back with the force of the new.)

Whatever the historical reasons for the emergence of the term "novel" to name in English a work of prose fiction of a certain length, it points directly to my concerns. Is novelty, real originality of the kind I have been talking about, constitutive of the type of writing (and reading) we generally call literary? Or is it an optional characteristic of the literary text, rather than a defining property? Or, a third possibility, should we try to distinguish between two varieties of literature (as we might two varieties of philosophy): that which gets its name from an adherence to existing formal and thematic norms, and that which earns the adjective "literary" precisely because of its refusal to be comprehended by those norms? None of these ways of treating the category is without its problems, and none without its merits; if I gravitate toward the third it is because it enables me to talk about the "literary" as a power possessed by certain works (not all of them, in fact, commonly classed as literature) in relation to a specific time and a place.

: II :

It was my reading of *The Master of Petersburg* that, on its publication in 1994, provoked the questions I have just raised in a peculiarly acute form. Having over a period of about fifteen years read all Coetzee's novels, from *Dusklands* to *Age of Iron,* in many cases on their initial appearance, I looked forward with pleasurable anticipation to the next novel—especially as it would be Coetzee's first novel written since South Africa began to refashion itself as a democratic state. I didn't indulge in any predictions, however, predictions being particularly, perhaps constitutively, problematic in the literary domain, and one of the remarkable features of Coetzee's oeuvre being its refusal to settle into a single mode. Each novel has entered new territory and used new fictional techniques. Coetzee has used both male and female first-person narrators, third-person narration tracking closely the consciousness of an individual, letters, journals, purely imaginary characters, characters with some basis in history or in fiction of the past, present-tense narration, past-tense narration, and so on.

Nevertheless, in reading these diverse works I, like many others, had formed a conception of a "Coetzee novel," without being fully conscious that I had done so. To take an obvious feature, all the earlier novels evinced a clear concern with contemporary South Africa, with the questions of otherness, oppression, and resistance that its political and social history raise so starkly—whether this concern was articulated in a narrative of South African life (past, present, or future) or one which allowed for translation into South African terms (Robinson Crusoe's Friday on the streets of London; the struggle of the Empire against the "barbarians"). Although refusing to adopt a simple political position, they could be read by those looking for a pronouncement about South Africa as indictments of apartheid and exemplifications of the human deformities it produced.

As anyone who has read *The Master of Petersburg* will know, this novel offers no such firm political or moral footholds. Temporally and geographically, the events are firmly fixed (and in fact announced in the novel's first three words): they take place in St. Petersburg in October, and later November, 1869. The novel uses third-person present-tense narration, and stays extremely close to the consciousness of the main character, with the inclusion of some interior monologue. This type of narration was not new for Coetzee: he used a form of it for the representation of Michael K, though as we noted in chapter 2 the reader was not allowed to experience any consistent intimacy with the character's inner life. The protagonist this time is very different: not an apparently simple mind cutting through the complex force-field of a collapsing totalitarian state but a highly sophisticated and hyperconscious mind wrestling with its own guilt, fears, losses, and desires. The name of the protagonist, one discovers after thirty-three pages (if one is reading for the first time, that is, and is unaided by the commentary of others or by one's own specialized knowledge of Russian cultural history), is Fyodor Mikhailovich Dostoevsky.

The fictional Dostoevsky has returned secretly from Dresden, where he and his wife and child are living, unable to enter Russia openly for fear of creditors. The reason for his return is the death in mysterious circumstances of his stepson Pavel—the son of his late first wife—whom he had been supporting in Petersburg. Dostoevsky is soon living in Pavel's apartment, trying to come to terms with his loss, while the narrative follows two major threads: his intense relationships with the landlady and her young daughter Matryona (or, more familiarly, Matryosha), and his equally intense relationship with Sergei Nechaev, a young revolutionary who turns out to have been a major influence on Pavel and who is in hiding from the authorities in the city.

The protagonist of *The Master of Petersburg* is very close to the historical Dostoevsky; much closer than, for instance, Foe in the novel named after him is to the historical Daniel Defoe (see above, chap. 3, n. 15). Coetzee takes pains to reward the reader who checks the historical record, as presented, for instance, in Joseph Frank's volume of biography dealing with the years 1865–71 (Coetzee's review of which appeared in 1995).[2] As in the novel, Dostoevsky was living in Dresden in 1869, under the watchful eyes of the Russian secret police, unable to return openly to St. Petersburg because of his debts there. If he did make a visit to the city in October of that year—for which there is no evidence—he would have to have done so incognito.[3] He did indeed have a stepson called Pavel whom he supported in Petersburg while he was outside the country. Sergei Nechaev is also a historical individual, and was in Russia at this time; he would soon become notorious for his involvement in the murder of a student who belonged to his revolutionary group. Well-known aspects of Dostoevsky's biography feature in the novel, such as his gambling and his epilepsy. And the tortured spirals of self-doubt, self-denigration, and self-exculpation that occupy so much of the protagonist's mental world are familiar from Dostoevsky's fiction and letters.

The reader is thus invited to treat *The Master of Petersburg* as an interpretation of the historical Dostoevsky's life and work—a project entirely different from anything Coetzee had attempted before. (While *Foe* is certainly in part about the founding of the English realist novel, it doesn't encourage the reader to take it as a considered account of Defoe's own life and creative activity.) Even more specifically, the novel asks to be read as a fictionalized account of the genesis of one of Dostoevsky's own novels: *The Possessed* (also known in English as *The Devils* and *Demons*). We know that he was beginning to work on this novel in December 1869, a month after the close of Coetzee's narrative. The fictional events provide personal sources for both the main characters of *The Possessed*, Peter

---

2. The review was reprinted in Coetzee's *Stranger Shores*, 134–48.

3. The impression given in *The Master of Petersburg* of a particular interest on the part of the police in Dostoevsky (evoked especially in the superbly Dostoevskian chapter "Maximov") is not mere fiction; Joseph Frank quotes a letter written by Dostoevsky in 1868 in which he complains from Dresden, "The Petersburg police open *all* my letters" (*Dostoevsky*, 299).

Verkhovensky (who, it has always been evident, was based on Nechaev) and Nicholas Stavrogin, to whom we shall return.[4]

At the same time as enforcing the connections between fiction and history, however, Coetzee makes the gap between the novel's protagonist and the historical Dostoevsky absolutely clear, at least to the reader who possesses, or obtains, a modicum of information about Dostoevsky's life—and this knowledge functions to *block* the reading of the novel as a commentary on an actual writer and his work. Apart from the lack of any evidence of a surreptitious visit to St. Petersburg (at a time when Dostoevsky's daughter Lyubov, not mentioned in the novel, was barely a month old), the basic premise on which Coetzee's work is built—Dostoevsky's painful coming to terms with Pavel's death—is glaringly contrafactual. The real Pavel outlived the real Dostoevsky.

A double discomfort, then. First, Coetzee's novel seems far removed from the preoccupations of South Africa in the early 1990s. (I want to emphasize that I'm not insisting that Coetzee, or any other writer living in South Africa, has an obligation to write "about South Africa"—Coetzee has resisted the limiting label "South African writer" [see chap. 3, note 7], a position with which one can sympathize. My point is simply that his novels before this one produced an expectation which the new novel failed to satisfy.) Second, insofar as it does situate itself in relation to history, it does so ambiguously and unsettlingly. Coetzee appears to be asking, "What could have led Dostoevsky to write a novel like *The Possessed?*" and at the same time saying, "My answer will not be of the order of the historico-biographical—except to the extent that the historico-biographical always partakes of the fictional."

Also disquieting on a first reading is that where the novel is most obviously concerned with issues of politics, of oppression, of the future of a nation in turmoil, there is very little that could be read as celebration of the triumphs and fresh beginnings that marked this period in South

---

4. Other elements in *The Master of Petersburg* which point to *The Possessed* include the story of Pavel's courtship of a woman named Maria Lebyatkin, who appears as a character in *The Possessed,* and the possibility (never confirmed) that Pavel's death is in fact Nechaev's doing, which would add a personal dimension to Dostoevsky's account of the killing of Shatov in *The Possessed,* an event based more obviously on the murder of the student Ivan Ivanov. But the picture is clouded again by the presence in *The Master of Petersburg* of a character called (pseudonymously) Ivanov, a police spy, who is also murdered, presumably by the Nechaevites, and by the absence of any reference to the historical murder of Ivan Ivanov, which took place on November 26, 1869, approximately when Coetzee's novel ends—as if the actual death has been displaced onto two separate fictional deaths.

Africa's history. Coetzee chooses as his central figure someone who, turning his back on a radical activist past (which brought exile to Siberia after a narrow escape from execution), had become by the 1860s an outspoken opponent of revolutionary political movements and a champion of the Russian Church as the foundation of a new, spiritually regenerated Russian nation. The novel that we see being born was intended as an onslaught on the Russian radical movements of the time, and was published in a conservative Russian journal.

Coetzee gives us, it is true, a Nechaev who is eloquent in his denunciation of poverty in Tsarist Russia and his demonstration of its source in the collusion of interests that benefit from it, but he is countered by an equally eloquent Dostoevsky, who willfully or blindly fails to comprehend the young man's proto-Marxist argument and proffers a more individualized view of the suffering of the poor (180–84). This is not to say that the novel espouses Dostoevsky's position as politically or even morally superior to Nechaev's. The young revolutionary, although he is an unappealing person whose political position is totalizing and single-minded (rather like the boy from the townships who calls himself "John" in *Age of Iron*), remains a force (like John) whom the protagonist is obliged, although finally unable, to take account of. But however forceful Nechaev's presentation of his case, and however much he succeeds in unsettling the convictions of Coetzee's Dostoevsky, he can hardly be read as a salute to the fighting members of the ANC or the South African Communist Party.

Coetzee has chosen, then, to view revolutionary activism through the eyes of a dedicated conservative; and to allow neither position to carry the day. However, this aspect of the novel—the clash between a politics that attempts to program the future and an ethics that attempts to do justice to the singularity of the other human being—is not in itself unprecedented in Coetzee's fiction, and I have already discussed a related opposition in *Age of Iron* (see chap. 4 above). We will return to the conflict between the political and the ethical, but if we want to go to the heart of the work's originality, to confront what is most gripping and most troubling about this book because most unfamiliar, we need to look elsewhere.

: III :

We can start by considering the unusual demands the novel makes on its readers. We expect momentum in a novel, a sense of direction, some principle of onward movement, involvement in the dilemmas and choices of characters, glimpses of a resolution ahead that will give meaning to short-term enigmas and apparent digressions. Coetzee's novels up to *The Master of Petersburg* are not exactly generous in fulfilling these require-ments, but they offer just enough to keep the willing reader engaged— the increasing physical dissolution which Mrs. Curren experiences in *Age of Iron,* for instance, coupled with the hope that she will achieve some kind of new understanding of the South African conflict before death; or the successive stages in the campaign by Susan Barton to have her story recorded for posterity in *Foe* together with her attempts to make contact with the speechless Friday. It is not clear, however, *what* Dostoevsky's project in St. Petersburg is, what his real choices are, where the novel is taking us. He is mourning his stepson Pavel, of course, but he does not have to stay in Petersburg for that; there is something that he is waiting for, or trying to bring about, but he seems not to know precisely what it is. He wants, he says, to find his way to Pavel, or to have Pavel come to him, but it is not clear what this means, nor how it could be achieved. He is living in Pavel's room, sometimes even wearing his clothes, in an attempt to effect a union with the dead stepson that will exceed anything attained in life. (The novel provides hints of a past relationship not very different from the one recorded in biographies of Dostoevsky: a child resentful of his mother's second marriage, and then, after her death, of his stepfather's second marriage to a girl his own age; a stepfather acknowledging to the full his responsibilities as sole guardian after the death of both the boy's parents, but finding many barriers to the relationship.)[5]

It's a novel of waiting, then, and waiting without any clear sense of what would constitute the longed-for arrival. A Beckettian situation, but not lightened by any Beckettian humor. Thanks to Derrida, we can propose a name for what Dostoevsky is waiting for: the *arrivant,* which we might translate into English as "one who arrives" or "arrival" (as in "the latest

5. Joseph Frank cites two of Dostoevsky's letters of 1868 to his friend Apollon Maikov which indicate the strength of the writer's sense of responsibility toward Pavel and the frustration he experienced in trying to fulfill it. In the first, he is explaining the sacredness of his obligations to his dependents: "In Pasha's case, he was entrusted to my care by poor Marya Dimitrievna [Dostoevsky's first wife] on her deathbed. And so how can I abandon him altogether? He is like a son to me" (285). And having heard that Pavel has left two jobs as a clerk because he felt insulted by his superiors, he writes, "What a mentality, what opinions and ideas, what braggadocio! It's typical. But then, on the other hand—how can I abandon him?" (*Dostoevsky,* 295).

arrival"). (It is also worth bearing in mind that the word *arriver* can mean "happen.") In *Aporias,* Derrida glosses the term as follows:

> *The new arrivant:* this word can, indeed, mean the neutrality of *that which* arrives, but also the singularity of *who* arrives, he or she who comes, coming to be where he or she was not expected, where one was awaiting him or her without waiting for him or her, without expecting *it,* without knowing what or whom to expect, what or whom I am waiting for—and such is hospitality itself, hospitality toward the event. (33, translation modified)

Derrida uses a word which, although singular rather than general, conveys nothing about the nature of what it is that arrives: he is as interested in the event of arrival as in the person or thing that arrives, and would regard any entity that could be delimited in advance (as human rather than animal, for instance) as to that extent less than a true *arrivant.* The *arrivant* is closely tied, therefore, to the *event,* understood as a happening that could not have been predicted (even if with hindsight its emergence from a prior state of affairs can be logically traced), a happening, that is, that brings otherness into being. As the quotation above indicates, it is also closely linked to *hospitality:* to welcome the *arrivant,* the other that arrives on your doorstep, is to be willing to remake your familiar world without setting any prior limits on how far you are willing to go.[6]

Most of Coetzee's novel occurs in the time before the advent of the *arrivant,* the "desert-like" time of the "messianic," perhaps, as Derrida describes it in *Specters of Marx* (28). Dostoevsky, in the novel, does know that he is waiting for some kind of ghost, a revenant, the specter of Pavel. Quite early on he asks himself, "Why this plodding chase across empty country after the rumour of a ghost, the ghost of a rumour?" (53); and much later the question recurs, "How long can he go on waiting for a ghost?" (154). At one point his attempt to summon up his son's image (in place of Nechaev's) is described as "conjuring" (49). But it is the living he becomes entangled with, the living who seem to be given the task of bringing Pavel back, back to where he in fact never was, united with his father. (Not, for example, the corpse of his stepson; Dostoevsky visits the grave soon after his arrival, promises to return the next day, but never goes back.) In particular, it is Pavel's generation, the "children," as

---

6. Derrida provides an account of hospitality—taking the concept to its implicit limits— in *Of Hospitality,* co-authored with Anne Dufourmantelle, and discusses some of its political consequences in *On Cosmopolitanism and Forgiveness.*

Dostoevsky thinks of them, who come in his place: Matryona, the young girl in the apartment whom Pavel had befriended, and Nechaev, the youthful revolutionary under whose spell he—and she—appear to have fallen. I'll return later to these characters and their importance in the novel.

: IV :

These intractable questions of waiting, of expectation, of hospitality, of giving oneself to the future, to the other, are articulated most fully and forcefully in a chapter entitled "Ivanov"—which is nevertheless (or therefore) a deeply puzzling chapter, whose relation to the plot, such as it is, is not evident. One night Dostoevsky hears, in his sleep, a voice calling him, but when he wakes up fully it turns out to be just the howling of a dog. His response engages movingly with the deconstructive logic (or alogic) of the *arrivant*:

> A dog, not his son. Therefore? Therefore he must throw off this lethargy! *Because* it is not his son he must not go back to bed but must get dressed and answer the call. If he expects his son to come as a thief in the night, and listens only for the call of the thief, he will never see him. If he expects his son to speak in the voice of the unexpected, he will never hear him. As long as he expects what he does not expect, what he does not expect will not come. Therefore—paradox within paradox, darkness swaddled in darkness—he must answer to what he does not expect. (80)

Here is the dilemma of the one who waits for the *arrivant;* the one, that is, who wishes to be open to the arrival of the other, the wholly new. The reader who wishes to do justice to the real originality of a new novel, for instance. The judge who wishes to respond justly to what is completely unique in a given case. The activist who wishes to be attuned to the stirrings of an entirely new social formation. If one *knows* what one is waiting for, it can only be the familiar. But even if one knows one is waiting for the *unfamiliar,* one has already constrained the unfamiliar by conceiving of it on the basis of the familiar—the thief in the night, for example, is the unexpected already defined against the expected, the proper, the orderly. The cry of the dog, however, is not the unexpected in this sense; it is the event that interrupts the order of the familiar and unfamiliar with absolute heterogeneity, an appeal from the other which comes from outside any structure of moral obligation. It carries no guarantees, fits into no program, is imbued with no particular significance. It is the easiest thing in the world to ignore. This is why it must be answered. (I need not labor the parallel with the exemplification of trust in *Age of Iron*, discussed in the previous chapter.)

But answering is not simple, because an answer presupposes an understanding of the demand being made. It is not just a question of kindness to animals; if that is all that is at stake (and it is not nothing) we cannot talk of the *arrivant*. The question is whether the howl in the night, as it affects Dostoevsky, has the potential to free up the jammed components of his world, to lead to the wholly new that fitfully beckons him—or whether it is merely a banal irritation. As Derrida says in *Specters of Marx*: "*One does not know* if the expectation prepares the coming of the future-to-come or if it recalls the repetition of the same.... This not-knowing is not a lacuna. No progress of knowledge could saturate an opening that must have nothing to do with knowing. Nor therefore with ignorance" (36–37). Dostoevsky leaves the house and eventually finds the dog, chained to a drainpipe, the chain wrapped around one leg. He frees the leg, but leaves the dog tied up, still howling.

> "*It is not my son, it is just a dog,*" he protests. *What is it to me?* Yet even as he protests he knows the answer: Pavel will not be saved till he has freed the dog and brought it into his bed, brought *the least thing,* the beggarmen and the beggarwomen too, and much else he does not yet know of; and even then there will be no certainty. (82)

Being wholly responsive to the new, the other, doing justice to it every time, is impossible. Even minimal adherence to its demands is an interminable task, with no sure reward, not to be thought of in terms of instrumentality or merit.

Let me juxtapose this passage from Coetzee with a passage from Derrida's *The Gift of Death* which I find extraordinarily powerful, like the whole discussion of which it is part:

> I am responsible to the other as other, I answer to him and I answer for what I do before him. But of course, what binds me thus in my singularity to the absolute singularity of the other, immediately propels me into the space or risk of absolute sacrifice. There are also others, an infinite number of them, the innumerable generality of others to whom I should be bound by the same responsibility, a general and universal responsibility (what Kierkegaard calls the ethical order). I cannot respond to the call, the request, the obligation, or even the love of another without sacrificing the other other, the other others. (68)

Dostoevsky knows that the demands of the other are unfulfillable. The responsible answer to this paradox, to this aporia, is not to throw up one's hands, of course, but to carry on, to increase one's attentiveness and one's responsiveness, recognizing that the aporia not only makes wholly responsible action impossible but also that it is a condition for any exercise of responsibility at all. Derrida writes of the necessity for "a sort of nonpassive endurance of the aporia" as the condition of responsibility (*Aporias*, 16), and also names it "passion" (19). Dostoevsky, in Coetzee's novel, does not bring the dog to his bed, but while he is outside he discovers, crouching in a corner, a beggar—or rather a police spy very convincingly disguised as a beggar—who has been keeping watch on the house.

"He starts to climb the stairs. But tediously the paradox comes back: *Expect the one you do not expect.* Very well; but must every beggar then be treated as a prodigal son, embraced, welcomed into the home, feasted?" (84). The obligations of hospitality, at their limit, answer yes. He does take the man into his room, listens to his pathetic story, gives him his own bed and his own breakfast, all with some degree of distance and distaste. Nothing seems to come from the gesture, no self-satisfaction, no useful information, no advance towards Pavel. In the evening he is faced with the question of whether he should seek the false beggar out to offer him shelter again. Clearly, by any normal moral standards, he is under no such obligation, but eventually he goes to search for the man, and is relieved that he is nowhere to be found. "I have done what I can, he thinks. But he knows in his heart he has not. There is more he could do, much more" (93). As Derrida stresses, there is always much more that could be done; the demands of the other are infinite, and every other is completely other, *tout autre est tout autre.*[7]

: V :

Dostoevsky does not, cannot, know what he is waiting for, under the name of Pavel. His mourning—for a stepson with whom he had a troubled relationship—seems excessive. (It could be said, however, that the absence of a blood relation between them in some ways makes the loss all the more difficult to cope with, reminded as he constantly is that his claim on

---

7. I have discussed the implications of Derrida's account of responsibility to the other, and the necessary sacrifice it involves, more fully in "On Mount Moriah."

Pavel's memory is an indirect one.) He allows his actions to be determined by impulses, attractions, obscure desires, though without fully trusting in any of them.

Continually through the novel his words and movements are described in terms that suggest a yielding to a force from outside; we encounter statements such as "His own next sentence is already emerging, in what sounds to him like a drone" (96), "The words come without premeditation" (122), and ". . . still following the words like beacons, seeing where they will take him" (140). (Here, of course, we find echoes of Michael K's and Mrs. Curren's unpremeditated actions, and the "new thick voice" which the Magistrate says "seems to be mine.")[8] The major figure for this yielding is Dostoevsky's epilepsy, which manifests in stark terms his subjection to forces over which he has no control. Its first manifestation is described in characteristic terms, puzzling to the first-time reader: "Something is on its way, something whose name he is trying to avoid" (27). He renames it—a germ of the book that lies ahead in his career as a novelist—*possession* (213), and proceeds to allegorize it, though complaining as he does so that he is "making his own sordid and contemptible infirmity into the emblematic sickness of the age" (235).[9]

All this makes the reading uncomfortable, motorless, rudderless. Readers who hook on to the political plot or the sexual plot as the main hope of narrative direction and conclusion, like some of the early reviewers, find the rewards meager. With no plan, following up whatever impinges on his existence from outside, Dostoevsky lets himself become embroiled in the political activities of Nechaev and his group, culminating in the writing of a statement about his stepson's death for publication on the group's illegal press. He begins a sexual relationship with the landlady, Anna Sergeyevna (although he takes the initiative, it is soon she who is in charge), but it is her daughter Matryona who exerts the strongest erotic influence on him. Though he makes no overt sexual approach to the young girl, his inner world is suffused with her sexual presence, and one does not feel that Anna Sergeyevna is wrong when she accuses him of using her as a route to her child (231). He himself, in a particularly repellent passage, names his outward act of physically comforting her after having reduced

---

8. See pp. 57, 95–96, and 45 above.

9. Another figure from Dostoevsky's life that Coetzee uses on several occasions is gambling. Gambling involves a future-oriented risk-taking, but it does not involve the work of achieving openness to the other. More generally, however, Dostoevsky does have to wager that a trust in the other will save rather than destroy him; there is no calculation possible.

her to helpless sobbing over Pavel's death a "violation," accompanied as it is by his imagining of her in orgasmic ecstasy with the corpse of his son (76).

The novel demands of the reader a willingness to wait, to keep alternatives open, to remain scrupulously attentive to details. Only in the last chapter does it fulfill the promise implicit in such demands: that there will be an end of waiting, that the time in the wilderness will be redeemed. Reader and character, perhaps writer too, are at last able to welcome the *arrivant*, even though the path to this moment remains obscure. But far from being the most satisfying, it is the most disturbing chapter in a disturbing book.

: VI :

The chapter is entitled "Stavrogin," although the name does not occur within it (unlike the earlier chapters, which are all given titles that are repeated in the subsequent text). Only knowledge of another text, the historical Dostoevsky's novel *The Possessed,* can give the title meaning. Coetzee is once again making considerable demands on the reader—more so than with *Foe,* since familiarity with at least the outline of *Robinson Crusoe* is much more likely than familiarity with Dostoevsky's long, difficult, historically embedded novel.[10] The character of Stavrogin in *The Possessed* is Dostoevsky's attempt to create a figure of peculiar evil, the talented, bored aristocrat who destroys others without any strong motivation or evident satisfaction. One reason why *The Possessed* is a difficult novel is that Stavrogin's worst offence, which Dostoevsky no doubt intended as a crystallization of his dark portrait, did not see the light of day, for the editor of the journal refused to publish it. That crime is the violation of his landlady's eleven-year-old daughter, Matryosha, and his subsequent failure to take any action to prevent her from hanging

---

10. There are also a number of intertextual connections with *Crime and Punishment,* which was written several years before the supposed incidents of *The Master of Petersburg.* For example, the fires, in the chapter of that name, seen by the fictional Dostoevsky on the other side of the river (229)—fires started by revolutionary students—sound very like the fires on the far side of the Neva which Raskolnikov finds reported in the newspapers he goes through in search of the account of his crime (*Crime and Punishment,* 205). Svidrigailov, a foreshadowing of Stavrogin in many respects, is also rumored to have raped a young girl, who then hanged herself (356).

herself. The novel we see being born in *The Master of Petersburg*, how-ever, is clearly the novel as Dostoevsky *wanted* to publish it, with Stavro-gin's confession of his offence a central feature. It is almost as if Coetzee has attempted to undo the act of censorship that removed this part of the book, and to reinstate Stavrogin's crime and confession as its main-spring.[11]

The title of the chapter therefore signifies that the culmination of this long wait, this so far sterile following of hints and urges, is in writing, the event of writing, writing *as* event, an occurrence neither fully active nor fully passive. The nonpassive endurance of the aporia. Writing as passion. Pavel comes, finally, not with a ghost's embrace but as the ghost-liness of writing, of letting words come, of giving them the initiative. But the *arrivant,* the other, the new, does not come from nowhere: the artist's inventive act that brings it into being—which is also an event that al-lows it to emerge—involves the deepest engagement with the cultural and social environment and with the inner, subjective embodiment of that ex-ternal reality, tracing its fractures, finding its contradictions, uncovering its occlusions.

At many points earlier in the novel Dostoevsky had set out his writing paraphernalia in Pavel's room, but written nothing. He now unpacks his writing-case once more, the day after a student rising that reveals the brute strength of Nechaev's movement, the day after Matryona has seen her mother sleeping with the lodger. A new understanding of his task has dawned on him, for which he again uses the figure of the falling-sickness, linking it to Pavel's deadly fall:

> There is a choice before him. He can cry out in the midst of this shameful fall, beat his arms like wings, call upon God or his wife to save him. Or he can give himself to it, refuse the chloroform of terror or unconsciousness, watch and listen instead for the moment which may or may not arrive— it is not in his power to force—when from being a body plunging into darkness he shall become a body within whose core a plunge into darkness is taking place, a body which contains its own falling and its own darkness.
> (234)

Giving himself to the fall—we may remember Mrs. Curren's "let-ting go"—involves a receptiveness to the *arrivant;* and Dostoevsky (or

---

11. *The Master of Petersburg* is thus one reflection of Coetzee's interest in the question of censorship; see his set of studies on the subject, *Giving Offense.*

Coetzee) is as clear as Derrida that there can be no guarantee that it will arrive. (Derrida refers in *Aporias* to "the guest who must be at once called, desired, and expected, but also always free to come or not to come" [11].) The fall may be just that, in all its negativity, or it may be a passage to a new condition: "Not to emerge from the fall unscathed, but to achieve what his son did not: to wrestle with the whistling darkness, to absorb it, to make it his medium; to turn the falling into a flying, even if a flying as slow and old and clumsy as a turtle's" (235).

In this process, Dostoevsky reaches a different appreciation of his relation to Pavel, of his project in Petersburg, one that abandons the commitment to the ethical, that stops asking what is the right way to behave with **regard** to Pavel, Anna, Nechaev, Matryona, his wife:

> No longer a matter of listening for the lost child calling from the dark stream, no longer a matter of being faithful to Pavel when all have given him up. Not a matter of fidelity at all. On the contrary, a matter of betrayal—betrayal of love first of all, and then of Pavel and the mother and child and everyone else. *Perversion:* everything and everyone to be turned to another use, to be gripped to him and fall with him. (235)

But he still cannot write. The other does not come, though he senses an indistinct presence in the room, which at first seems like a stick-figure version of himself. He remembers the episode with the dog and the aporia involved in the expectation of the unexpected. "If he is to be saved, it will be by the thief in the night, for whom he must unwaveringly be on watch. Yet the thief will not come till the householder has forgotten him and fallen asleep" (236). Unwaveringly on watch, yet without predetermining what will come.[12]

---

12. In *Youth*, the young Coetzee, intent on becoming a poet and longing for sexual fulfillment, faces the same problem: "Of course in his heart he knows destiny will not visit him unless he makes her do so. He has to sit down and write, that is the only way. But he cannot begin writing until the moment is right, and no matter how scrupulously he prepares himself, wiping the table clean, positioning the lamp, ruling a margin down the side of the blank page, sitting with his eyes shut, emptying his mind in readiness—in spite of all this, the words will not come to him. . . . Unless he wills himself to act, nothing will happen, in love or in art. But he does not trust the will. Just as he cannot will himself to write but must wait for the aid of some force from outside, a force that used to be called the Muse, so he cannot simply will himself to approach a woman without some intimation (from where?—from her? from within him? from above?) that she is his destiny" (166–67).

Let me cite another passage from Derrida, this time from "Psyche":

> One does not make the other come, one lets it come by preparing for its coming. The coming of the other or its coming back is the only possible arrival, but it is not invented, even if the inventiveness of the greatest genius is needed to prepare to welcome it: to prepare to affirm the chance of an encounter that not only is no longer calculable but is not even an incalculable factor still homogeneous with the calculable, not even an undecidable still caught up in the process of decision making. Is this possible? Of course it is not, and that is why it is the only possible invention. (341–42)

If invention is the preparation for the coming of the other, Dostoevsky is still too locked within himself to invent: "He cannot think, he cannot write, he cannot mourn except to and for himself. Until Pavel, the true Pavel, visits him unevoked and of his free will, he is a prisoner in his own breast. And there is no certainty that Pavel has not already come in the night, already spoken" (239). But it is precisely faith in the impossible that opens the way to the other: "What he listens for, therefore, is Pavel's second word. He believes absolutely that he does not deserve a second word, that there will be no second word. But he believes absolutely that a second word will come" (239).

Gradually the specter in the room, the *arrivant*, takes shape, "a phantasm . . . whom it has been given him to bring into being" (240) (the verbs, we may note, imply both passivity and action). It is himself, it is Nechaev, it is Pavel, but it is also none of these—we know that it will eventually reach written form in the pages of *The Possessed* as Stavrogin. "Is the thing before him the one that does the fathering," he asks himself, "and must he give himself to being fathered by it? . . . If that is what must be, if that is the truth and the way to the resurrection, he will do it. He will put aside everything. Following this shade he will go naked as a babe into the jaws of hell" (240–41). Stephen Watson, in one of the most acute published responses to the novel, comments on this moment: "To write one has to transgress, to be divided, even double. But to be double is to open oneself to the possibility [one might say the necessity] of being overtaken by another voice. This voice may be anything but benign; it may even be that of the Devil himself" ("The Writer and the Devil," 56).

Soon Dostoevsky is writing, letting the writing happen, falling into writing. He depicts the apartment, and sketches a version of Pavel (who is also a version of himself) arousing the sexual curiosity of a girl-child. His writing is a form of treachery to everyone and everything he has known in Petersburg; they are used, abused, revealed, distorted. Nothing is left secret, but nothing is truthfully told. As the novel closes, he remembers a moment when Matryona had quoted Pavel: "*They pay him lots of money for writing books,* said the child, repeating the dead child. What they failed to say was that he had to give up his soul in return" (250).

Nor is the betrayal simply something that happens on the page, a theoretical or paper betrayal; in this chapter Dostoevsky finds himself deliberately writing a sketch that will corrupt Matryona's memory of Pavel—her most treasured possession, perhaps—and leaving it for her to see. Thus he, in effect, brings about the violation of the girl by Stavrogin that is to be the fictional core of *The Possessed*. And, knowing that novel, or rather its excluded core, we are invited to project beyond the end of Coetzee's novel to a further possible event: Matryona's suicide.

How are we to understand this figure of the *arrivant* at the end of the novel, to which Dostoevsky finds himself answerable? It is not God: although Coetzee continually and effectively evokes the Christian context of Dostoevsky's thought, he does not reduce the ending to an acknowledgment of the divine, as the historical Dostoevsky might have done.[13] Clearly, for Coetzee, what is important about Dostoevsky's works is that they go further than their own explicit doctrines; Dostoevsky's Christianity is not sufficient to account for the intense power of a character like Stavrogin. If we had to give a name to this *arrivant*—and all names are misleading here, "not because the name is hidden but because the figure is indifferent to all names," thinks Dostoevsky (238)—one possibility would be "Russia." In *The Possessed* the historical Dostoevsky attempted a diagnosis of the sickness he believed had beset his country, and Coetzee's Dostoevsky tells Anna: "I am required to live—what shall I call it?—a Russian life: a life inside Russia, or with Russia inside me, and whatever Russia means. It is not a fate I can evade" (221). He had earlier strongly resisted Nechaev's identification with Russia, and claimed for himself the burden of "Russia's madness" (202), and in the final chapter he formulates as his task, "To live in Russia and hear the voices of Russia murmuring within him. To hold it all within him: Russia, Pavel, death" (235). It is as a manifestation of Russia, that is to say of his place and time (but for the reader of Coetzee's new novel, our place and time), of its darknesses and tensions, that the figure of the other emerges.

---

13. In "Confession and Double Thoughts," Coetzee argues that confession in Dostoevsky is interminable, except when faith and grace intervene to put a stop to its endless redoublings. See chap. 6 below.

We can now understand more fully the clash between Nechaev and Dostoevsky in the novel. It is not merely the opposition between an absolutist politics and an ethics of responsibility to the singular other of the kind Coetzee had staged in *Age of Iron;* it is specifically as a *writer* that Dostoevsky cannot afford to accept Nechaev's totalizing and rationalizing position. His investment has to be in the other as absolutely singular, exceeding all political programs—but exceeding too all moral notions of responsibility to other human beings. Nechaev's "Everything is permitted for the sake of the future" (200) may sound like a transgression of all moral laws, but is a strict moral calculation, the subordination of the means to what is taken to be the greater good of the end. Dostoevsky's obligation, to repeat Derrida's words, is to "prepare to affirm the chance of an encounter that is no longer calculable but is not even an incalculable factor still homogeneous with the calculable." This obligation presents itself not as a simple *alternative* to moral behavior, but as a responsibility that stubbornly remains when all the needs of morality have been answered. If we call it ethical, it is an ethics that makes demands even beyond those that Vercueil and John make on Mrs. Curren as individuals entering her life at its close.[14]

The contest between generations is also clearer in the light of the last chapter. It has already become evident that it is a contest between a certain kind of innocence—shared by Pavel, Nechaev, and Matryona (and by implication, Dostoevsky's young wife back in Dresden)—and a certain kind of experience, above all the awareness of death, shared by Dostoevsky and the landlady, Anna Sergeyevna. Dostoevsky articulates the opposition as "The children against those who are not children, those old enough to recognize in their lovemaking the first foretaste of death" (63), and he finds himself thinking of Anna's body as "Fullgrown and therefore open (that is the word that insists itself) to death" (131). They make love "as though under the sentence of death" (225). The young are single-minded in their politics and sexuality, they love and act spontaneously, and they are not subject to the corrosive and inhibitory self-consciousness of their elders. Their spontaneity is a very different thing from the effortfully achieved openness to the event that we see in Dostoevsky. The writing of the young—we have the example of Pavel's draft of a story found among his papers—is morally and politically admirable, but only the older generation can achieve the inventiveness of the *arrivant,* which is never

14. Looking ahead to *Disgrace* and *The Lives of Animals,* we see that Coetzee will return to an ethics that goes beyond obligations to human others.

dissociable from death.[15] Yet as we have seen, the path to the *arrivant* in the novel lies through the younger generation, who exert an irresistible fascination on Dostoevsky. It now becomes apparent that what is required for writing, for literature, to begin is the sacrifice of their innocence.

It is a bleak view of the price to be paid for inventiveness, for being receptive to the other, for admitting the *arrivant*. It forces us to reinterpret the entire book; we now see Dostoevsky moving slowly and painfully through a series of betrayals—betrayal of the political utopianism he once embraced and now rejects in Nechaev, betrayal of the innocence of childhood, betrayal of the obligations of fatherhood—to the final betrayal, the madness, the inhumanity or ahumanity that enables a great work of fiction to come into being. It is not simply betrayal in the sense of the inevitable violence done to the other in apprehending and representing it; it goes deeper than that. About to write in the new novel of what he regards as the "possession" that has overtaken Nechaev and his associates, the nihilists whose creed he is determined to ridicule into nonexistence, Dostoevsky is himself possessed, he has indeed given up his soul to the devil. "Stavrogin" names the absolute otherness that has taken him over, obliterating every human and social responsibility, everything that is normally called ethical, replacing the need to mourn with another kind of need. This otherness is the completely new, but it is also the very ancient, the ahuman that preexists the human. Dostoevsky makes a comparison as he acknowledges the presence of the Stavrogin-spectre in his room:

> Confronting it is like descending into the waters of the Nile and coming face to face with something huge and cold and grey that may once have been born of woman but with the passing of ages has retreated into stone, that does not belong in his world, that will baffle and overwhelm all his powers of conception. (240)

Here, above all, is what disturbed me most when I read *The Master of Petersburg* as a newly published novel, and which disturbs me each time I re-read it: not that the reader's reward for patient attentiveness occurs so late, and is so far from the conventional political/sexual conclusion—the tying up of the plot—that might have seemed promised, but that it presents a vision of the writing process, and more generally of creativity, of inventiveness, of the achievement of the new, as having nothing to do with

---

15. Derrida writes: "This border [the border always already crossed by the *arrivant*] will always keep one from discriminating among the figures of the *arrivant,* the dead, and the *revenant*" (*Aporias,* 35).

traditional understandings of ethics, or with human responsibility—only responsibility to and for the new, unanticipatible, thing that is coming into being. In his previous novel, *Age of Iron,* Coetzee pitted a certain kind of human responsibility, which I termed ethical, against a certain kind of politics, the reductive politics of closed certainties and programs. Writing was there a way of negotiating between the two, and opening the writer to the unexplored possibilities of the ethics of otherness. Writing in that book, however, meant the writing of a deeply personal letter. In the new book, writing is the creation of public fiction, and this hard-won sense of the ethical is what now has to be sacrificed.

Though less obviously concerned with the conflicts and contradictions of South Africa's past and present than Coetzee's earlier novels, this novel stages a drama that can hardly be said to be irrelevant to that country's pressing needs and problems as it moves into the uncharted territory beyond apartheid and the euphoria of its ending. If Dostoevsky, in *The Master of Petersburg,* succeeds finally in giving voice to Russia, or at least attending to and bodying forth one—or some—of its voices, not through conscious note-taking but through a giving up of himself to his place and time, isn't Coetzee, also letting his fiction take him beyond the known and the familiar, doing the same? Rather than attempting to represent other voices, the voice of the other, by mimicry and ventriloquism, he has let his own voice be taken over by a strange and at times dismaying mode of utterance. It doesn't speak to us of South Africa, but it speaks of the role of literature, of art, in a country like South Africa, a country struggling to be born anew. It is not a reassuring account.

But Coetzee's novel is to be welcomed precisely for the discomfort it causes, for the hypothesis it tests without flinching. No doubt our cultural institutions are busy massaging the novel into a more appealing, and probably less powerful, shape than the sinister, Stavrogin-like work I am describing here. Though I find myself resisting the novel—*because* I find myself resisting it—I hope that this process of accommodation will not be entirely successful. I would also like to think, though this is probably a fond hope, that my account of the novel will not contribute to it.

: VII :

Let me return to my original question: what is my responsibility as the reader of a new work? *The Master of Petersburg* is itself concerned with the question of responsibility toward the wholly new (or the unrecognizably old come back with the force of the new), of doing justice to what is original and singular in one's time and therefore barely to be perceived or understood, of the proper attitude to and engagement with that which arrives unheralded to challenge norms and expectations. The entire work is part of Coetzee's attempt to do justice to the disturbing singularity of *The Possessed*, his countersignature to Dostoevsky's unique signature in that novel, and within the narrative the character Dostoevsky, in his response to the dog's howling, to the beggar, to the emerging figure of Pavel/Stavrogin, stands for the reader as well as the writer in his struggle to welcome the *arrivant*. The reader's responsibility towards the new work, the novel suggests, is to give oneself attentively to it, expecting the unexpected without even determining the unexpected *as* unexpected, neither passively yielding to its seductions nor actively managing its meanings, knowing—but without being inhibited by the knowledge—that one's efforts will always be inadequate, will always involve sacrifice and betrayal. It enjoins me to focus my attention on the opaque or disturbing passages, not pass them by to concentrate on the familiar.

Coetzee himself puts in Dostoevsky's mouth a description of one kind of reading (in contrast to the kind of reading characteristic of his interrogator, Councillor Maximov, who treats fiction—Pavel's draft of a story—in purely instrumental terms, looking through it for treasonable sentiments): "Reading is being the arm and being the axe *and* being the skull; reading is giving yourself up, not holding yourself at a distance and jeering" (47). Maximov is not wrong when he replies, in another reference to Dostoevsky's next novel, "You speak of reading as though it were demon-possession" (47): reading, like writing, in full responsiveness to the other is a kind of madness.

The Master of Petersburg thus poses a question to the thinking of the other that we find in many of Derrida's works, in "Psyche," in *Aporias,* in *The Gift of Death,* in *Specters of Marx*. If I am enjoined to be open to the other's coming, without any attempt at preprogramming it or limiting its possible violence, accepting the risk of the unknown, asking for no guarantees, might the cost not be my own humanity, and the human other or others that I sacrifice with it?[16] As early as his essay "Structure, Sign, and Play" Derrida acknowledged the necessarily dismaying character of the *arrivant* (though not under that name), referring to "the as yet unnamable

---

16. Elizabeth Costello makes this point in her lecture on the problem of evil: "I take seriously the claim that the artist risks a great deal by venturing into forbidden places: risks, specifically, himself; risks, perhaps, all" (*Elizabeth Costello,* 173).

which is proclaiming itself and which can do so, as is necessary whenever a birth is in the offing, only under the species of the nonspecies, in the formless, mute, infant, and terrifying form of monstrosity" (293).[17] And in a 1990 interview Derrida returned to this subject, noting—in terms that foreshadow the final chapter of *The Master of Petersburg*—that the monster "shows itself in something that is not yet shown and that therefore looks like a hallucination, it strikes the eye, it frightens precisely because no anticipation had prepared one to identify this figure" (*Points,* 386), and adding, "All experience open to the future is prepared or prepares itself to welcome the monstrous *arrivant,* to welcome it, that is, to accord hospitality to that which is absolutely foreign or strange" (387).

But is the monstrous new birth always to be welcomed? If it is a work of art (or for that matter a work of philosophy or science, or even of political and social refashioning) that opens up the new, the absolutely heterogeneous, will this achievement always be worth the price that has to be paid for it? These questions are, strictly speaking, inadmissible; they imply a calculus, a weighing of profit and loss, which is precisely what openness to the other, the event, the *arrivant* exceeds. As soon as we attempt to categorize the newcomer, to apply terms like "good" and "evil," "welcome" or "unwelcome," we begin the inevitable process of appropriation and domestication—a process whose inevitability requires that the preparation for the other never cease.

POSTSCRIPT: CONFESSION

Coetzee, like Dostoevsky, is fascinated by confession. He has written one of the best essays on the subject ("Confession and Double Thoughts") and much of his fiction partakes of the confessional, presenting characters who experience the need to reveal in language their histories, thoughts, feelings and desires, however private and shameful (Eugene Dawn in *Dusklands,* Magda in *In the Heart of the Country,* Mrs. Curren in *Age of Iron,* to name only three examples). In the same decade as he was writing his essay on confession he was translating from the Dutch an 1894 novel by Marcellus Emants entitled *A Posthumous Confession,* in which a first-person

---

17. A similar comment occurs near the end of the "Exergue" to *Of Grammatology:* "The future can only be anticipated in the form of an absolute danger. It is that which breaks absolutely with constituted normality and can only be proclaimed, *presented,* as a sort of monstrosity" (5).

narrator bearing a strong resemblance to Dostoevsky's Underground Man
(as Coetzee notes in his introduction) relates a life of bitterness and anger
culminating in the murder of his wife. In the following chapter, I shall argue that his two memoirs, *Boyhood* and *Youth,* are revealing of his earlier
life in a manner that engages directly, if complexly, with the tradition of
the confession.

Confessions are also prominent in Dostoevsky's fiction, and Coetzee
focuses on some of these in his essay on confession—the extended confession of *Notes from Underground,* the many confessions in *The Idiot,*
and Stavrogin's confession in the censored section of *The Possessed.* Towards the end of *The Master of Petersburg,* the fictional Dostoevsky sums
up his existence as a writer as "a life without honour; treachery without
limit; confession without end" (222). Coetzee seems to be inviting us to
read *The Possessed* as a confession, in which Dostoevsky betrays his own
crimes and in so doing betrays all those whose lives have touched his.
Although there seems to be no foundation to the story that Dostoevsky
confessed to Turgenev that he was guilty of something like Stavrogin's act,
he was all his life haunted by the memory of the rape of a nine-year old
girl he played with as a child.[18] What then of *The Master of Petersburg?*
Does it invite a further novel about a character called Coetzee who betrays his human ties in answering an imperative demand from an absolute
other? Has Coetzee already written such a novel, a novel about its own
genesis, inviting us to change the names of people and places? What significance do we place on the fact that the novel was written soon after his
own son's untimely death? (Nicholas Coetzee's death, along with those
of Coetzee's father and mother, are registered in the dedication of *Age of
Iron.*) Not being a novelist, I feel no urge (this is my confession, no doubt
concealing as much it reveals) to follow through this train of thought, and
carry out the betrayals it would entail. But by bringing me to the edge of
such writing, I confess, Coetzee has begun to dislodge some of my own
preconceptions about fiction, about the act of literature.

Of course, for Coetzee, as for Dostoevsky, confession is never simple
or direct, it is always what Derrida calls a circumfession, an avoidance as

---

18. According to Joseph Frank, following V. N. Zakharov, the stories of Dostoevsky's
sexual involvement with a young girl stem from the author's reading of his rejected chapter
to friends, compounded by Turgenev's malice (*Dostoevsky,* 432n). Frank quotes a reported
conversation in the 1870s about the worst possible crime, in which Dostoevsky is said to
have proposed that nothing is worse than the violation of a child, and to have recounted
the story of his sexually murdered playmate (22).

well as an admission, a staging of confession as well as a confessing. (Just as the kind of writing which eschews the confessional mode—philosophy, for example—is all the more subject to its effects.) Perhaps that is what saves the inventive novelist and the deconstructive philosopher from the betrayals that would destroy both them and those they love: the endless relays and mediations of which writing consists, and by means of which—even at its most unguardedly open—it continues to guard its secrets.

CHAPTER SIX

Confessing
in the Third Person

Boyhood and *Youth*

: I :

As a novelist, Coetzee is not known for confessional self-revelation. In a series of nine works, from *Dusklands* in 1974 to *Elizabeth Costello* in 2003, he has honed a fictional style that, whatever the mode of narration, offers no hint of a personal authorial presence. The characters through whose consciousness the narrative is relayed, whether they are represented in the first or third person, occupy the entire affective and axiological space of the fiction. If, as I speculated in the previous chapter, *The Master of Petersburg* may be understood as a confession by Coetzee, it is a thoroughly disguised one. Coetzee's substantial body of critical commentary, too—which includes the books *White Writing, Giving Offense,* and *Stranger Shores,* as well as the articles collected in *Doubling the Point*—while moving away from the highly technical stylistic analyses of the early essays to issues of more autobiographical relevance like censorship and animal rights in the later work, is not to any great degree self-revelatory. When he does give expression to extreme personal views—on the treatment of animals, for instance, or on the achievements of the humanities—these are not his but those of invented characters such as Elizabeth Costello and her sister Blanche. His reluctance to account for his fictions in the terms provided by his own life reaches a somewhat bizarre extreme in the written interview that was published in the 1994 special issue of the *South Atlantic Quarterly* devoted to Coetzee: questions that occupy some thirteen pages in all receive answers that add up to little more than a page.[1]

It's not really as simple as that, of course—and Coetzee would be the first to agree. At the beginning of the series of endlessly suggestive interviews that make up part of the volume *Doubling the Point,* published in 1992, he answers David Attwell's first question, which concerns just this issue of the absence of autobiographical writing from his output, as follows: "Let me treat this as a question about telling the truth rather than as a question about autobiography. Because in a larger sense all writing is autobiography: everything that you write, including criticism and fiction, writes you as you write it" (17). Coetzee's biographers, when they draw their connections between the life and the fiction, will have a mass of material to work with: even with the small amount of biographical information that is currently in the public domain it is clear that the novels are woven out of personal experiences and obsessions at least to the same degree as the majority of novels and probably more so.

The picture is not, however, one of complete resistance to overt personal revelation. Occasionally in interviews and short pieces (such as "Remembering Texas" and "Meat Country") Coetzee has made private experiences public, and the interviews with Attwell in *Doubling the Point* provided a vehicle for an extended meditation on his own intellectual development. The last of the interviews in that book ends with a rather extraordinary passage in which Coetzee tells the story of his life up to the years 1982–83. Not the least remarkable feature of this passage is that Coetzee chooses to speak of himself as a boy in the third person and the present tense. Here is his description of part of his early boyhood:

> His years in rural Worcester (1948–51) as a child from an Afrikaans background attending English-medium classes, at a time of raging Afrikaner nationalism, a time when laws were being concocted to prevent people of Afrikaans descent from bringing up their children to speak English, provoke in him uneasy dreams of being hunted down and accused; by the age of twelve he has a well-developed sense of social marginality. (393)

The sense of marginality continues into his teenage years:

> His years in Worcester are followed by adolescence in Cape Town, as a Protestant enrolled in a Catholic high school, with Jewish and Greek

---

1. Philip R. Wood, "Aporias of the Postcolonial Subject."

friends. For a variety of reasons he ceases visiting the family farm, the place on earth he has defined, imagined, constructed, as his place of origin. All of this confirms his (quite accurate) sense of being outside a culture that at this moment in history is confidently setting about enforcing itself as the core culture of the land. (393–94)

It is only in recounting when, in 1965, at the age of twenty-five (that is to say, halfway through his life up to the time of the interview), he went to the University of Texas as a graduate student that he says "*he* now begins to feel closer to *I: autre*biography shades back into autobiography" (394).

None of this, however, could have prepared his readers for the book that appeared in 1997. *Boyhood,* subtitled *Scenes from Provincial Life,* is a short (and very selective) account of the young John Coetzee's life in Worcester and Cape Town. The major events of the book occur when John is between the ages of ten and thirteen (which is to say between the years 1950 and 1953); the background (seen only through the eyes of the young boy) is that of the early years of D. F. Malan's Afrikaner Nationalist government (elected in 1948) and of the family's slide from middle-class respectability into something approaching poverty (a family history that recalls one of the book's major forebears, *A Portrait of the Artist as a Young Man*). My point of departure for this essay is that it is told, like the passage on his boyhood in the *Doubling the Point* interview, in the third person and the present tense.[2]

The result of this choice of presentational mode is a singular immediacy, one might almost say a depthlessness, in the recounting of events, but not the sense of intimacy we gain from confessional autobiography of a more orthodox sort. Here is a sample of straightforward narrative, in which the effect of Coetzee's choice of person and tense is evident:

Once a year Boswell's Circus comes to Worcester. Everyone in his class goes; for a week talk is about the circus and nothing else. Even the Coloured children go, after a fashion: they hang around outside the tent for hours, listening to the band, peering in through gaps.

They plan to go on the Saturday afternoon, when his father is playing cricket. His mother makes it into an outing for the three of them. But at the ticket booth she hears with a shock the high Saturday afternoon prices: 2/6 for children, 5/- for adults. She does not have enough money

2. Coetzee himself comments on the effect of the third-person perspective: "To rewrite *Boyhood* and *Youth* with *I* substituted for *he* throughout would land you up with two books only remotely related to their originals" (Interview with David Attwell, forthcoming).

with her. She buys tickets for him and his brother. "Go in, I'll wait here," she says. He is unwilling, but she insists. (47)

This style of narration, I scarcely need to say, is unusual for autobiography. *The Education of Henry Adams* and *A Portrait of the Artist as a Young Man*, to take two obvious precursors that narrate the childhood of a writer with exceptional gifts, both use the third person (Joyce's work, of course, is a deliberate mixture of fact and fiction), but are written in the past tense—and both, as a result, can introduce an adult irony to complicate the naiveté of the boy's outlook.[3] Most of Coetzee's fiction makes use of first-person narrators—Jacobus Coetzee, Eugene Dawn, Magda, the Magistrate, Susan Barton, Mrs. Curren—and of the four exceptions, one, *Life & Times of Michael K*, uses the past tense. It is in his more recent work, from *The Master of Petersburg*, the last novel to be written before *Boyhood*, to *Elizabeth Costello*, that he makes use of both the third person and the present tense.

Turning to the content of *Boyhood*, we may note that it calls to mind a number of well-known autobiographies, whether genuine, fictional, or semi-fictional, that are presented, to a greater or lesser degree, as confessions. As with the young Augustine in his *Confessions* and the young Marcel in *A la recherche du temps perdu*, the most potent presence in young John's life is that of his mother, even when he is rebelling against her; and the admission of this degree of attachment has a confessional ring to it. As in Rousseau's *Confessions* and in many of Dostoevsky's fictional confessions, the life that is narrated is marked by fiercely kept secrets and an acute sense of shame. The very shock of autobiographical explicitness after so many years of tight-lipped resistance is also suggestive of the confessional mode. But one of the questions *Boyhood* poses is this: is confession *possible* in the third person and in the present tense?

: II :

Coetzee himself is the author of an acute analysis of confession that will throw light on this question, the lengthy essay I have already mentioned entitled "Confession and Double Thoughts" first published in 1985 and

---

3. The importance of Adams for Coetzee's autobiographical writing, however, is clear from a comment in one of the *Doubling the Point* interviews: referring to his short memoir "Remembering Texas," he says "I took as my sounding board the prose of *The Education of Henry Adams*, especially its affectless irony" (26).

reprinted in *Doubling the Point* (251–93). (It is the composition of this very essay in 1982–83 that Coetzee, in the final interview of *Doubling the Point*, sees as the pivotal moment in his twenty-year writing career, marking the beginning of what he describes as "a more broadly philosophical engagement" with his situation in the world [394].) In discussing Tolstoy's *Kreutzer Sonata*, Rousseau's *Confessions*, and Dostoevsky's *Notes from Underground*, *The Idiot*, and *The Possessed*, Coetzee demonstrates the structural interminability of confession in a secular context. Every act of confession is subject to self-reflexive scrutiny: its motivation can be questioned, and its impurity (or the inevitable falsehood of any claim to purity) confessed, and the motivation for this further questioning questioned and its imperfection confessed, and so on without end. (In the larger scheme of Coetzee's writings one might perhaps see the essay on confession as itself an instance of this skeptical self-reflexivity on the part of the person attempting to confess.)[4] Only confession in the sacramental context, an act of faith confirmed by the operation of grace, can have a conclusion that is not arbitrary. The fullest development of this logic of interminability is in the chapter excised from the original published version of *The Possessed*, in which Stavrogin—who, as we have seen, features importantly in the closing pages of *The Master of Petersburg*—confesses an abhorrent deed to the monk Tikhon.[5]

For a different kind of exemplification of this argument, one can turn to a historical event that was part of nearly every South African's mental landscape during the years in which *Boyhood* was written. The Truth and Reconciliation Commission, set up as part of the 1994 agreement establishing a multiracial democracy in South Africa, was conducting hearings across the country, in a remarkable attempt to achieve a national coming-to-terms with the terrible years of repression under apartheid. The Commission heard testimony from victims and confession from perpetrators, in the hope of bringing to light the concealed crimes of the last thirty-four years of the Nationalist era. The Commission had vested in it the power to put an end to potentially endless confessions, to decide in each case

---

4. In an interview in *Doubling the Point*, however, Coetzee finds in the essay a dialogue between two views of the possibility of truth in autobiography, and identifies the skeptical position with the person he was ceasing to be at the time. The belief in the possibility of truth-telling he associates with "a person I desired to be and was feeling my way toward" (392).

5. For a further elaboration of Coetzee's argument, with particular emphasis on the role of confession in the American law courts, see Peter Brooks, *Troubling Confessions*.

whether the truth had been attained; its power to grant amnesty when it was satisfied that the confession was genuine and full—that the whole truth had been exposed—was the major inducement it had to offer those in whose interest it would otherwise have been to remain silent. But it was officially a secular body, not a religious one, so its judgments necessarily had an element of the arbitrary in them, and the result was a great deal of controversy. At a certain point, it had to effect closure, put a stop to the potentially endless spinning of stories, make a decision—inevitably with a certain violence—about motivation, conscience, honesty, sincerity, and other imponderable and inaccessible human attributes. The termination of hearings—a winding-up which was postponed more than once—was more a matter of expediency than an indication that all the stories had been told, all the voices heard.

In *Boyhood,* it is primarily Coetzee's choice of person and tense that prevents the interminable spiraling of confession by short-circuiting it before it even gets going. The use of the third person implicitly dissociates the narrative voice from the narrated consciousness, telling us that this was another person—that we are reading, to use Coetzee's term, an *autre*biography, not an autobiography. At the same time, the use of the present tense both heightens the immediacy of the narrated events and denies the text any retrospection, any place from which the writer can reflect on and express regret about (or approval of) the acts and attitudes described. In other words, Coetzee achieves the same effect that we find in his works of fiction: the reader is refused the comfort of a metanarrative level or perspective from which authorial judgments (here, judgments on his earlier self) could be made. If anyone is to take responsibility for judgments on the boy of *Boyhood,* it is the *reader,* and the reader is thus implicated in the ethical web spun by the work.[6]

Coetzee, that is to say, avoids the problem he identifies in his essay on confession by avoiding the self-reflexivity that produces the problem, but in so doing he makes any attempt to relate the work to the genre of confession more difficult. We can imagine what would happen if a past supporter of the apartheid government had described a series of criminal acts to the Truth Commission in the third person and the present tense. The Commissioners would no doubt have concluded that, however accurate and complete the account, there could be no question of an

---

6. In a brilliant discussion of Joyce's short story "Clay," Margot Norris makes a similar argument vis-à-vis the judgments made on the story's central consciousness, Maria; see *Joyce's Web,* chap. 6.

amnesty. Although overt repentance was not required by the Commission, implicit in its demand for accounts of their deeds by perpetrators was both identification of person (it was I who did these things) and distance in time (I did them then; I would not do them now).

What is it about *Boyhood,* then, that leads the reader—and I'm sure I'm not alone in this—to relate the work to the tradition of confession, and speaking less academically, to experience it, in some way, *as* a confessional text?

In "Confession and Double Thoughts," Coetzee lays particular emphasis on the connection between confession and *truth*. Focusing his attention on secular confession, he proposes the following distinction: "We can demarcate a mode of autobiographical writing that we can call the *confession,* as distinct from the *memoir* and the *apology,* on the basis of an underlying motive to tell an essential truth about the self" (252). This "essential truth" is not a matter of historical or factual truth, which is the domain of the *memoir,* nor is it a matter of explaining or excusing the construction or deformation of the self, which is the function of *apology.*[7] But in his first interview with Attwell in *Doubling the Point* (17–18), Coetzee makes it clear that the purpose of the distinction is not to lay claim to a "higher" or "deeper" truth to which the confession, if it is made in good faith and with sufficient courage, may penetrate. He describes the process of attaining to the truth of autobiography (he doesn't use the term *confession* here, but the connection is clear) as a process of *writing,* and writing understood in a particular way:

> It is naive to think that writing is a simple two-stage process: first you decide what you want to say, then you say it. On the contrary, as all of us know, you write because you do not know what you want to say.... Writing, then, involves an interplay between the push into the future that takes you to the blank page in the first place, and a resistance. Part of that resistance is psychic, but part is also an automatism built into language: the tendency of words to call up other words, to fall into patterns that keep propagating themselves. Out of that interplay there emerges, if you are lucky, what you recognize or hope to recognize as the true. (18)

And he adds: "I don't see that 'straight' autobiographical writing is any different *in kind* from what I have been describing. Truth is something that comes in the process of writing, or comes from the process of writing"

---

7. Coetzee derives this tripartite distinction from an essay by Francis R. Hart, "Notes for an Anatomy of Modern Autobiography."

(18). The "essential truth about the self" that is the goal of confession, then, is not just the revelation of what has been known all along by the author but kept secret for reasons of guilt and shame; rather, it is something that emerges in the telling, if it emerges at all. Nor can it be "read off" by the reader, as a series of facts hitherto unrevealed; it can be experienced only *in the reading,* or in a certain kind of reading. The text does not *refer to* the truth; it produces it.[8] Confession is, that is to say, a variety of literature, perhaps even a variety of fiction.

Now, as Coetzee points out in his essay, confession is usually thought of as one element in a series: transgression, confession, penitence, and absolution. But, in discussing Augustine's story of the stealing of pears from a neighbor's garden, he argues that "transgression is not a fundamental component" (252). What needs to be confessed is not the crime but something that lies behind it. Augustine is searching for a truth about himself that would *account* for the theft, a "source within the self for that-which-is-wrong." For Augustine, there is no possibility of finding this source before he is admitted to God's grace: discovery of the truth will be, at the same time, absolution. But in the realm of secular confession, such absolution is not possible; even self-forgiveness, Coetzee demonstrates in his discussion of Stavrogin and Tikhon, is subject to further self-doubt. "The end of confession," states Coetzee near the close of his essay (and the subject is clearly still secular confession), "is to tell the truth to and for oneself" (291). At first sight, this may seem a surprising statement: is confession not premised upon telling the truth to another, or the other, a making public of what has hitherto remained secret? This would seem to be the basis of Rousseau's *Confessions,* and of many confessional works that have followed in its powerful wake.

But Coetzee's assertion is of a piece with his understanding of truth as something arrived at in the process of articulation, not a hidden fact finally revealed. If the struggle to articulate that which is not yet known by the writer is complicated by the consciousness of an audience, by the need to convince another party, it will be weakened, turned aside from its goal.

---

8. Compare Mrs. Curren's words in *Age of Iron* cited in chapter 4 above, which are ostensibly written to her daughter as part of the long letter that constitutes the novel: "If Vercueil does not send these writings on, you will never read them. You will never even know they existed. A certain body of truth will never take on flesh: my truth: how I lived in these times, in this place" (130). Brooks, in commenting that "Coetzee's brilliant reading of Rousseau and Dostoevsky leaves me unsatisfied ... in its traditional notion of 'truth'" (*Troubling Confessions,* 49), is perhaps taking the word too much at face value.

Earlier in the essay, Coetzee had said, following Tolstoy, that "the condition of truthfulness is not perfect self-knowledge but truth-directedness" (261), and taking the presence of an interlocutor into account can only deflect and dissipate this overriding concern with the truth.[9] (It is interesting that Stavrogin's confession in *The Possessed* is *written* and handed, as a printed document, to Tikhon, not spoken to him.) One does not need to read Bakhtin or Derrida to be aware that the attempt to write only for oneself is doomed to failure; articulated language is always already premised on the existence of an interlocutor or potential interlocutor, and the "self" for which one writes is not some hermetically sealed space but a site of constant traffic with that which is not the self. Confession is, inescapably, public, because language is. But the impossibility of the project of telling the truth to and for oneself is not a reason for its not being desirable; on the contrary, desire is at its most powerful in the face of the impossible. The impossibility of this project is, however, one more reason for the interminability of confession.

If the articulation of the truth of oneself to oneself is the goal of secular confession, it is evident that the next in the series of traditional components, penitence, is not an essential accompaniment. (We have seen already that the first component, transgression, is not wholly necessary, and that the final component, absolution, is not even available.) To feel and express regret for what it is that one has discovered (or produced) in one's articulation will add nothing to the truthfulness, or truth-directedness, of the confession; and it will provoke a further round of self-interrogation as the subject doubts the genuineness of his or her emotion. (This will hold true all the more if the confession is being made to another or to others, when there is everything to gain from an appearance of remorse.) It may

---

9. The structure of confession bears a close relation to the structure of the gift, as described by Derrida: the intention to confess, with the accompanying consciousness of a hearer or reader and the possibility of absolution, annuls the pure act of confession, just as the intention to give and the consciousness of the gift annul the pure act of giving. See, for instance, *Given Time 1*, 10–30 (where Derrida makes it clear that the impossibility of such a "pure act of giving" renders it neither unthinkable nor undesirable). In a discussion of *Age of Iron*, Head points out that Mrs. Curren's confession to Vercueil is made possible *because* he is useless as a confessor, even though Mrs. Curren has the opposite fear. (She asks, "Is a true confession still true if it is not heard? Do you hear me, or have I put you to sleep too?" [*Age of Iron*, 151].) Head comments, "Because Vercueil does not respond as confessor... he cannot elicit or encourage double thought from her" (*J. M. Coetzee*, 140).

be that repentance—or what is of value in repentance—only repeats what is already implicit in confession in the fullest sense. For if to confess is to discover in language a truth of the self that had eluded one, that one did not know, and did not know one did not know, it would seem to involve a kind of *taking responsibility for* that truth. *It is* my *truth I confess, and mine alone. In giving it form, and thus bringing it into being as truth, I acknowledge it as true and as mine.* The Truth and Reconciliation Commission, in declining to demand verbal repentance from perpetrators, in not making it a requirement that the speaker convince the commission of his or her remorse but requiring rather that the speaker unfold the truth, may have been acknowledging this fact.

Moreover, it would appear that an inevitable component of confession is *shame*. Shame is not the same as repentance; it is inflected by no possibility of self-deceit; it requires no formal articulation. It is as much a physical response—a coloring of the cheeks, an increase in body temperature, a tightening of the stomach muscles—as an emotional one (insofar as this distinction is a tenable one). Augustine, in recounting the theft of the pears (this is where Coetzee begins his essay on confession), says that he and his friends were "seeking nothing from the shameful deed but the shame itself" (quoted by Coetzee, 251), as if a desire for shame is the urcondition of all acts of evil, associated in some way with the inaccessible source of that-which-is-wrong in the self.

The "essential truth about the self" which confession tries to tell, then, is always a shameful truth, not because human beings are indelibly tainted with original sin (at least not in the secular context within which we are considering confession), but because the most difficult task in articulating the history and condition of the self is admitting that of which one is ashamed, that which one's very body resists admitting. And it is only in its grappling with this material that a confession can gain authority (primarily with the self, and secondarily with its external audience). Tolstoy's story *The Kreutzer Sonata* illustrates for Coetzee the fact that "whatever authority a confession bears in a secular context derives from the status of the confessant [i.e., the one who confesses] as a hero of the labyrinth willing to confront the worst within himself" (263). Shame is a component not only of the truth that is confessed and of the act of confession (which is always, as we've seen, a public act, however private its intentions); it also accompanies each stage in the interminable process of skeptical self-examination, as the revelation of a further truth shamefully exposes the inadequacy of what has been revealed so far (273).

: III :

Now let us return to our question about *Boyhood* and confession. Although it lacks the trappings of a conventional confessional work—notably, as we've seen, in its use of the third person and the present tense—the book exemplifies the project of confession as presented by Coetzee in the essay we've been discussing and in the interviews of *Doubling the Point*. Of course, that project cannot be judged by the reader, insofar as the goal of confession is "to tell the truth to and for oneself"; but the reader can testify to what we might call, following Roland Barthes on the subject of realism, a *confession effect*—the *experience*, in the reading, of a truth-directed articulation of an author's past life. This is not to say that the work reads as artless; on the contrary, the way in which (as with Coetzee's fictional writing) every sentence seems to have been sculpted into maximal effectiveness is part of the experience of a struggle to shape and thus discover the truth, of that interplay between "the push into the future" and the resistance of the psyche and of the medium that Coetzee himself describes. That earlier self seems both alien to the adult author and yet vividly present; and both these features are communicated powerfully to the reader.

The use of the present tense and third person doesn't convey a desire to avoid responsibility or the absence of any sense of remorse; rather, it signals that the author has no interest in *making a case,* in convincing the reader of the unimpeachability of his motives or the fullness of his repentance. And rather than indicating a lack of self-reflexivity, they suggest, especially if the essay on confession is taken into account, a subtlety of self-reflection beyond the scope of most autobiographies. Coetzee provides an intimation of the way he sees his task in an interview given seven or eight years before the publication of *Boyhood:*

> We must see what the child, still befuddled from his travels, still trailing his clouds of glory, could not see. We—or at least some of us, enough of us—must look at the past with a cruel enough eye to see what it was that made that joy and innocence possible. Forgivingness but also unflinchingness: that is the mixture I have in mind, if it is attainable. First the unflinchingness, then the forgivingness. (*Doubling the Point,* 29)

What kind of truth, then, does *Boyhood* lay claim to? One indication that Coetzee was not overridingly concerned with the detailed accuracy of historical truth is the fact that at the insistence of the American publisher—who feared litigation—he changed many of the original, historically accurate proper names in the book to invented names.[10] Yet, these enforced changes aside, there is nothing to suggest that the work is deliberately unhistorical; and part of its singular power undoubtedly comes from the reader's sense that this is not fiction (in the narrow sense of the word).[11] Fiction, it might be said, is always involved in a certain avoidance of responsibility: *these things haven't actually happened, I make no claims for them, I am just trying them out.* Coetzee's series of short fictions involving the character Elizabeth Costello exploits just this avoidance, as I have already suggested: he is able to articulate arguments in forceful terms without taking direct responsibility for them.[12] Historical writing (including biographical and autobiographical writing), however, cannot avoid responsibility to the past. And when the character on which the history is focused, and through whose consciousness it is witnessed, is identifiably the author—even more obviously so here than in the case of Proust or Joyce[13]—we intuit that a process of self-examination is going on, and that the essential truth being exhibited is not of the historical, factual kind.[14]

But is this self-examination of such a nature that we can call it a confession? Many of the passages which divulge boyhood secrets or reveal a

---

10. The first proofs of *Boyhood* contain the original names.

11. The reality presented is, of course, highly selective, and in the selection one can again sense the adult author at work: the incidents chosen are those that have stuck in the memory, no doubt, but also those that came to him, those that seemed appropriate to the task in hand, in the act, or the event, of writing. There is also the selectiveness of the boy's response to his surroundings; you would never guess from the dispiriting descriptions of *Boyhood* that the view from the front door of No. 12 Poplar Avenue, Worcester, takes in the magnificent range of the Hex River Mountains.

12. I shall argue in chapter 8 that this avoidance of responsibility does not inhibit the fictions' ethical force.

13. One indicator that the narrator and the boy are identifiable is the consistent use of the third-person pronoun in referring to the latter, never "John" or "the boy"—a consistency more characteristic of the first-person pronoun.

14. Coetzee gives an interesting account of the place of truth in autobiography: "What if young William Wordsworth never *in fact* stole a boat and went rowing on Ullswater? There are two things to say in response to this question. One is that, barring the discovery of fresh historical evidence, we will never *know for a fact* whether Wordsworth actually stole the boat. The other is that, while it does not matter, with respect to our response to *The Prelude,* that we *know for a fact* whether he actually stole the boat, *knowing for a fact* that he did *not* steal the boat, and therefore facing the fact that a pact we assumed to be in operation has been violated, might very well alter that response" (interview with David Attwell, forthcoming). In other words, historical knowledge can only disturb our confidence in autobiographical truth; it cannot create such confidence, which is a given of the genre.

sense of shame seem to belong more to the tradition of the novel than the mode of confession. For instance, the boy experiences shame at not being what he is made to think is a "normal" child:

> The very idea of being beaten makes him squirm with shame. There is nothing he will not do to save himself from it. In this respect he is unnatural and knows it. He comes from an unnatural and shameful family in which not only are children not beaten but older people are addressed by their first names and no one goes to church and shoes are worn every day. (6)

This passage operates like the famous moment in *Huckleberry Finn* when Huck decides to defy his conscience and aid Jim, the runaway slave: the reader has no doubt about the adult author's position and relishes the resultant irony. What we have is not confession, but rather the relieved acknowledgment that some childhood traumas—whose potent effects are not thereby denied—turn on comic misunderstanding. There are many other examples in *Boyhood*, often extremely funny, including the boy's secret preference for the Russians over the Americans (largely because of his liking for the letter R) (27), his assertion at school that he is a Roman Catholic rather than—the other choices offered him—a Christian or a Jew (again the attraction to that letter R, combined with his admiration for Horatius on the Tiber bridge) (18–19), and his belief that only he among his contemporaries has erotic stirrings (57).

Even closer to the example of Huck Finn is the embarrassment he experiences in many of his encounters with the coloured people of the Cape, an embarrassment which we (and we must assume his adult self) take as a laudable sign of his instinctive discomfort with the ingrained racism of white South African society. At other times, the boy's unquestioning reproduction of racist thinking—like his assertion that "One can dismiss the Natives, perhaps.... They are men without women, without children, who arrive from nowhere and can be made to disappear into nowhere" (61–62)[15]—can be read as sadly inevitable; an indication of the potency of the ideology rather than any failing in the boy. If it is a confession, it is a confession of having been, without realizing it, all *too* "normal."

Many other experiences are not so easily placed in the past with an amused adult knowingness, however. Let us continue with the passage

---

15. "Natives" in the 1950s was the common term for black Africans in South Africa. The contrast being made is with the coloured people of the Cape (see chap. 1, n. 27).

about the circus, as a small but characteristic example. (It will be recalled that the two boys have gone inside the tent while their mother, unable to afford the entry price for all three, has stayed outside.) In reading it, consider how different the same passage would seem if one came across it in a novel:

> Inside, he is miserable, enjoys nothing; he suspects his brother feels the same way. When they emerge at the end of the show, she is still there. For days afterwards he cannot banish the thought: his mother waiting patiently in the blazing heat of December while he sits in the circus tent being entertained like a king. Her blinding, overwhelming, self-sacrificial love, for both him and his brother but for him in particular, disturbs him. He wishes she did not love him so much. She loves him absolutely, therefore he must love her absolutely: that is the logic she compels upon him. Never will he be able to pay back all the love she pours out upon him. The thought of a lifetime bowed under a debt of love baffles and infuriates him to the point where he will not kiss her, refuses to be touched by her. When she turns away in silent hurt, he deliberately hardens his heart against her, refusing to give in. (47)

In a novel, this passage would be part of the construction of a character's psyche; it might seem a little exaggerated in its not-too-original portrayal of the sacrificing mother and the indebted, resentful son. But if we take the "he" to be the *author* of the sentences we are reading, they come across very differently. Fiction becomes recollection; the intensity of the related experience becomes a mark of its power as memory, as lasting imprint on the same psyche that is producing the words we read.

The bitter acknowledgment of a mother's destructive love now has the character of a secret revealed in these very sentences, and although there is no retrospective commentary to give us the adult author's views (we don't know if he *has* had a lifetime bowed under a debt of love), we read in the distanced prose the struggle required to make such a self-revelation.[16] It is something very like confession. A confession without any overt acceptance of responsibility, one that the Truth Commission

---

16. It is characteristic of confessions that they are enabled by the deaths of individuals who figure prominently in them and might have been hurt by them; and above all by the death of the confessant's mother (or in the case of Derrida's "Circumfession" her mortal illness, rendering her incapable of recognizing her son; see Geoffrey Bennington and Jacques Derrida, *Jacques Derrida*). It requires only a glance at the dedication of *Age of Iron* to deduce that Vera Coetzee died in 1985.

would not recognize, perhaps—but this very avoidance of the show of responsibility might, at least in the realm of the literary, be read as itself a mark of the confessional mode, in all its secular uncertainty, an uncertainty which the Truth Commission cannot afford to acknowledge. *I tell you these things that I did and experienced, but I know all too well that if I start apologizing you will suspect my motives—I will suspect my motives—and if I reveal my suspicions you will suspect my motives for this revelation, and we will get nowhere. So here it is, without reflection, judgment, apology. I challenge you to guess at what it cost me to write these words.*[17]

A more general critique of the use of childhood as a confessional vehicle is presented by Michiel Heyns in an essay that deals with what he calls the "rite of passage novel" in recent white South African fiction. The use of the child's voice, he argues, correctly I believe, avoids issues of confession and absolution because "it is granted absolution through the legal fiction that the child is not accountable, and the related fictional convention that children are 'innocent' in a generally unspecified sense" ("The Whole Country's Truth," 50). This proposition is fully borne out in Mark Behr's novel *The Smell of Apples,* one of the works which Heyns considers, and one which provides an illuminating comparison with *Boyhood.* Published to great acclaim in South Africa in 1993 (as *Die Reuk van Appels*), the novel is told largely in the present tense and the first person by an eleven-year-old boy growing up in an Afrikaner family in the Western Cape. The narrative is "confessional" in a weak sense: it shows how a boy can be lured into participation in the dominant racism of his culture in spite of a confrontation with some of its darkest manifestations. Though the novel is not overtly autobiographical in the way *Boyhood* is (as I have noted, we learn that the "he" of the narrative is named "John Coetzee"), the reader is certainly invited to make some identification of the boy with the author, and to read the work as offering an explanation for his own

---

17. By demonstrating the possibility of confessing in the third person, *Boyhood* helps us read the confessional in all Coetzee's fiction, and it is perhaps only an apparent paradox that someone who is known as an extremely private individual should reveal so much (without overtly doing so, of course) in the novels he writes. As I have noted, *The Master of Petersburg,* which was written in the aftermath of Coetzee's son's death, can be read as not only about the confessional mode but also as an instance of it, and much of the thinking of Magda, of the Magistrate, and of Mrs. Curren can be connected to the childhood related here. The relationship of Michael K to his mother (who, like Vera Coetzee, had a strong connection to the small Karoo town of Prince Albert) also takes on a new and more personal resonance.

involvement in the nefarious work of the apartheid government (which included—as Behr "confessed" during a 1996 conference on the Truth and Reconciliation Commission—being a paid informer for the South African security forces while holding a senior position in a left-wing student organization).[18]

The contrast with *Boyhood* is striking: Coetzee's text is in no sense an apology for his internalized prejudices, nor does it attempt to take any credit for the moments of resistance to apartheid ideology. There is no ulterior motive at work that we can fathom, no design on the reader that we can sense, as we can in Augustine and Rousseau.[19] It is true that the complicity with apartheid that the young John shows is rather run-of-the-mill, though no less reprehensible for being that; but even the occasional moments of personal inhumanity are presented with a stark absence of explanation or justification.

One instance where unconscious racism is obviously at work is the treatment of Josias, the African man who delivers groceries from the local store and whom the family refer to, typically for whites at the time, as "Schochat's boy." If he arrives with an order including a can of condensed milk while their mother is out of the house, John and his brother steal it and lay the blame on him (63). It's not difficult to imagine the additional sweetness imparted to the unctuous liquid by the boys' sense of their own wickedness, but if there is any guilt involved in the act its causes do not include the unjust accusation against Josias. John is unsure whether their mother believes their lie; but, he adds, "this is not a deceit he feels particularly guilty about." The contrast with the famous "Marion" episode in Rousseau's *Confessions,* in which the young Jean-Jacques lays the blame for his theft of a ribbon on a maidservant, couldn't be clearer: Rousseau writes of "the unbearable weight of a remorse which, even after

18. Behr's more recent novel, *Embrace* (another exercise in pseudo-autobiography) further testifies to the force of Heyns's critique, trading as it does on a combination of childhood innocence and eroticism. For a very different fictional treatment of a young South African boy's exposure to adult homosexuality, see Heyns's own novel, *The Children's Day.*

19. In an essay on his confessional autobiography *Manhood* (an autobiography written in the traditional first-person past-tense mode), Michel Leiris comments on the failure of his attempt to write without such a motive: "What I did not realize was that at the source of all introspection is a predilection for self-contemplation, and that every confession contains a desire to be absolved. To consider myself objectively was still to consider myself—to keep my eyes fixed on myself instead of turning them beyond and transcending myself in the direction of something more broadly human" (*Manhood,* 156).

forty years, still burdens my conscience" (86), whereas we can only guess at the guilt felt by the adult Coetzee at his early freedom from any such emotion.

The most salient and disturbing example of purely personal cruelty occurs not in the present-tense narrative but as a memory while John and his younger brother are playing with a book press in their Aunt Annie's storeroom. The two boys, visiting a farm, had come upon a machine for grinding mealies (that is, maize):

> He persuaded his brother to put his hand down the funnel where the mealie-pits were thrown in; then he turned the handle. For an instant, before he stopped, he could feel the fine bones of the fingers being crushed. His brother stood with his hand trapped in the machine, ashen with pain, a puzzled, inquiring look on his face. (119)

The younger boy, we learn, was rushed to hospital, and half the middle finger was amputated. We wait for some psychological elaboration here, the confession of deep hatred, or of a taste for casual violence, or of a desire for shame and punishment, or perhaps a premonition of decades of remorse, but all we get is this: "He has never apologized to his brother, nor has he ever been reproached with what he did. Nevertheless, the memory lies like a weight upon him, the memory of the soft resistance of flesh and bone, and then the grinding" (119).

The "memory" referred to here is, literally, of an event only two or three years earlier, but it is impossible not to read it also as a memory which has retained its potency up to the time of writing. However, one can only speculate on the possible effects upon the author of its public exposure, since in this present-tense narrative there can be no equivalent of Rousseau's account of his desire to free himself from the burden of the never-before-revealed ribbon episode by putting it in print (*Confessions*, 88). The chiseling of language that the reader senses here is part of the experience of a struggle to articulate a truth that could only be diminished by explanation or justification. That there is no attempt to account for or excuse the horrifying action described does not diminish the passage's truth-directedness. The reverse is the case, in fact: as Paul de Man notes in discussing the ribbon episode, the act of explicit confession can never be judged "true" since it is always contaminated by the possibility that it is motivated by the desire to excuse (*Allegories of Reading*, 280).

That the memory is exclusively of the physical experience and not its emotional or mental dimensions also removes any suspicion that the account is meant to exculpate—and again, there is a clear contrast with

Rousseau, who shifts from a description of the unjust accusation of Marion to a revelation of his "inner feelings" and in so doing moves unmistakably into the mode of excuse. And the use of the third person and the present tense as the basic mode of the book is part of this attempt to be true: we've seen that in narrating the same period of his life in an interview Coetzee falls into just this way of speaking. Such is the sense of integrity that the book has conveyed up to this point that the spareness of the passage comes across not as a withholding but as a sign of the adult author's continuing bafflement, of an essential truth that he, like Augustine, cannot penetrate. Heyns makes the valid point that there is something contradictory in the notion of confessional fiction, because of the novel's tendency to explain, contextualize, and provide motives ("The Whole Country's Truth," 50). This may be less true of Coetzee's novels than of many others, and it does not apply at all to the spare prose of *Boyhood*.

The truth that *Boyhood* offers, then, is first and foremost that of testimony: a vivid account of what it was like to grow up as a white male in the 1950s in South Africa as the Nationalist government set about institutionalizing its particular brand of racism and entrenching the power of Afrikanerdom, an account that combines general truths about that experience (and having shared it, I can vouch for its accuracy and penetration) and of singular truths about one highly unusual child, at the interface of English and Afrikaans cultures, in the specific location of the Western Cape, undergoing the trials of a father's declining economic status and a family permanently damaged by the upheavals of the Second World War.[20] But *Boyhood* is a literary as well as a documentary work, and to the extent that it is the former, its object is not the conveyance of historical truth.

---

20. Its subtitle is not *A Memoir* (although the American paperback carries this phrase on its cover), but *Scenes from Provincial Life*. The subtitle sounds like some descriptive Russian prose-work, such as Turgenev's *Sketches from a Hunter's Notebook;* though it also echoes two of George Eliot's titles, *Scenes of Clerical Life* and *Middlemarch: A Study of Provincial Life*. (Eliot's titles are designed, of course, to claim historical weight and accuracy for her fictions.) Other echoes are Balzac's *Comédie humaine*, which included a group of novels entitled *Scènes de la vie de province*, and Flaubert's *Madame Bovary*, subtitled *Moeurs de province*. In a review of *Boyhood*, David Attwell discusses a lesser-known precursor: the influential neo-realist novel *Scenes from Provincial Life* by William Cooper, nom-de-plume of H. S. Hoff, published in 1950. This dense web of allusion (to which one might add the main title's echo of two memoirs, Leiris's *Manhood*, already mentioned, and Tolstoy's *Boyhood*, the second volume of his semi-autobiographical trilogy) places the book firmly within a long European tradition even while it asserts its marginality.

Literature may, however, be deeply involved in an exploration of *truth-telling,* of what it means, and what it feels like, to articulate sentences governed by an obligation to be accurate and honest. *Boyhood* enacts the truth of confession, and writing as confession, without transgression, repentance, or absolution.

: IV :

The consequences for the reader of the choice of the third person and the present tense for a memoir became particularly apparent with the publication in 2002 of Coetzee's second autobiographical work, *Youth,* which uses the same mode of narration to recount some of the significant events of his life between 1959 and 1964 (from the age of nineteen—he is a student at the University of Cape Town when the book opens—to twenty-four). In the U.S.A., the book appeared with the subtitle *Scenes from Provincial Life II,* which made its connection with *Boyhood* clear, but in the U.K. there was no addition to the single word of the title.[21] Nevertheless, British readers familiar with the earlier book, or with the bare facts of Coetzee's life, should have had no difficulty in identifying the work's genre; and even those without these advantages would have noticed that the main character is a young white South African called John with an Afrikaner background and aspirations to be a writer.[22] But the third person and present tense (and perhaps the difficulty of associating the self-deceived, uncreative, blundering antihero with the internationally admired author) caused even reviewers in prestigious periodicals to treat

21. The existence of two other well-known works with the same title, by Tolstoy and by Conrad, provide complex intertexts. Tolstoy's *Youth,* the third part of the trilogy *Childhood, Boyhood, Youth,* is, like Coetzee's work, based on the author's own experience, though it is at once more autobiographical in presentation, since it is in the first person and past tense, and less autobiographical in its relation to facts, since Tolstoy feels free to invent names (including the name of the narrator) and other details. It is, however, similar to Coetzee's *Youth* in presenting a highly unappealing earlier self, and in losing a great deal if read without an awareness of its autobiographical nature. Conrad's *Youth* is a complete contrast: a tale about testing at sea and coming through into manhood, derived from an episode in Conrad's early career at sea but fictionalized via the narrator Marlow. The relation between Coetzee's work and Conrad's can only be a highly ironic one.

22. The book's epigraph, from Goethe's *West-Östlicher Divan,* also gives a clue: "Wer den Dichter will verstehen muß in Dichters Lande gehen" (Whoever wants to understand the poet must visit the poet's country).

the work as a novel—and, inevitably, given the string of disasters without development or denouement that it retails, as a botched novel.[23]

Here, for instance, are a few sentences from Peter Porter's record of his disappointment in the *Times Literary Supplement,* which reveal clearly how the failure to appreciate the autobiographical nature of the work results in the application of inappropriate standards and the invention of irrelevant intentions:

> In the remainder of the novel, John is immersed in England's uncomfortable bedsitter land. With an internal colloquy knowledgeable about Ingeborg Bachmann and Hans Magnus Enzensberger, and an ambition to write the definitive study of the novels of Ford Madox Ford, is it feasible that he should be also naive, imperceptive and overwhelmed by simple events? It becomes clear that Coetzee's real intention is to provide the right crucible for youthful discontent and that this will be England. London as the hub of a world-wide network of English-speaking artists seeking a proper apprenticeship for genius is over-familiar by now. It has seldom been rendered so remorselessly and humourlessly. There are no picaresque adventures, no comic interludes, not even much in the way of illustrative *faux pas.* (22)

Although many readers would disagree with Porter about the implausibility of a well-read and intellectually ambitious youth being at the same time hopelessly incompetent in the world of practical and emotional affairs, questions of probability are (as Aristotle understood) more appropriate for fiction than for history. It is true that, even more than is the case with *Boyhood,* Coetzee has selectively concentrated on the most shaming events of these years (only one experience of real happiness is related—a few moments of half-consciousness on Hampstead Heath [117]—an experience that is all the more intensely conveyed for the contrast it creates), but as we have seen, confession is above all confession of that of which one is ashamed.

Porter, reading the work as fiction, states, "We leave John in his mid-twenties obviously intending (or doomed) to return to South Africa." In fact, Coetzee ends his memoir not long before the move that turned out to be a highly productive one for his career as a writer ("a life-saving

---

23. In defense of British reviewers, it appears that prepublication copies were sent out with an accompanying note that implied the work was a novel—part, perhaps, of Coetzee's double strategy, evident also in the choice of tense and person, of simultaneously baring himself and hiding himself in these two works.

decision," he called it in a *Doubling the Point* interview [393]): not back to South Africa, but to the U.S.A. to undertake a Ph.D. at the University of Texas. (This is the moment, we recall, when in an earlier recounting of his life story, *autre*biography begins to shade into autobiography—making it improbable that there will be a third volume of this kind.) He thus chooses to deny the reader any sense of light at the end of the tunnel of fruitless, miserable endeavor. Toward the end of the book, however, there are hints at what is to come, discernible only by those who are familiar with Coetzee's personal history. The young man's fascination with accounts of travels in South Africa ("stories of ventures into the interior, reconnaissances by ox-wagon into the desert of the Great Karoo" [137]) contains the seeds of the second part of *Dusklands*, published ten years later. The conversation with his fellow-worker Ganapathy about the possibility of gaining a fellowship at an American university (151–52) can be understood as bearing fruit just beyond the (mordantly defeatist) final words of *Youth*, since, in order to begin his studies at the University of Texas in September 1965, Coetzee would have had to submit an application a few months after the summer of 1964 with which the book ends. And the chance discovery of Beckett's *Watt* (155) clearly marks the end of Pound's stranglehold over the aspirant writer and a new influence which will have a profound effect on his future writing—Coetzee's Texas Ph.D. dissertation will focus on Beckett's fiction, and his own early fiction will be marked (as we saw in chapter 3) by Beckettian echoes.

Youth is as much (and as little) a confession as *Boyhood:* an unflinching admission of the faults of self-centeredness, cruelty, ineptitude, and callousness—most painfully evident in a series of disastrous sexual encounters. The most that can be said in the young Coetzee's defense is that these failings are born mainly out of naiveté, timidity, and an agonizing incapacity to open himself to others. Dostoevsky's conviction at the end of *The Master of Petersburg* that inventive writing requires the "betrayal of love, first of all" is implicit throughout the work, but without the creative payoff we take for granted in the case of the Russian writer. There is the betrayal of motherly love, a continuation of one of the central themes of *Boyhood:* as a student in Cape Town, John has cut himself off completely from his mother, and in England he is exasperated by the letters that arrive each week from her. And there is the betrayal of sexual love: sex is something John urges himself toward as a necessary enterprise for an artist, but with very little awareness of the human responsibilities it entails.

This is a riskier and darker book than *Boyhood*, then, exposing the self more radically yet continuing to withhold the crucial moment of self-reflection and regret. This confession of earlier sins against love, against people he encounters, and (though within the work he remains blind to this dimension) against art has quite a different ring from the revelation of childhood weaknesses and prejudices in *Boyhood*. The tendency to exculpate the child observed by Heyns is no longer operative: in his twenties, a man must be held fully responsible for his actions and attitudes, and even when he is looking back from the vantage point of his sixties it is difficult to dissociate him completely from his earlier self. We as readers are required to provide the perspective from which the young man is being regarded, the perspective of the older and more worldly-wise author looking back at the illusions and errors of his youth, and we can't be sure what proportions of amusement and dismay make up that backward gaze.[24] In Coetzee's terms, we sense the unflinchingness more strongly than the forgivingness.

If this perspective is not granted as the enabling principle of the work—if it is taken to be a novel rather than a memoir—it reads, as we have seen, as a pointless rehearsal of inadequacy, wrongdoing, and failure. Granting this perspective, on the other hand, it is in many places an extremely funny book. John stumbles into one hilariously calamitous situation after another, situations to which one can imagine a writer like Kingsley Amis doing ample comic justice (in a very different style). Next to the moments of mature reflection are moments of simple-minded misapprehension reminiscent of the humorous misunderstandings of *Boyhood*, justifying the American subtitle "Scenes from Provincial Life" even though the larger part of the work is set in metropolitan England. Thus, to take just one example, John, aged twenty-three or twenty-four, still has as strong an emotional attachment to the communist side in the Cold War as he did in *Boyhood*, and when the U.S.–Vietnam conflict increases in intensity he toys with the idea of joining the Vietcong (apparently forgetting that by his own admission he is not very good in "the real world" or at "real life" [22, 45]). But he decides to write instead to the Chinese Embassy

24. There is only one moment, I believe, when retrospective narration is hinted at: a sentence beginning "In a poetry magazine—*Ambit* perhaps, or *Agenda*—he finds an announcement" (72). That "perhaps" sounds like the product of the uncertain memory of the time of writing, unless the young John is confused about of the name of the magazine he is reading.

in London offering his aid in the struggle against the Americans—and then lives in fear that the British secret services have intercepted his letter (153). At moments like these, it is hard not to hear the author chuckling, though the writing itself gives nothing away.

In spite of the fact that John's self-communings on the subject of women and sex are for the most part hilariously deluded, his actual encounters are often painful to read. It is here that the protocols of confession are most severely tested, where the awkwardness and shame experienced by the young man cry out for the complement of later regret and repentance. The abortion procured by a partner in Cape Town, in which he plays what he admits is an ignominious role (32–36); the affair with the seventeen-year old Austrian au pair in London, a "mistake" for which he feels guilty (86–87, 101–2); and the bloody deflowering of his cousin's friend Mari-anne, which he calls "a sorry business" (127–31): these are all described in language which conveys the shame and distaste felt at the time but gives no hint of how the author now regards them. Yet there can be no doubt of the truth-directedness of the writing: these passages expose the moral failings of the author as a young man all the more unblinkingly for not including anything that could be taken to be excuse or extenuation—and, as I have argued, there is, structurally speaking, no form of retrospection that can avoid being suspected of an ulterior motive.

Youth has less value as testimony than *Boyhood*: we get some insight into the impact on white South Africans of the Sharpeville massacre, an intense sense of London's inhospitability to foreigners in the early 1960s, and glimpses of the early stages of the computing industry and of Britain's part in the Cold War, but these are viewed through the eyes of such a limited and self-absorbed witness that readers are unlikely to learn a great deal. Paradoxically, perhaps, the even greater naiveté of the boy in *Boyhood* provides a cleaner page on which the effects of the historical situation and its mutations are written. Moreover, if we com-pare the life narrated in *Youth* with the biographical facts available, we find that the commitment to a negative view of this period of Coetzee's life has resulted in rather startling omissions and distortions. For exam-ple, Coetzee received his master's degree from the University of Cape Town in 1963, whereas John in the book is still toiling away at his study of the novels of Ford Madox Ford in 1964 (his "third summer in Eng-land") (159–60). More striking still is the absence of any mention of Coet-zee's marriage to Philippa Jubber in 1963 (see Goddard and Read, *J. M. Coetzee: A Bibliography,* 15), an absence which makes possible a re-morselessly self-denigrating picture of the narrator's sexual relations, but which renders the notion of autobiographical "truth" particularly problematic. The urge to confess may itself distort the representation of the past, producing an exaggeration of one's failings, and *Youth* certainly provokes the thought that by giving us so little in the way of compensatory moments of generosity or joy Coetzee has succumbed to this tendency. By contrast, the narrator of Tolstoy's *Youth* reports in detail an act of confession—according to the rites of the Russian Orthodox Church—but keeps from us its content, including the "shameful sin" which he realizes afterwards he has concealed, necessitating a trip to the confessor's monastery.

In both *Boyhood* and *Youth* the power of this exposure of the self, of this drive for the truth, can be felt only if the author of the words we read is identified with the "he" of the narrative. This power is not reduced by the undismissable possibility that Coetzee has woven fictional episodes into a framework of autobiography, carrying out, that is, the experiment outlined in *Youth* of writing a work with the "aura of truth" that will get it "into the history of the world" (138). For in the end, this possibility can never be more than that, since, like Wordsworth's stealing of the boat on Ullswater, many of the episodes are private and thus beyond any possibility of confirmation or disconfirmation, and any comments Coetzee himself might make on the subject (whether to assert or deny the presence of fictional elements in the work) could always be part of a deliberate strategy of deception.[25] This doubt haunts all autobiography, however, a genre that hovers permanently at the borders of the literary and the nonliterary. Confessional autobiography does not escape this condition: as we have seen, confession is always, in a sense, staged, and these two works are no exceptions. It is in that staging, however, that confession becomes of interest to others; we read *Boyhood* and *Youth* not in order to dispense forgiveness or blame, but to experience the pleasures of language being shaped and arranged to capture, for its author, for its readers, a certain form of truth.

25. As Coetzee himself observes in discussing Dostoevsky's *Notes from Underground*: "The more coherent such a hypothetical fiction of the self might be, the less the reader's chance of knowing whether it is a true confession. We can test its truth only when it contradicts itself or comes into conflict with some 'outer,' verifiable truth, both of which eventualities a careful confessing narrator can in theory avoid" (*Doubling the Point,* 280).

CHAPTER SEVEN

Age of Bronze, State of Grace

Disgrace

: I :

"The age of iron. After which comes the age of bronze. How long, how long before the softer ages return in their cycle, the age of clay, the age of earth?" (*Age of Iron,* 50). Mrs. Curren, writing to her daughter about the South Africa of the mid-1980s in which she is slowly dying of cancer, views the grim panorama of devastated communities, callous authorities, and armed children through the lens of classical myth, Hesiod's account of the successive ages of men. She performs an odd reversal on the traditional sequence, however: she places the age of bronze *after* the age of iron in which she feels she is living, and which provides J. M. Coetzee with the title of his novel.[1] Unlike every previous novel by Coetzee, *Age of Iron* is set entirely in his native country at the time of its composition, the years of emergency laws and township warfare which in retrospect we see as the

---

1. In Hesiod's *Works and Days,* echoed by Ovid in the *Metamorphoses,* the ages come in the order gold, silver, bronze, and iron (with the age of demigods coming between the bronze and iron ages in Hesiod's scheme). The men of the age of bronze, according to Hesiod, were "a terrible and fierce race, occupied with the woeful works of Ares and with acts of violence" (*Works and Days,* 145).

death throes of apartheid but which then felt for many like a nightmare without foreseeable end.

In the late 1990s, we find Coetzee at work on another compelling novel set in the South Africa of the time of composition.[2] The struggle against the repressive, racist state is finally over, apartheid is a discredited policy of the past, and democratic government has finally been established. The age of iron is no more. Has South Africa reentered at last one of those "softer ages" longed for by Mrs. Curren in her reinvention of Hesiod's creation narrative? The new novel, *Disgrace,* published in 1999, certainly suggests that the ten or twelve years that have passed since Mrs. Curren's dying days have indeed wrought a transformation in the country, but it's not easy to say what age we find ourselves in now. A time of rampant crime, inefficient police services, middle classes barricaded into their fortress-homes: have we followed Mrs. Curren's inverted sequence and moved beyond iron only to reach bronze?

Coetzee's fiction has, as we have noted, always had a mixed reception in South Africa, and its very success elsewhere in the world has increased the suspicion felt among some groups in his native country. Coetzee himself has insisted on the complexity of the relation between fiction and history, and his most astute critics have read the novels as in part exploring precisely that relation.[3] Nevertheless, there can be no doubt that a ceaseless, intense engagement with the country, and more specifically with its political and social history, has marked his writing. Nor should there ever have been any doubt about his strong opposition to the policies and practices of the Nationalist government in power between 1948 and 1994, and the older colonial traditions on which they were built, even though his fiction did not take the form of straightforward "resistance writing." In such works as "The Narrative of Jacobus Coetzee," with its memorable descriptions of colonial brutality, *Waiting for the Barbarians,* with its representation of a state apparatus relying on torture and cross-border raids, *Life & Times of Michael K,* with its imagined state of war in a future South Africa, and *Age of Iron,* with its vivid depiction of the violence

2. We can date the events of *Disgrace* to 1997 or 1998. The main protagonist, David Lurie, who is fifty-two when the novel opens and whose age is given (presumably incorrectly) as fifty-three by the press, was born in 1945 (46).

3. See, in particular, David Attwell, *J. M. Coetzee.*

in the townships and the systematic viciousness of the police, Coetzee, quite as much as any South African author, has registered for his time and for future generations the brutality, the anger, and the suffering of the apartheid era (even though, as I have been arguing, the most valuable and rewarding qualities of his writing, as literature, lie elsewhere). After the democratic elections of 1994 and the sweeping ANC victory that brought Nelson Mandela from prison to the presidency, one might well have expected from his pen a novel with at least a tinge of celebration and optimism.

It's hardly surprising, then, that mixed in with the huge acclaim that greeted Coetzee's far from affirmative novel there were expressions of annoyance and anger, especially from South African commentators.[4] The overriding question for many readers is: does this novel, as one of the most widely disseminated and forceful representations of post-apartheid South Africa, impede the difficult enterprise of rebuilding the country? Does the largely negative picture it paints of relations between communities hinder the steps being made toward reconciliation? Is it a damagingly misleading portrait of a society that has made enormous strides in the direction of justice and peace? Even readers whose view of the artist's responsibility is less tied to notions of instrumentalism and political efficacy than these questions imply—and I include myself among these—may find the bleak image of the "new South Africa"[5] in this work hard to take.

Nor is it possible to argue that the novel makes no claim to represent or criticize ANC-governed South Africa, that it's fundamentally the story of a group of individuals who happen to live in a particular place and time, the place and time in which the work was written. Quite apart from the fact that a novel dealing with relations between racially defined groups set in immediately post-apartheid South Africa could hardly be

---

4. One example (admittedly among the least considered if among the most colorful): in a profile by Christopher Goodwin in the (London) *Sunday Times,* Athol Fugard, without having read the novel, expresses outrage that "we've got to accept the rape of a white woman as a gesture to all of the evil that we did in the past. That's a load of bloody bullshit. That white women are going to accept being raped as penance for what was done in the past? Jesus. It's an expression of a very morbid phenomenon, very morbid." For discussion of the novel's reception, including its citation by the ANC in the latter's submission to the South African Human Rights Commission hearings on racism in the media, see Attridge, "Introduction"; Attwell, "Race in *Disgrace*" and McDonald, "*Disgrace* Effects."

5. Although I shall drop the quotation marks around "the new South Africa" from now on, their invisible presence may be assumed: the phrase has too many complex connotations to be used in a simple referential way.

read as having no interest in national issues, there are repeated references to the changed times and their impact on the way lives are now being lived (just as in *Age of Iron* there are many references to "the times," fleshing out the title's implication that the portrayal of a particular period of South Africa will play an important part in the novel). But what *is* new in this picture as Coetzee paints it, what *are* the changes that are making themselves felt in the workplace, on the farm, in the classroom? To what extent, in particular, are the assessments of the changes offered by characters in the novel interpretable as criticism of ANC policies, and of the national effort of reconciliation and regeneration more widely, as they filter through to the local level? What I propose to do by way of an introduction to some further questions about the novel and its relation to its historical and political context, and also as a way of recalling its narrative outline, is to devote some pages to an examination of a number of these references in the text to "the times" in which the characters find themselves living.

The first such moment occurs near the beginning of the novel when David Lurie—the university professor through whose consciousness the entire work is presented—is speculating on the life lived by "Soraya," the coloured prostitute with whom he has a weekly arrangement: she may, he realizes, work for the escort agency only once or twice a week, and otherwise have a respectable suburban existence. "That would be unusual for a Muslim," he thinks, "but all things are possible these days" (3). Lurie is articulating what sounds like a common experience of old certainties gone, of little left to wonder at in a rapidly altering landscape. It is hardly an expression of regret at religious breakdown—in fact, Lurie is perfectly happy to profit from such breakdown, if this is indeed what makes it possible for a Muslim woman to work as a part-time prostitute. But it does suggest at the very opening of the work that it will be concerned with "these days" in South Africa, with changed surroundings, a new mentality, different ways of doing things. In the spheres of both religion and sex, passion and commitment appear to be giving way to organization and efficiency.

Then we learn of the contour of Lurie's career as an academic, which signals another, related, aspect of the altered world:

> Once a professor of modern languages, he has been, since Classics and Modern Languages were closed down as part of the great rationalization, adjunct professor of communications.... He has never been much of a

teacher; in this transformed and, to his mind, emasculated institution of learning he is more out of place than ever. But then, so are other of his colleagues from the old days, burdened with upbringings inappropriate to the tasks they are set to perform; clerks in a post-religious age. (3–4)

The implicit critique here is aimed not at a local issue but at a global phenomenon of the end of the twentieth century; those who work in educational institutions in many parts of the world can tell their own stories of the "great rationalization," and of course the syndrome goes well beyond the walls of the academy. If a specific attack on official South African educational policy is implied here, it's only because those who control this policy have failed to resist a much broader shift in attitudes and expectations. In this domain the change from a racist to a democratic political system has made little difference.

The arrangement with Soraya breaks down because Lurie can't sustain his attempt—perfectly in keeping with the times—at a rational solution to what the novel's first sentence calls "the problem of sex" (1). In the wake of this breakdown, he takes the new, young departmental secretary, to whom Coetzee gives (with nice irony) the name Dawn, to lunch; it is the opening move in a new (and as it turns out, short-lived) erotic undertaking. We are made privy to very little of their conversation, but Dawn's views on post-apartheid South Africa are highlighted: "I mean, whatever the rights and wrongs of the situation, at least you knew where you were. . . . Now people just pick and choose which laws they want to obey. It's anarchy" (8–9). Lurie's response is withheld from us, but the comment is presented as significant: presumably because it is typical in both registering an increase in social disorder and remaining blind to its causes.

Soraya's disappearance and Lurie's subsequent sexual deprivation—he wonders if it possible to request castration (9)—also play a part in precipitating the event that sets in motion the unfolding of the central plot: Lurie's seduction of Melanie Isaacs, a twenty-year-old student in one of his classes. During the brief affair, Lurie surreptitiously watches a rehearsal of the play in which Melanie is acting, a play which presents a startlingly different vision of "the times":

Sunset at the Globe Salon is the name of the play they are rehearsing: a comedy of the new South Africa set in a hairdressing salon in Hill-brow, Johannesburg. On stage a hairdresser, flamboyantly gay, attends to two clients, one black, one white. . . . Catharsis seems to be the presiding principle: all the coarse old prejudices brought into the light of day and washed away in gales of laughter. (23)

Even before the official dismantling of apartheid, Hillbrow had become known as a suburb of Johannesburg in which middle-class "racial mixing" occurred freely.[6] Lurie's somewhat jaundiced description of the play's premise no doubt reflects his view that the process of coming to terms with the legacy of apartheid will be much more painful and long drawn out than is suggested by this cheerful divertissement with its racial and sexual liberties—a view which the novel does nothing to counter.[7]

After the brief liaison has come to a nasty end, Lurie, now the subject of an official sexual harassment enquiry, dines with his ex-wife. "Don't expect sympathy from me, David," she warns him, "and don't expect sympathy from anyone else either. No sympathy, no mercy, not in this day and age" (44). Again, a fairly commonplace statement hints at the bitterness of the white South African who has lost the privileges her race conferred on her, but perhaps there is an echo, too, of the dehumanizing effects of the "great rationalization" of end-of-century global capitalism: there are many places other than South Africa where Rosalind's comment would not have seemed unusual.

Forced to resign from the university, Lurie seeks refuge with his daughter Lucy on a smallholding in the Eastern Province, where she grows flowers and vegetables for the market in nearby Grahamstown and runs dog kennels. He meets Petrus, the African man who assists Lucy and has recently become her co-proprietor, and expresses his concern about her isolation. "Yes," replies Petrus, "it is dangerous.... Everything is dangerous today" (64). If this is an age of bronze, it is not just those who have lost their privileges who experience it as such. Locked as we are into Lurie's view of things, we don't gain much sense of what the new South Africa means to those who are poor or black or both—for the most part the new South Africa to them would seem to be much the same as the old South Africa—but this moment is a telling exception, and it

---

6. A novel that uses a Hillbrow setting to explore some of the social changes in South Africa during the transition from apartheid to democracy is Ivan Vladislavic's *The Restless Supermarket;* unlike Coetzee, however, Vladislavic chooses as a focalizing hero someone who sees only the decay of norms and distinctions—he is a retired proofreader—and none of the effects of the increasingly administered society. A rather different view of the area is offered in Phaswane Mpe's *Welcome to Our Hillbrow.*

7. In her roughly contemporaneous novel *The House Gun,* Nadine Gordimer also uses a group of young people of varying races and sexualities as a paradigm of the new South Africa, a paradigm that the older couple at the center of the novel find hard to stomach. However, Gordimer appears to take such instances of the new sexual and racial order more seriously than Coetzee, or at least than Lurie.

introduces a new layer to the accumulating meanings of "the times." To black as well as white, there are new fears about personal safety. Petrus, however, remains almost entirely inscrutable, and could merely be giving polite assent to Lurie's comment; as so often in Coetzee's fiction, the racially or socially privileged character can gain virtually no understanding of the inner world of the other who has been excluded from such privilege.[8]

A little later, Lurie and his daughter are discussing his disgrace, and his refusal to gain a reprieve by complying with the committee's demands that he make an acceptable public confession and undergo counseling.[9] What has precipitated Lurie's public shaming is not his submission to the desire to fuck Melanie Isaacs—"It must go on all the time," comments Lucy, no doubt with some justice—but his refusal to submit to these demands, a submission that in his eyes would constitute acceptance of the newly asserted institutional rights and newly emergent collective mores that he finds deeply repugnant. "These are puritanical times," he says. "Private life is public business" (66). He explains to Lucy that he can't mount a public defense of his actions: "The case you want me to make is a case that can no longer be made, *basta*. Not in our day" (89). In this new age, hitherto private details of sexual intimacy have become matter for daily public discourse, but rather than heralding a greater acceptance of sexual diversity and sexual needs, this shift marks an increase in puritanical surveillance and moralistic denunciation. (A perfect emblem of the paradox is, of course, the Clinton-Lewinsky affair that engrossed the U.S.A.—and the world—in 1998.) Once more, then, the issue is not

---

8. Among the pairs of characters already discussed in earlier chapters are Magda and Hendrik in *In the Heart of the Country*, the Magistrate and the barbarian girl in *Waiting for the Barbarians*, the medical officer and Michael K in *Life & Times of Michael K*, Susan Barton and Friday in *Foe*, and Mrs. Curren and Vercueil in *Age of Iron*. Gayatri Spivak (forthcoming) argues interestingly that *Disgrace* invites the reader to resist the novel's consistent focalization through Lurie's consciousness by "counterfocalizing," but she suggests Lucy, not Petrus, as the alternative center. This is a reading strategy that might be extended to other characters and other novels, although failure would be as revealing as success.

9. Mark Sanders points out the resonances here with the Truth and Reconciliation Commission, referring to "the confusion between the legal requirement of perpetrators to make a full disclosure, and the unlegislated moral pressure to express remorse, make repentance, and even ask forgiveness of victims" ("Disgrace"). For a discussion of the question of reparation in the TRC and in *Disgrace*, see Elleke Boehmer, "Not Saying Sorry." See also chap. 6, sect. 2 above.

simply one of changes arising from the end of apartheid, but of shifts elsewhere—notably in the United States—impacting upon a South Africa becoming increasingly absorbed into a global milieu. In an essay on the intellectual in South Africa, Coetzee writes of "a process of intellectual colonisation going on today that...originates in the culture factories of the United States, and can be detected in the most intimate corners of our lives, or if not in our own then in our students' lives" ("Critic and Citizen," 111).[10]

There's little to suggest that at the time he makes it Lurie intends his stand as a principled challenge to the entire establishment in the name of desire (the novel opens, after all, with his carefully calculated sexual regimen), nor that he is consciously and deliberately embarking on a complete reinvention of his way of living. In its emotional resonance it seems more like a matter of pique, irritation, and hurt pride taking him willy-nilly down a road whose destination is obscure. Much of this early section of the novel reads, unusually for Coetzee, as satire, not difficult to connect with its author's situation at the time as professor of literature in the University of Cape Town.[11] The mood begins to shift and deepen when Lurie reaches the Eastern Cape, as both he and the reader begin to understand the scale of his gesture of opposition; and it is transformed when one day the smallholding is attacked by two men and a boy, all black. The dogs in the kennels are shot, Lurie is burned and his car stolen, and Lucy is gang-raped.

After this event, the novel's representation of "the times" becomes much darker. Lurie, as he tries to wash off the ash that is all that remains of his hair, formulates his sense of a changed moral and social landscape with characteristic angry sarcasm, which we must not be too quick to

---

10. Sanders, in "Disgrace," notes the common ground between Coetzee's and Njabulo Ndebele's public pronouncements on this issue, and relates them interestingly to the novel.

11. In "Critic and Citizen," Coetzee comments that the "old model of the university finds itself under attack as an increasingly economistic interrogation of social institutions is carried out" (110). Sanders gives some details of the changes in Coetzee's own institution, the University of Cape Town, which the novel echoes closely ("Disgrace"). John Banville, in his review of *Disgrace*, calls the opening section "hardly more than an overture to the main events of the novel," and complains that there is a "new note of authorial irritation" in it (23). While this observation seems to me to underestimate the skill with which this section prepares for the remainder of the novel, there is undoubtedly some truth in it. Coetzee's resignation from the University of Cape Town in 2001 and his move to Australia may not be unconnected with the views implicit here.

attribute to the author, but which we cannot completely dissociate from him either:

> A risk to own anything: a car, a pair of shoes, a packet of cigarettes. Not enough to go around, not enough cars, shoes, cigarettes. Too many people, too few things. What there is must go into circulation, so that everyone can have a chance to be happy for a day.... That is how one must see life in this country: in its schematic aspect. Otherwise one could go mad. Cars, shoes; women too. There must be some niche in the system for women and what happens to them. (98)

With bitter irony, Lurie applies the rationalizing mode of thought characteristic of the times to the increasing incidence of crime—including rape—in the country; the alternative, he feels at this moment, would be madness.

To a greater degree than anything else in the novel, it is the attack by the three intruders—combined with the generally negative light in which black characters are presented—that has angered readers concerned with the image of post-apartheid South Africa.[12] For Lurie, certainly, it is entirely representative of what has happened in the past ten years: the coming of majority rule has also meant rising expectations which can't be met, a reduction in the efficiency of the forces that previously kept criminals as well as political opponents in check, and a new sense that whites, once all-powerful, are now exposed and vulnerable. If we were to use some measure of "realism" to judge the novel, there is nothing implausible about the scene of rural crime that Coetzee introduces. More important,

---

12. See, for instance, McDonald's discussion of the criticism by Jakes Gerwel ("*Disgrace* Effects," 325–26). Intriguingly, Coetzee himself, in a review published at about the same time as the novel, takes Breyten Breytenbach to task for repeating "gruesome reports . . . of attacks on whites in the new, post-apartheid South Africa." He continues: "These stories make disturbing reading not only because of the psychopathic violence of the attacks themselves, but because the stories are repeated at all. For in a country plagued with violent crime which the national police force—undermanned, underfunded, demoralized—is utterly unable to control, horror stories have become a staple, particularly among whites in the countryside, where farmers have died in murders that are commonly read in the most sinister light: as politically directed, as aimed at driving whites off the land and ultimately out of the country" ("Against the South African Grain," 52).

Coetzee reminds us that it is by no means only whites who suffer from criminal violence in the new South Africa, while white paranoia is fueled by such stories, and asks the question which has been asked of him: "Why then does Breytenbach lend himself to the process?" (Coetzee, "Against the South African Grain," 52). Breytenbach's answer, Coetzee surmises, is that such violence has an ancient history, going back to the earliest colonial settlements.

however, is the question of its place in the novel and the responses to it that seem to be endorsed.

Lurie is in many ways a typical white South African of the generation that grew up with apartheid (he would have been three years old when the Nationalist government won power), even though his relatively liberal views mark him as belonging to a particular sector of the white population (predominantly English-speaking, and perhaps, in his case, Jewish).[13] In the attack he can see only a crime that deserves punishment, oblivious of any parallel with his own recent sexual behavior. Lucy, to his astonishment, has a different attitude and a different sense of the new South Africa. She refuses to lay a rape charge against the men, explaining: "What happened to me is a purely private matter. In another time, in another place, it might be held to be a public matter. But in this place, at this time, it is not. It is my business, mine alone." When Lurie asks "This place being what?" she answers, "This place being South Africa" (112).

Lucy is, like Petrus, a figure of the other for Lurie, though in some ways more unsettlingly so since she is a daughter to whom he has in the past, by his own account (which we have no reason to doubt), been a loving and attentive father. Where he clings to the values and habits of a lifetime, regretting their erosion or rupture, she seeks a new accommodation, even to the extent of a willingness to become Petrus's third "wife." Perhaps "seeks" is the wrong word, belonging to the Romantic vocabulary her father still tries to rely on; she *allows* a new accommodation to occur, fully conscious of the enormous price she is paying.

David Lurie's experience of changed times grows stronger as Petrus comes to play a larger and larger role in their lives, and in Lucy's future. It comes to seem likely that his absence during the attack was no coincidence, and that his long-term plan is to reduce Lucy to a condition of dependency, a *bywoner* on his expanding farm. Lurie finds to his exasperation that in the new South Africa he has no way of dealing with this challenge. "In the old days one could have had it out with Petrus. In the old days, one could have had it out to the extent of losing one's temper and sending him packing and hiring someone in his place.... It is a new world they live in, he and Lucy and Petrus. Petrus knows it, and he knows it, and Petrus knows that he knows it" (116–17). This is the closest we get to

---

13. He is closer to the Magistrate in *Waiting for the Barbarians* than to any character in the intervening novels; like the Magistrate, he has a strong sense of justice which seems not to extend to his own sexual activities.

an expression from Lurie of discontent with the passing of apartheid and its benefits to the likes of him. The distribution of power is no longer underwritten by racial difference, and the result is a new fluidity in human relations, a sense that the governing terms and conditions can, and must, be rewritten from scratch.

Although much of the discomfort Lurie experiences on the smallholding arises from traditional African farming practices that have been unaffected by the political transformation, Petrus does not represent the old ways of doing things. The story of post-apartheid South Africa we are being told is emphatically *not* the story of the technologically advanced but oppressive state sliding into backwardness under majority rule. Petrus borrows a tractor and makes short work of the plowing, and Lurie reflects, "All very swift and businesslike; all very unlike Africa. In olden times, that is to say ten years ago, it would have taken him days with a hand-plough and oxen" (151). Although this example is a benign one, there is a hint once more of the startling pace of global change in which even rural South Africa is now participating.

One last reference to the times occurs in the final pages of the novel, when Lurie, having been for a while back in his house in Cape Town (ransacked during his absence), returns to Lucy's smallholding, then takes lodgings in Grahamstown. Lucy is pregnant from the rape and has refused an abortion, and Lurie feels more cut off from her than ever. "I am determined to be a good mother, David," she tells him, "A good mother and a good person. You should try to be a good person too." Whatever the ironies playing through this last sentence (ironies that are heightened by the memory of Mrs. Curren's confession that she is "a good person" in times when "to be a good person is not enough" [165]), there is clearly some seriousness in Lurie's answering thought: "A good person. Not a bad resolution to make, in dark times" (216).

: II :

The outline I've sketched with the aid of this necklace of references to "the times"—there are others, but this selection will suffice—has enough ingredients to make a compelling novel, with both a personal and a political dimension: the story of a man's self-destructive opposition to a new collective insistence upon accountability and moral rectitude, of the unhappy consequences of sexual frustration and uncontrolled impulse, of the terrible aftermath of the use of sex as a weapon, of the inevitable—and inevitably painful—process of distancing whereby a daughter makes her life her own, of the difficult renegotiation of relations between communities and individuals struggling free of a historical stranglehold. I have attempted to show that this narrative is not an attack on the new nation that emerged from the elections of 1994, and that it expresses no yearnings for the system of apartheid, but rather that it portrays with immense distaste a new global age of performance indicators and outcomes measurement, of benchmarking and targets, of a widespread prurience that's also an unfeeling puritanism; and that it explores, by means of one invented life, some of the pains and strains of a social and economic order reinventing itself against this background.[14]

Such a novel would be almost unrelievedly grim, lightened only by the satiric side of its hero's reflections. Like all Coetzee's novels, it offers the temptation of an allegorical reading (a reading, for instance, that would interpret the number of relatively unsympathetic black characters as a comment on racial differences)[15] and at the same time undercuts it, exposing such readings as part of the mechanistic attitude it finds

14. Another novel about sexual relations between an aging white man with academic pretensions and a young girl with wide cheekbones and closely cropped black hair that is set in the new South Africa is André Brink's *The Rights of Desire,* published a year later than, and with a title taken from, *Disgrace.* Although the catalogue of corruption, destruction, rape, murder, and mutilation is longer than in Coetzee's work, it functions more as a continuous background to the major events of the novel and is thus both easier to read as a negative portrait of post-apartheid South Africa and less devastating in its impact on the reader.

15. Such a reading would need to take into account the many details suggesting that the Isaacs family are, according to apartheid race classifications, "coloured," including Melanie's facial appearance (11), her vivid *Kaaps* accent in the play (*Kaaps* being the dialect of Afrikaans spoken by the Cape coloured community) (24), her boyfriend's warning "Stay with your own kind" (194), Lurie's phrase "the dark one" (18), and Dr. Rassool's comments on "a case with overtones like this one" (50) and "the long history of exploitation of which this is part" (53). The name Isaacs is common among the Cape Muslim community (though there is some irony in the fact that, like Lurie, it is also common among South African Jews.) The resultant allegorical scheme is probably something that only South African readers schooled in the niceties of apartheid thinking would be tempted into. Perhaps the most significant feature of Lurie's mental representations of Melanie is the *absence* of any direct reference to her race, given the fact that their sexual relationship (like Lurie's sex with Soraya) would have been a prosecutable offence for most of his life. We are, however, allowed to surmise that her appeal derives in part from a certain exoticism (he thinks, for instance, of her cheekbones as "almost Chinese" [11]).

wanting.[16] Its relation to the condition of post-apartheid South Africa could be better expressed, in Adorno's terms, as the "determinate negation" of the "administered world" out of which it emerges—a capacity which, for Adorno, art possesses thanks to its formal shapings of historical materials.[17] But my brief survey of the novel has left out two major strands that don't entail reflection on "the times," and that make it a somewhat different (if no less problematic) work than the one just summarized. These strands don't soften the work's blows or provide a way out for any of its characters, but they do lead the ethical and political issues raised by the fictional events I've sketched into different, and less summarizable, territory. One strand is the chamber opera which Lurie is contemplating at the beginning of the book and on which he is working in earnest when it ends; the other is the role played by animals, especially dogs, in the book's latter part. Both these subjects increase in importance as the novel goes on, the space given to them on the pages reflecting their growing role in Lurie's daily existence. The main questions I want to pose in the remainder of this chapter are the following: can these elements of the novel be read as a response to the private and public events that it so powerfully and dishearteningly presents in its central narrative? And if so, is it a response which *literature* is especially competent to make?

Let me summarize each of the two strands. Having published three books of criticism, Lurie is seized—several years before the novel opens—by the idea of writing a musical work based on the life of a poet with whom he identifies (an identification that is hardly surprising given his history of sexual adventuring): "*Byron in Italy:* a meditation on love between the sexes in the form of a chamber opera" (4). He explains to Lucy that he will borrow most of the music (63), though for a long time he has been hearing in his mind snatches of the sung lines (4, 121). The opera, as he plans it, deals with Byron during his final years, when he was living in Ravenna with his young mistress Teresa Guiccioli and her husband (87). It is only after the assault on the smallholding that Lurie starts to work

16. The headline provided by the *New York Times* for Michael Gorra's review is typical of many readings of the book that fail to appreciate its undermining of allegorical modes: "After the Fall: In J. M. Coetzee's novel, one man's humiliation mirrors the plight of South Africa." For a discussion of allegorizing readings of Coetzee's fiction, see chap. 2.

17. For the fullest elaboration of this argument, see Adorno's *Aesthetic Theory.*

on the opera, however; and once he does so, it refuses to remain in the form in which he had imagined it, as if in his new state the idea of the "Byronic" has lost some of its savor.

Back in Cape Town, in his wrecked house, he begins yet again; this time pitching the work long after Byron's death, when Teresa is "a dumpy little widow installed in the Villa Gamba with her aged father" calling sadly to her one-time lover, whose faint replies can just be heard (181–83). Instead of the borrowed music he had planned, the two characters, one alive, one dead, "demand a music of their own," and the music slowly and fitfully comes to him. Finding the piano producing too rich a sound, he drags from the attic a township banjo bought as a child's present, and creates for Teresa a music based on the contrast between yearning song and the instrument's "silly plink-plonk" (184). When he returns to the Eastern Province, he continues to compose with the aid of the banjo. The opera "consumes him night and day," but shows no sign of developing beyond this "long, halting cantilena hurled by Teresa into the empty air, punctuated now and then with groans and sighs from Byron offstage" (214). The last we hear of the opera is when Lurie wonders if he could add another lamenting voice to the duet: that of a dog (215).

This thought is a link to the other strand I omitted from my earlier summary. Apart from a reflection on the apparent sadness of castrated animals (9), there is no sign of any particular feeling for (or against) animals on Lurie's part until he reaches his rural retreat. The first animals we meet are the dogs being kept for their owners in Lucy's kennels. They are all watch-dogs—not a new phenomenon in South Africa but one which testifies to the general state of anxiety about crime.[18] At first, they impinge on Lurie merely as a nuisance: barking that keeps him awake in the night (67)—an echo of the howls that wake Dostoevksy in *The Master of Petersburg* (see chap. 5, sect. 4 above). His affection is, however, gained by one of the dogs in the kennels: Katy, an abandoned bulldog, with whom he senses an obscure empathy (related, no doubt, to his feeling of affinity with the widowed and loverless Teresa Guiccioli.) There is no conscious change of heart; without warning, events and feelings simply overtake him. In a moment which combines absurdity and pathos (a moment typical of Coetzee's narrative imagination at its most telling), he falls asleep in Katy's cage, stretched out on the concrete beside her. The ironic parallel with all the women he has slept with needs no underlining.

18. These dogs are trained selectively: Lurie reflects that South Africa is "a country where dogs are bred to snarl at the mere smell of a black man" (110).

The change of attitude crystallized in this event becomes more marked when Lurie meets an acquaintance of Lucy's, Bev Shaw, who runs an animal clinic. On hearing about this enterprise from Lucy, his initial response is a rancorous outburst at which he himself is surprised, suggesting some deeper psychic disturbance of which he is unaware: "It's admirable, what you do, what she does, but to me animal-welfare people are a bit like Christians of a certain kind. Everyone is so cheerful and well-intentioned that after a while you itch to go off and do some raping and pillaging. Or to kick a cat" (73). But before long he is helping Bev Shaw regularly, "offering himself for whatever jobs call for no skill: feeding, cleaning, mopping up" (142).

His altered relation to animals is further evidenced by his response to the two sheep Petrus brings back for a party to celebrate the transfer of some of Lucy's land: he can't stand seeing them tethered at a barren patch, and moves them to a place where there is grass. Again, he realizes only in retrospect that something has happened to him, and is puzzled by it:

> A bond seems to have come into existence between himself and the two Persians, he does not know how. The bond is not one of affection. It is not even a bond with these two in particular, whom he could not pick out from a mob in a field. Nevertheless, suddenly and without reason, their lot has become important to him.
>
> He stands before them, under the sun, waiting for the buzz in his mind to settle, waiting for a sign. (126)

The powerful but baffling claim made by the sheep on him is, it seems, far from either the emotional pull experienced by the animal lover or the ethical demand acknowledged by the upholder of animal rights. Like Michael K, like Mrs. Curren, like the fictional Dostoevsky, he finds himself relinquishing intellectual control in obedience to a dimly perceived demand that comes from somewhere other than the moral norms he has grown up with.

Animals and art provide the substance of Lurie's new existence. After his return from Cape Town, and until the novel ends, we see him spending most of his days at the animal clinic, waiting out the time of Lucy's pregnancy among the dog-pens, carrying out chores or plucking Teresa's childish banjo. As always with Coetzee's fiction, there is no identifiable authorial voice, nothing overt to stop us from taking this culmination as a sign of Lurie's defeat, his total irrelevance to the new South Africa. By the standards of the great rationalization, he has learned nothing and is contributing nothing. There is no chamber opera to surprise the world, and his work with animals has no value whatsoever when measured against the human needs in the country. (Lucy comments, "On the list of the nation's priorities, animals come nowhere" [73].) For a novel which has shown itself to be so aware of the demands of its time and place, the ending provides very little by way of solution or resolution.

The two strands I've separated out not only seem to exist at a tangent to the other concerns of the novel; they also seem to have very little relation to one another. I wish to argue, however, that they are connected, both to one another and to the rest of the work—not because I wish to transform the novel into an organic whole or to flourish some triumphant interpretative key, but in order to show that its engagement with its times, however unpalatable one may find it, and however little it offers by way of remedy, is serious, committed, and responsible. It must be said that it would be very easy to misrepresent these connections, to succumb to the ever-powerful desire for reassurance, for silver linings, for utopian moments. Thus, having identified these two motifs there is a temptation to argue that Coetzee is offering two related "solutions" to the multiple problems of the age his novel delineates: the production of art and the affirmation of human responsibility to animals. My argument, however, is that one of the novel's striking achievements (which is also one of the reasons for its undeniable rebarbativeness) lies in its sharp insistence that neither of these constitutes any kind of answer or way out, while at the same time it conveys or produces—in a way that only literature can do—an experience, beyond rationality and measured productivity, of their fundamental value.

: III :

I want to approach the question I've raised by means of a term that might seem to court exactly the danger I've just warned against. Buried in the novel's title, with its specific references to the experiences of David Lurie and his daughter, and its vaguer reference to the prevailing conditions in which they occur, is the word *grace*.[19] Its actual occurrences in the novel

---

19. A misprint in a critical work highlighted for me the multiple resonances of *Disgrace* as a title: in Robert Fraser's *Lifting the Sentence*, the novel is called *Disgraced* (137), a title which could only refer, in a limiting way, to Lurie.

are not underlined: Lurie's ex-wife misremembers Lucy's lover's name as "Grace" (187), and a particular dog at the clinic is said to have a "period of grace" during which it may be adopted (though it isn't). We might add the *coup de grâce* that the intruder fails to give the dog he has shot in the chest (95), and Lurie's reflection on castration as a possible escape from the sexual drive—"Not the most graceful of solutions, but then ageing is not a graceful business" (9). Among the many verbal doublets in the novel—a tic of Lurie's somewhat academic mental style (compliant/pliant [5], moderate/moderated [6], purgation/purge [91], kin/kind [194], drive/driven [194], and so on)—we don't find disgrace/grace. Yet it seems to me that the term is present in a ghostly way through much of the text.[20]

"Grace" is not, as it happens, the opposite of "disgrace." The opposite of disgrace is something like "honor"; the OED definition of "disgrace" links it frequently with "dishonor." Public shame, in other words, is contrasted with, and can only be canceled by, public esteem, disgrace redeemed by honor. Lurie spurns the opportunity to escape disgrace by means of public confession, and he makes little attempt to regain a position of public honor after his shaming. (His visit to the Isaacs family is his most significant effort in this direction, but his appeal for forgiveness is constantly undercut by the uncontrollable reassertion of desire—he even imagines Melanie and her schoolgirl sister together in bed with him, terming it "an experience fit for a king"! [164].) Yet his behavior after the committee finding against him is by no means an endeavor to shrug off what has happened, to rebuild his life on another conventional, bourgeois basis. It is as if in retrospect the experience with Melanie and its immediate aftermath (in particular, the stand he has found himself taking) have crystallized and clarified all his disgust at the "times"—and I must

---

20. Coetzee uses the word several times in the interviews in *Doubling the Point.* Moments of intense responsiveness to a writer like Kafka he terms "grace, inspiration" (199), and the charity which he hopes he exhibits in his writing he also associates with grace (249). "Grace," too, is the term he uses to oppose to "cynicism" in presenting opposed views of the possibility of achieving truth in autobiography, views represented for him by Stavrogin and Tikhon (392; and see above, p. 142). (It will be evident that a number of the topics discussed in earlier chapters of this book conjoin here.) Elizabeth Costello's son John proposes that she teaches people how to feel "By dint of grace. The grace of the pen as it follows the movements of thought" ("As a Woman," 12), combining the sense of blessedness with the sense of comeliness. However, when Attwell proposes the word to designate the state achieved by Mrs. Curren by the end of *Age of Iron,* Coetzee demurs: he feels he cannot lay claim to it since, unlike Dostoevsky, he is not a Christian (250).

stress once more that this has much wider reference than the political and social order of post-apartheid South Africa—and taken away any remaining urge to find a compromise way of life, of the sort represented by his earlier "solution" to the problem of sex. He sees no point in attempting to wash away the public disgrace, to regain honor in the eyes of the community: that would involve capitulation to the very standards he has now rejected. He declares to Isaacs: "I am sunk into a state of disgrace from which it will not be easy to lift myself. It is not a punishment I have refused. I do not murmur against it. On the contrary, I am living it out from day to day, trying to accept disgrace as my state of being" (172).

Although there is an element of self-dramatization here, Lurie's acceptance of his condition is not belied by his acts. With Bev Shaw he is more straightforward, if less acquiescent, telling her that he is "in what I suppose one would call disgrace" (85). And he wants to learn from his invented Teresa how to manage, as she does, in a condition "past honour" (209). The disgrace into which Lurie feels himself to be sunk cannot be equated with the public disgrace his actions and words have produced, however: he never wholeheartedly regrets his seduction of Melanie, the memory of whom continues to stir flickers of desire, and he has no regrets at all about his behavior before the committee. What he experiences is a deeper sense of being unfit for the times in which he lives.

What is left for Lurie after his fall? Sexual relations being at an end (the inconsequential sex with Bev Shaw seems to mark the exhaustion of this aspect of Lurie's life), there remain family relations. Lurie spends the rest of the novel in a stumbling but tenacious endeavor to be a good father to Lucy, and although his protection of her is without value and his advice to her is ignored, although he understands very little of her feelings and motives, his fidelity and persistence are not to be dismissed. On their last meeting she invites him in for tea as if he were a visitor, and he thinks, falling back on one of his verbal doublets, "Good. Visitorship, visitation: a new footing, a new start" (218).[21] This is one of the few positive mentions of the new in the novel.

---

21. The word *visit* and its cognates cannot be used without irony by this point in the novel, given its previous appearances: on the one hand, Lucy feels lucky to be visited every year by wild geese (88), on the other hand, the word is used repeatedly in connection with the attack (107, 115, 159). (The ironic contrast is heightened by the fact that Lucy's elation at being "the one chosen" by the geese occurs during the morning of the day on which she is raped.) Lurie is also described as a "visitor" when he calls on Mr. Isaacs and his family (165, 168). Rita Barnard, while aware of these ironies, brings out the tentatively affirmative elements in this moment ("Coetzee's Country Ways," 390).

But one would not call this intimation of a new relationship the achievement of grace. Grace is by definition something given, not something earned, in the way that Lurie has earned this moment of optimism in his relationship with his daughter. Grace is a blessing you do not deserve, and though you may seek for grace, it comes, if it comes at all, unsought. This sounds like a recipe for doing nothing, or doing whatever you like, but the paradox of the theological concept of grace which I'm borrowing is that it is not a disincentive to good works, but a spur.[22] Coetzee makes no attempt to resolve, on this secular plane, the ancient quarrel between Augustine and Pelagius—echoed in many a later controversy—as to whether a prior gracious gift from God is necessary to make the individual fit to seek and receive grace, or whether the human freedom to accept or reject the offer of grace is primary. If Lurie achieves something that can be called grace—which it is my purpose to argue—we cannot say either that he finds it or that he is found by it. Rather, we have to say both.

In his reaching for a register that escapes the terminology of the administered society Coetzee has often turned to religious discourse, and there is a continuity among several of his characters who find that, although they apparently have no orthodox religious beliefs, they cannot talk about the lives they lead without such language. Lurie, who makes it clear to Mr. Isaacs that he doesn't believe in God (172), recalls the church fathers' conclusion that the souls of animals "are tied to their bodies and die with them" (78; see also 161), but by the end of the book he is moved to depict the canine soul with visual and olfactory vividness; and he insists—against his daughter's commonsense skepticism—that "We are all souls. We are souls before we are born" (79). When he dreams that Lucy is calling to him to save her, he speculates that her soul might have left her body and come to him (104). This talk of souls—there is much of it in the novel—has many precedents in Coetzee's fiction. The Magistrate in *Waiting for the Barbarians* often speaks of his "soul" (118, 125, 126), and the medical officer in *Michael K* sees K as "a human soul above and beneath

22. Grace is certainly not a matter of obeying every impulse one experiences: the novel represents many impulses acted upon without thought, and they are not always productive. We may note the ironic rhyming between the moment when "on an impulse" Lurie touches Bev Shaw's lips (148) and the even more blackly comic moment when "on an impulse," prompted by the observation of a physical similarity between Mr. Isaacs's mouth and Melanie's, Lurie "reaches across the desk, tries to shake the man's hand, ends up by stroking the back of it" (167). The impulse that leads to Melanie's seduction, and which Lurie describes in terms of the power of Eros over him (52, 89), is more complicated.

classification, a soul blessedly untouched by doctrine, untouched by history, a soul stirring its wings within that stiff sarcophagus, murmuring behind that clownish mask" (151). Mrs. Curren, who expresses her skepticism about God in vivid terms—"God is another dog in another maze" (138)—also frequently uses the word: see, in particular, her description of the children with stunted souls (7), her fancy that her soul's "spirit" will reach her daughter through the letter (130), and her depiction of Vercueil and his dog by her side waiting "for the soul to emerge . . . neophyte, wet, blind, ignorant" (186).[23]

There is also a recurrent concern with "salvation," once more without any particular religious belief being implied: Magda in *In the Heart of the Country* asks herself, "How shall I be saved?" (16), while the Magistrate regards his break with the Empire as "salvation" (78) and later thinks, "I cannot save the prisoners, therefore let me save myself" (104). Mrs. Curren echoes Magda in asking, "How shall I be saved?" (136), and Elizabeth Costello says of her vegetarianism that it does not come out of moral conviction, but "out of a desire to save my soul" (*Elizabeth Costello*, 89). Lurie does not raise the question of salvation, just as he does not formulate a concern with grace; but in searching for terms to discuss his behavior and state of mind toward the end of the book, they come readily to mind. Although Lurie's motives for doing what he does seem as obscure to him as they are to us, something leads him in his "state of disgrace" to undertake a life of toil in the service of others. The "others" in question, moreover, are not other people, they are, on the one hand, the partly historical, partly imagined characters in an artistic work he is inventing, and, on the other hand, animals.[24] It is as if the conventional

23. Coetzee also uses the word "soul" outside his fiction, but with noticeable hesitation: "A contest is staged . . . within Elizabeth's—what shall I say?—soul" (*Doubling the Point*, 250). Elizabeth Costello, however, has no hesitation in using the word.

24. It is interesting to note that Elizabeth Costello uses the former type of "other" to reinforce her point about the latter. Reminding her audience that she is the author of a novel called *The House on Eccles Street,* in which Joyce's Molly Bloom is the main character, she says, "If I can think my way into the existence of a being who has never existed, then I can think my way into the existence of a bat or a chimpanzee or an oyster" (*Elizabeth Costello,* 80). I suspect I'm not alone in finding the logic here specious, but the strength of Costello's performance does not depend, for reasons she is very explicit about, on her rational arguments (see note 30 below). Coetzee's willingness to associate aesthetic creativity with other-directed acts in the world might be seen as a challenge to the view—perhaps most powerfully expressed in modern times by Thomas Mann in "Death in Venice" and *Doctor Faustus*—that the former tends inevitably toward amorality.

moral injunctions about the human community are themselves too com-
promised, too caught up in the age's demands, for his newly stark vision
of what is truly important.

This other-directed toil is not, therefore, a question of choosing a good
cause on rational grounds and getting on with it, secure in the knowledge
that one is bettering one's world. It is very different from either Bev Shaw's
wholehearted commitment to the cause of animal welfare or Lucy's survival strategy of pragmatic accommodation at any price. It goes with a
certain openness to experience and to the future, an openness which is not,
as Coetzee's Dostoevsky finds, simply a matter of expectation, nor even of
expecting the unexpected. The arrival of the unexpected, the visitant, the
arrivant, may not be an event you welcome—it can take the form of three
men who one day force their way into your house, set you on fire, and
rape your daughter. It may even, when it comes, have the feeling of something expected—locked in the toilet by the attackers, Lurie thinks, "So it
has come, the day of testing" (94).[25] It can be uncertain and ambiguous,
like the desire that suddenly strikes you for the young student on the path,
or the yet-to-be-born offspring of a rape. The event I am calling "grace" is
the arrival of the unexpected in unexpectedly beneficent form (we remember Lucy's joy at being "the one chosen" by the wild geese [88])—though
I have to add immediately that classification into "good" and "bad" belongs to the system of accounting that the *arrivant* eludes and exceeds.[26]

Lurie's (and Coetzee's) phrase "state of disgrace" clearly evokes the
theological notion of a "state of grace," the name for a condition of
receptiveness to the divine. To claim that by the close of the novel Lurie
achieves something approaching a state of grace is to claim that his daily
behavior testifies to some value beyond or before the systems—moral,
religious, emotional, political—of reward and punishment, of blueprint
and assessment, of approbation and disapprobation, that have brought
about his disgrace; that he is true to an excess, an overflow, an alterity
that no calculation can contain, no rule account for. (Grace, like its close
companions mercy and forgiveness, has, since Paul at least, always been
opposed to law.) One symptom of his state is that, in spite of the trials he
faces, he does not fall into despair—in its theological sense a loss of faith

---

25. In his memoirs, Coetzee vividly relates the experience of being tested, whether in
the repeated terrors involved in playing cricket (*Boyhood,* 53) or in the soul-destroying
routine of his London existence (*Youth,* 47, 66, 113–15). These particular experiences do
not, however, herald the advent of the other.

26. See above, chap. 5, sects. 3 and 4.

in the capacity of God's grace to exceed human deserving—but exhibits an obscure tenacity of will, not even strong or clear enough to be called faith or optimism. Although he may have forfeited the reader's moral sympathy early in the novel, he is far from being a dismissable figure at the end.

We may now return to the music and the animals. Countless artists, including Coetzee, have testified to the role of something like grace in the act or event—it is, of course, both—of aesthetic creation, though it is usually given different names, such as "inspiration." (Blanchot, in his fine pages on inspiration in *The Space of Literature,* calls it "this grace which is given and taken away" [182]).[27] David Lurie is no exception. Although he expends great effort on his musical composition, it seems to emerge, when it does so in a form which he feels is worth preserving, without his willing it (and the word *blessedly* suggests that the religious register is not inappropriate here):

> And, astonishingly, in dribs and drabs, the music comes. Sometimes the contour of a phrase occurs to him before he has a hint of what the words themselves will be; sometimes the words call forth the cadence; sometimes the shade of a melody, having hovered for days on the edge of hearing, unfolds and blessedly reveals itself. As the action begins to unwind, furthermore, it calls up of its own accord modulations and transitions that he feels in his blood even when he has not the musical resources to realize them....
>
> So this is art, he thinks, and this is how it does its work! How strange! How fascinating! (183–85)[28]

It is important to insist once more that the novel is not proffering the work of art as a solution to or a compensation for the ills of its time. Coetzee makes *Byron in Italy,* as it comes into being, anything but a masterpiece, and Lurie has no illusions about his odd, monotonous, often ludicrous work: "It would have been nice to be returned triumphant to society as the author of an eccentric little chamber opera. But that will not be" (214). Nor is it even a matter of the artist's personal satisfaction

27. For a full and revealing study of this topic, see Timothy Clark, *The Theory of Inspiration.*

28. I have explored this aspect of artistic creation in *The Singularity of Literature,* which could well have had as an additional epigraph a sentence from this part of *Disgrace:* "He is inventing the music (or the music is inventing him)" (186).

that something genuinely new or beautiful has been created. The most he hopes for is that "somewhere from amidst the welter of sound there will dart up, like a bird, a single authentic note of immortal longing." However, he is aware that if it should, he would not recognize it: "He knows too much about art and the ways of art to expect that" (214). Art, the novel implies, may provide all sorts of pleasures and remedies and enhancements for its society, it may bring all sorts of satisfactions and insights to its creator, but these, ultimately, are not why it matters. Indeed, there is no "why," a word which belongs to the accountants and rationalizers. Art matters, and Coetzee's powerful novelistic evocation of Lurie's experience of musical creation shows, twice over, that it does.

Then there are the animals. There is much, too much for a single chapter, to be said about the animals in *Disgrace,* and about their relation to the animals in Coetzee's earlier fictions and other writings. If Lucy and Petrus are others for David Lurie whom he struggles to know, if Melanie is an other whom he wrongs by not attempting to know, animals are others whom he knows he cannot begin to know. I want to focus on just one aspect of this relation to the absolute other of the animal, to bring out its links with what I have just said about art, and with many of my earlier comments on Coetzee's writing. In doing so, there will not be space to elaborate at any length on the many interrelations between the attention given to animals in *Disgrace* and Coetzee's roughly contemporaneous Tanner Lectures, *The Lives of Animals,* nor the striking similarities between both of these and Derrida's numerous discussions of animals and animality, most notably in "The Animal that Therefore I Am."[29]

Although Lurie's growing attachment to animals, his increasing awareness of their own singular existences, can be traced in a number of narrative developments—the two Persian sheep, the abandoned bulldog, the many animals he helps Bev Shaw treat at the clinic—the most telling and fully realized exemplification of this new attitude is his handling of the dogs which have to be killed. As with his treatment of artistic creation, Coetzee strips away all the conventional justifications for kindness to animals—implying not that these are empty justifications, but that they are part of the rational, humanist culture that doesn't get to the heart of

---

29. Other works of Derrida that discuss the animal/human boundary include *Of Spirit* (47–57), "'Eating Well'" (111–17), and "Force of Law" (18–19), as well as *Aporias* (see note 31 below).

the matter.[30] Indeed, the heart of the matter, the full and profound registering of animal existence that Coetzee is using his own art to evoke, constitutes, like art, a fierce challenge to that culture. In this respect, Coetzee's novel has some affinities with what Margot Norris, in *Beasts of the Modern Imagination,* terms the "biocentric tradition" in modern art: not that Coetzee creates in the manner of the writers she discusses, "with their animality speaking" (1), but that his work like theirs (and like hers) tries to imagine a relation to animal life outside of the worthy but limited concept of what Norris calls "responsible stewardship" (24). In one respect, his vision is even more extreme than those of Norris's chosen authors, since the most powerful writing in the novel involves the relation not to animal life but to animal death.[31]

Let us look at a couple of relevant passages. (As always with Coetzee, it's in the writing that the most important things happen.) After the attack, Lurie helps Bev Shaw at the animal clinic as often as he can, but it is Sunday afternoons that are the most intense, for it is then that she administers lethal injections to the large numbers of dogs who can't be cared for. Lurie is as mystified by his emotional involvement in this procedure as he is in the emergence of Teresa's yearning music or the sudden coursing of sexual desire at a memory of Melanie Isaacs's young body:

> He had thought he would get used to it. But that is not what happens. The more killings he assists in, the more jittery he gets. One Sunday evening, driving home in Lucy's kombi, he actually has to stop at the roadside to recover himself. Tears flow down his face that he cannot stop; his hands shake.
>
> He does not understand what is happening to him. (142–43)

Lurie's total absorption in the animals' dying is vividly described, but it his care of the corpses that marks the extreme limit of this theme in the novel. If a dog is an absolute other, what is a dead dog, and what response does it demand? It would be easy to dump the carcasses in their black bags at the incinerator on the same day, but he feels he can't simply discard them

---

30. Elizabeth Costello—who is, significantly, a novelist—also feels that all rational arguments about the treatment of animals are, finally, beside the point. She urges her audience to read the poets, "and if the poets do not move you, I urge you to walk, flank to flank, beside the beast that is prodded down the chute to his executioner" (*Elizabeth Costello,* 111).

31. Animal death is one of the subjects treated by Derrida in *Aporias.* In this work, Derrida troubles the distinction Heidegger tries to draw between human dying *(sterben)* and animal dying *(verenden);* see especially 30–42.

with all the other garbage: "He is not prepared to inflict such dishonour upon them" (144). (We are reminded, by contrast, of the casual slaughter of the dogs in the kennels by the intruders [95].) So, having bought a truck for the purpose, he takes the load of dead dogs to the incinerator on Monday mornings, where he loads the bags on the feeder cart, one at a time, and cranks them into the flames, while the crew whose job this is stand back and watch.

This degree of attention to the corpses is excessive by any rational accounting, but Coetzee's description of what had happened when the crew did the furnace feeding gives the reader—this reader, at least—a shudder of understanding:

> Rigor mortis had stiffened the corpses overnight. The dead legs caught in the bars of the trolley, and when the trolley came back from its trip to the furnace, the dog would as often as not come riding back too, blackened and grinning, smelling of singed fur, its plastic covering burnt away. After a while the workmen began to beat the bags with the backs of their shovels before loading them, to break the rigid limbs. It was then that he intervened and took over the job himself. (144–45)

The compulsion to intervene that Lurie experiences is all the more powerfully conveyed because it is represented in Coetzee's unemotional, precisely descriptive prose. As in Lurie's reaction to the tethered sheep, this can't be termed an ethical response, nor is it really an affective reaction; it's an impulse more obscure if no less commanding than these. One can't call it a biocentric attitude in the sense of taking on the animals' perspective: the dogs feel nothing at this point, and the values that Lurie is safeguarding on their behalf—honor, dignity—are products of human culture through and through. Yet in this absurd misapplication of the terms of human culture to dead animals there is an obstinate assertion of values more fundamental, if more enigmatic, than those embodied in the discourses of reason, politics, emotion, ethics, or religion—those discourses that govern the new South Africa and much else besides.

Lurie himself puzzles over what makes him undertake this task every Monday, incidentally modifying his earlier explanation of why he comes to the incinerator at all:

> Why has he taken on this job? To lighten the burden on Bev Shaw? For that it would be enough to drop off the bags at the dump and drive away. For the sake of the dogs? But the dogs are dead; and what do dogs know of honour and dishonour anyway?

For himself, then. For his idea of the world, a world in which men do not use shovels to beat corpses into a more convenient shape for processing. (145–46)

The last sentence comes as close as any in the novel to an articulation of the value that most deeply informs it, and perhaps Coetzee's fiction from its beginnings. It must be read with the previous sentence, however: this is not a practical commitment to improving the world, but a profound need to preserve the ethical integrity of the self. Lurie's "for himself" is very close to Elizabeth Costello's "out of a desire to save my soul," and echoes Magda's, the Magistrate's, and Mrs. Curren's desire to be "saved"—those other characters in Coetzee's fiction whose actions, though objectively good, are ultimately grounded in a profound personal need. It's this experience of finding oneself personally commanded by an inexplicable, unjustifiable, impractical commitment to an idea of a world that has room for the inconvenient, the non-processable, that I'm calling *grace,* though it's not, nor could it be, a word that occurs to Lurie.

Another word which doesn't occur to Lurie in his protracted self-examination is *penance:* it would be a misreading of his behavior to suggest that he is taking on an existence of suffering and service as expiation for his sin.[32] Nor does he ever make a connection between his forcing himself on Melanie on the second of the three occasions on which they have sex—"Not rape, not quite that, but undesired nevertheless, undesired to the core," he reflects (25)[33] —and the sexual attack on his daughter. Only in his little speech to Isaacs does he talk of his new life as a punishment, and his suspiciously rhetorical language at this point is not corroborated by any of the thoughts we are made privy to then or at other times. Whatever pain he has caused (it turns out that Melanie and her family seem to

32. "Humility" doesn't seem quite the right word either, although Mike Kissack and Michael Titlestad make an interesting case for it ("Humility in a Godless World"): something of the stubborn sense of worth that animated his resistance to the rationalized university remains to the end. However, I share their view that he becomes "completely divested of any transcendent or optimistic expectation" (137).

33. Since we have only Lurie's version of this sexual encounter, we aren't able to judge the accuracy of his disclaimer; although Melanie's overt objection is to the time and place—" 'No, not now,' she says, struggling. 'My cousin will be back!' "—the profound unwillingness with which she endures the act makes it hard not to call it rape. Our judgment is complicated by the fact that on the first occasion (19), she is passive but not, it seems, as reluctant, and on the third and last she is an active participant in the lovemaking, "greedy for experience"—Lurie remembers how "she hooks a leg behind his buttocks to draw him in closer" (29).

have dealt with the episode quite efficiently), Lurie's commitment to the dead dogs can't be thought of as an attempt to counterbalance the sexual wrong which began the sequence of events it concludes.

Lurie is quite clear-eyed about his dedication to a cause that, measured on any rational scale, would register as of no value, lacking even the tiny potential that his work on the opera might be said to possess:

> Curious that a man as selfish as he should be offering himself to the service of dead dogs. There must be other, more productive ways of giving oneself to the world, or to an idea of the world. One could for instance work longer hours at the clinic. One could try to persuade the children at the dump not to fill their bodies with poisons. Even sitting down more purposefully with the Byron libretto might, at a pinch, be construed as a service to mankind. (146)

While he is back in Cape Town, he tries not to think about the dogs. "From Monday onward the dogs released from life within the walls of the clinic will be tossed into the fire unmarked, unmourned. For that betrayal, will he ever be forgiven?" (178). Here his service to the dead animals is understood as *marking* and *mourning,* that is to say as registering the individuality of each dog's death, of contesting the reduction of dead animals to mere accumulations of matter. Like Derrida ("The Animal," 400–402), he resists the generalization implicit in the category "animal," preferring the impossible task of acknowledging the singularity of each individual creature. Ian Hacking, in a review of *The Lives of Animals* which also discusses *Disgrace,* describes very well the non-systematic ethical charge of these works: "Coetzee feels the force of almost all the ideas and emotions that his characters express. He is working and living at the edge of our moral sensibilities about animals. Much is fluid, changing, being created. One positively ought to hold incompatible opinions as one works and lives one's way through to their resolution" (22).

I trust it is clear that the two strands I have isolated, the two tasks Lurie undertakes in his state of disgrace, although each can be seen as bizarre, and as bizarrely conjoined in his mode of living at the end of the novel, do have a common thread. Both manifest a dedication to a singularity that exceeds systems and computations: the singularity of every living, and dead, being, the singularity of the truly inventive work of art. (And this is continuous with the collapse of his sexual routine when he tries to individualize "Soraya" and his resistance to the committee whose task it is to reduce a singular erotic experience to a classifiable category.) In this dedication we find the operation of something I've called *grace,* and perhaps—whatever ungainliness and awkwardness we associate with Lurie ("ageing," he thinks early in the novel, "is not a graceful business" [9])—even a touch of its derivatives, *gracefulness* and *graciousness*. Where Coetzee differs from many others who have taken similar positions is his unblinking acceptance of the non-instrumental nature of this stance. On the last pages of *Disgrace*, Lurie considers what he will do for the dog to which he has become particularly attached when the time comes—"caress him and brush back the fur so that the needle can find the vein, and whisper to him and support him . . . ; fold him up and pack him away in his bag, and the next day wheel the bag into the flames"— and comes to the difficult conclusion: "It will be little enough, less than little: nothing" (219–20). At most, these elements of the novel might be understood as an exemplification of the minimal hope of which Coetzee speaks in one of his interviews with Attwell: "I am someone who has intimations of freedom (as every chained prisoner has) and constructs representations—which are shadows themselves—of people slipping their chains and turning their faces to the light" (*Doubling the Point,* 341).[34]

What, however, of the main narrative of seduction and disgrace? Can we see in the operation of desire, so central to the unfolding of the plot, a similar dedication, a similar path to possible grace?

Just as Coetzee resists the conventional narratives of "artistic genius" and "devotion to animals," so he resists the tale of profound love blossoming out of mere lust. It would be no surprise to find Lurie, steeped as he is in Romantic poetry, shaping the story of his seduction of Melanie to fit this model; yet in spite of occasional hints of a temptation to do so the force he acknowledges over and over, referring to it as a god, naming it Eros, ascribing it to Aphrodite, is that of sheer physical desire, the desire of a fifty-two-year-old deprived of sexual satisfaction for an attractive, provocative twenty-year-old. This remains true even when the affair is over and the opportunity for romanticizing on Lurie's part is at its greatest. One example: strolling near Lucy's smallholding he encounters some children coming from school: "Without warning a memory of the girl

---

34. In his public statements, Coetzee appears to be more positive: he insists that "the new economic world order is not a reality" but "a huge confidence trick," which it is the duty of intellectuals to confront "in an active, David-and-Goliath spirit" ("Critic and Citizen," 110).

comes back: of her neat little breasts with their upstanding nipples, of her smooth flat belly. A ripple of desire passes through him. Evidently whatever it was is not over yet" (65). The words convey both the physical intensity of the desire and the puzzled helplessness of the man who experiences it. "Evidently" captures both the attempt and the failure to analyze the moment, "whatever it was" its lasting mystery. When, triggered only by the memory of Melanie's beauty, the sensation recurs—"Again it runs through him: a light shudder of voluptuousness"—there is a similar self-observing quality to Lurie's thoughts: "He does not appear to be able to conceal it. Interesting" (78).

Even if the story of the seduction is, like those of the opera and the dogs, a story of a man overmastered by a power that exceeds and disrupts the rationalizations of his age, and even if it is the immediate cause of Lurie's new mode of life, we can't say that, like numberless other fictions, it is about love as a path to grace. *Love* is used of the very different relation Lurie has to the dogs about to be put to death (219), and it also seems appropriate to his commitment to his daughter and her unknown future. It is a word he imagines on Teresa's lips, too, long after her lover is dead.[35] The story of Lurie and Melanie, however, is a story of desire, and desire, throughout Coetzee's fiction—we think of Magda, of the Magistrate, of Susan Barton, of Dostoevsky—seems to be an *arrivant* that remains permanently ambiguous, testing the boundaries between "good" and "bad," enrichment (a term Lurie finds himself using) and impoverishment. Any temptation to exaggerate the positive side of this force is challenged by its other significant manifestation in the novel, the desire which stiffens the penises entering Lucy Lurie's unwilling body.

The novel ends on one of the killing Sundays. All I have said about a dedication to singularity, both in Lurie's new mode of existence and in Coetzee's art, is exemplified in these final pages, as Lurie brings in the dog of whom he has grown particularly fond and gives him up to the waiting needle. Coetzee offers no explanation of Lurie's loving dedication to surplus dogs, and certainly doesn't proffer it as a model for the new South Africa, or for any reader's own conduct. If the novel succeeds in conveying something of the operation and importance of what I've been calling "grace," it conveys also that it is not a lesson to be learned or

---

35. For a reading of *Disgrace* that resists the redemptive implications of "love," see Michiel Heyns, " 'Call No Man Happy.' "

a system to be deployed.[36] In this way, *Disgrace* presents—by means of its forcefulness as a literary work, through its writing, and our reading, sentence by chiseled sentence—its own justification for not making a direct contribution to the building of the new South Africa.[37] It would not be inaccurate to say that the novel conveys something of the cost of that necessary process of national and communal construction, but to leave it at that would be—as I've tried to argue—to see only its negative, and least literary, aspects. It's precisely the notion of *cost,* the measurement of profit and loss, that Coetzee questions in *Disgrace* and that literature puts to the test. If there is a political challenge staged in this novel, and in all Coetzee's novels to date, it is to find a way of building a new, just state that is not founded on the elimination of unpredictability, singularity, excess. A state that recognizes the importance of the literary, which is to say of an inventive responding to the other that is also a responding to what has made the other other—a traceable past and a constituting present—and a wagering on, a trusting in, a different future. We might call it, should it ever come into existence, a state of grace.

36. This is just one of the affinities between "grace" and a number of terms Derrida has explored, including the "gift," "forgiveness," "hospitality," and "love"; it also resonates with Margot Norris's striking argument in *Beasts of the Imagination* that "biocentrism has no real practical effects" (24). Gareth Cornwell, in "*Disgrace*land," makes an interesting connection between the incomprehensibility of Lurie's action in rational terms and the condemnation by Elizabeth Costello's sister Blanche of the entire tradition of the humanities (in Coetzee's *The Humanities in Africa,* reprinted in *Elizabeth Costello*).

37. For a subtle engagement with the question of the work's effectiveness as literature, see Michael Holland, " 'Plink-Plunk.' "

A Writer's Life

Elizabeth Costello

: I :

I was lucky enough to be in the auditorium at Princeton University on October 15, 1997 when Professor John Coetzee rose to deliver "The Philosophers and the Animals"—the first of two Tanner Lectures on Human Values he was giving that year under the general title "The Lives of Animals." This was, of course, J. M. Coetzee the novelist, but his presence in an academic setting made one particularly conscious of his status as Professor of General Literature at the University of Cape Town. There had been indications in a few of Coetzee's publications of a concern with the question of human responses to animal suffering, most notably the passage about the chained dog in *The Master of Petersburg* we have already looked at (see chap. 5, sect. 4). Readers of *Doubling the Point* would have been struck by a moving passage in parentheses in one of the interviews: "Let me add...that I, as a person, as a personality, am overwhelmed, that my thinking is thrown into confusion and helplessness, by the fact of suffering in the world, and not only human suffering" (248). (*Disgrace* had, of course, not been published at this point.) There was also the fact, known to many, of his vegetarianism, comically represented in "Meat Country." Now, it seemed, he was going to spell out in two lectures his views on animal rights and the ethics of human-animal relations.

Although I don't recall any audible reaction from the audience, there could be no doubt about the surprise produced by Coetzee's opening words, spoken in his quiet, grave voice: "He is waiting at the gate when her flight comes in." No preliminary explanation, no introduction to prepare us for this clearly fictional statement, couched in the third-person present tense familiar from *The Master of Petersburg* (his most recent novel at the time); and for those of us who thought this might be the familiar lecturer's strategy of beginning with a quotation from another author, no break in the fictional tissue from henceforward to the end of the presentation. What made the event in which we were participating all the more disquieting was our gradual realization that it was being mirrored, in a distorted representation, in the fiction itself: the central character was revealed to be a novelist from the Southern Hemisphere who had been asked to give a lecture at an American college, and who had chosen to speak on the human treatment of animals.[1] We listened to the lecture given within the fiction—itself a testing of the norms of academic debate—and to the fictional account of the formal dinner that followed. Coetzee's final words, spoken in his fiction by the college president, could have been spoken by the chair of the real lecture we were attending: "We look forward to tomorrow's offering." Coetzee's second lecture, "The Poets and the Animals," did indeed follow the next day; it was a continuation of the story of Elizabeth Costello's visit to Appleton College, including a seminar led by the visiting novelist, entitled, as the audience were now primed to expect, "The Poets and the Animals."

The two "lectures" were published two years later as *The Lives of Animals,* accompanied by "reflections" offered by four scholars in various disciplines (revisions of the responses they gave in Princeton); and were reprinted in 2003 in *Elizabeth Costello: Eight Lessons,* without the responses and shorn of the academic footnotes that in the original publication contributed to the uncertainty of genre. Unrecorded in print, however, are the questions from members of the audience after the "lectures"; here, too, Coetzee tended to avoid the customary first-person consideration of points made to him, preferring locutions like: "I think what Elizabeth Costello would say is that . . ."

---

1. One commentator on the published lectures, Douglas Cruikshank, is so bemused by the mirroring process that he states that the visiting novelist in the fiction "has been asked to take part in the Tanner lectures, sponsored by the University Center for Human Values at Princeton University" ("Beastly Lectures," 1)! Fact and fiction became even harder to disentangle when Coetzee subsequently moved from South Africa to Australia.

The Princeton occasion was not the first time Coetzee had presented a fiction about Elizabeth Costello as a public lecture, though it became the best-known such event after the publication of *The Lives of Animals*. In November 1996 he had delivered the Ben Belitt Lecture at Bennington College, in which, under the title "What is Realism?," he had read a fiction with a very similar framework: as in "The Lives of Animals," Elizabeth Costello visits Appleton College in Waltham, Massachusetts (which sounds more like Bennington College than Princeton University), on this occasion to receive a literary award and make an acceptance speech entitled, it goes without saying, "What is Realism?"[2] We may surmise that Coetzee had no long-term plan when writing these early Costello pieces of combining them into something on a larger scale, and that when he was invited to deliver the Tanner Lectures at Princeton he decided to re-use the framework that had been successful at Bennington the previous year without worrying about overlap or inconsistencies—even having his protagonist discuss the same Kafka story, "Report to an Academy."[3] Costello's son John, who is a crucial focalizing presence in both pieces, lives in Australia in "What is Realism?" (he "teaches in the department of astronomy at the Australian National University" [60]) but in the U.S. in *Lives of Animals* (he is "assistant professor of physics and astronomy" at Appleton College). When Coetzee brought the pieces together in *Elizabeth Costello* he had to make some slightly awkward adjustments to achieve consistency: in the earlier piece, with which the book begins (now called just "Realism"), John is said to be on leave in Australia for a year from his college in Massachusetts, and has accompanied his mother from that country to a newly invented institution—Altona College, Pennsylvania—for the presentation of her award.[4]

2. The lecture was published in *Salmagundi* the following year.

3. She does, however, make a somewhat apologetic reference to an earlier lecture in the United States in which she had used the Kafka story, placing it two years in the past rather than one; and a footnote scrupulously refers us to the published version—not of Costello's lecture, of course, but Coetzee's.

4. Coetzee appears to have overlooked a couple more places where adjustments needed to be made: he has John, who lives permanently in the U.S.A., still referring to North America as a "foreign continent" (23) and an "unexplored continent" (27). There is also the puzzle of John's marriage: what does he mean when he tells the woman he has slept with in Pennsylvania that he has, or is, "Married and unmarried," when in "Lives of Animals" and "As a Woman"—a Costello piece published after *Elizabeth Costello*—he lives with his wife and children?

Elizabeth Costello incorporates two later lectures in which Coetzee asked his audience to accept a fiction in place of the expected first-person presentation. He delivered the Fall 1998 Una's Lecture at the Doreen B. Townsend Center for the Humanities at the University of California, Berkeley, under the title "The Novel in Africa," placing his protagonist on board a cruise ship and devoting much more space to a lecture by a (fictional) Nigerian novelist than to Costellos's own lecture. In March 2001 he read "The Humanities in Africa" at the Carl Friedrich von Siemens Stiftung in Munich, moving the location to South Africa and focusing on Elizabeth's sister Blanche. On a third occasion, a Nexus Conference on "Evil" in Tilburg, Holland, in June 2002, he once again challenged his audience with a self-referential presentation: he offered a fictional account of Elizabeth Costello's participation in a conference on the question of evil in Holland. This time, however, his contribution was announced on the program not as a lecture but as a "Reading," under the heading—the organizers no doubt had two of his novels in mind—"The Possessed; Crime and Punishment; Guilt and Atonement."[5] In Coetzee's fiction, however, itself first published in *Salmagundi* under the title "Elizabeth Costello and the Problem of Evil," Costello does not give a reading but a talk entitled "Witness, Silence, and Censorship" under the general rubric "Silence, Complicity, Guilt." Fact and fiction are further mixed in the talk itself, which centers on a real novel, Paul West's *The Very Rich Hours of Count von Stauffenberg.*[6] When she arrives at the conference, Costello is alarmed to find that West is among the conference participants, and one almost expects to find his name among the participants in the Tilburg conference when one looks it up on the web. In this respect, however, reality fails to conform to fiction.

There is a good deal of new material in *Elizabeth Costello*. The original published text of "The Humanities in Africa" ends with the triumph of the antihumanist, Christ-imitating Blanche: "You went for the wrong Greeks, Elizabeth" (89). The "lesson" with the same title in *Elizabeth Costello* gives us Elizabeth's uncommunicated response to this charge, taking up another ten pages. There are also three new pieces: the final two lessons,

---

5. Details of the conference can be found on the Nexus website; see spitswww.uvt.nl/web/nexus/nl/home/instituu/confero7.htm.

6. Costello refers to him as an "Englishman, but one who seemed to have freed himself of the more petty concerns of the English novel" (157). Although born in England, the real Paul West has lived and worked in the U.S.A. for most of his life.

"Eros" and "At the Gate," which make no use of the lecture format that has played through all the previous chapters, and a postscript in the form of a letter written by the imaginary wife—another Elizabeth C.—of Hugo von Hofmannsthal's imaginary Lord Chandos.[7] (As in "The Problem of Evil," Coetzee injects reality into his fiction in "Eros" by having Costello fancy the poet Robert Duncan, who may well have toured Australia with Philip Whalen in 1963 and read his well-known "Poem Beginning with a Line by Pindar.") A further episode in the life of Elizabeth Costello appeared a few months after the publication of the book; entitled "As a Woman Grows Older," it was read at the New York Public Library and printed in the *New York Review of Books* early in 2004. Not quite consistent with the pieces in the book—Costello's daughter in Nice is now running an art gallery there, and not "the guest of a foundation" as she was in "The Problem of Evil" (*Elizabeth Costello*, 160), and her son now lives in Baltimore—it consists largely of conversations between Costello and her two children, anxious about their now seventy-two-year-old mother's refusal to change her mode of life.

The fiction-as-lecture format returned in a remarkable guise in 2003, when Coetzee received the Nobel Prize for Literature and gave the obligatory address to an invited audience in Stockholm. Once again, instead of the expected format, his lecture took the form of a story, but this time without any of the traditionally novelistic, sometimes deliberately clichéd, openings of the Costello pieces. "He and His Man" begins with a quotation from *Robinson Crusoe*—which misleads the hearer or reader into thinking that the title refers to Crusoe and Friday—but then plunges into a report of a report: "Boston, on the coast of Lincolnshire, is a handsome town, writes his man. The tallest church steeple in all of England is to be found there; seapilots use it to navigate by."[8] We may recognize the style of Defoe's *Tour Through the Whole Island of Great Britain*— much of the address is made up of quotations, with slight variations, from this work and from the same author's *Journal of the Plague Year*[9]—but if

---

7. See Hugo von Hofmannsthal, *The Lord Chandos Letter*. This postscript, extending Hoffmansthal's depiction of a man who has given up writing because he has found that language fails before the revelations he experiences in his daily life, reads like a nightmarish version of some of Costello's fears about writing.

8. This lecture, which appears on the Nobel website, was reprinted in several places; *The Guardian Review*, for example, published it as "The Castaway."

9. For instance, the charmingly far-fetched account of the Lincolnshire "duckoys," who are trained to fly to Holland and Germany and tell the ducks there in their own language about the superior conditions in England, comes from letter 7 of the *Tour* (97–100), and the

"his man" doing the reporting is Defoe, not Friday, who is "he" who is being reported to? Only when we hear of his parasol and his parrot, which used to squawk "Poor Robin Crusoe," are we sure. Defoe sending reports to Crusoe (we hear of "his man" writing in a "quick, neat hand"): this is curious enough as it is, but it later emerges that the reports, and the man who sends them, are inventions of Crusoe's, who spends his evenings in the Jolly Tar on the Bristol waterfront making up these fictions. Soon the style changes to reflect the creative process itself: "Let him be a man of business.... Or else let the man be a saddler with a home and a shop and a warehouse in Whitechapel." But the man seems to become increasingly independent of the one who is supposed to be inventing him, and the piece ends with a fantasy, Crusoe's but also Coetzee's, in which "he" and "his man" pass one another, unhailing, on ships crossing a stormy sea.

: II :

One negative response to *Elizabeth Costello* has been to complain that Coetzee uses his fictional creations to advance arguments—about the human relation to animals, about the value of the humanist tradition, about the morality of representing evil in fiction—without assuming responsibility for them, and is thus ethically at fault. To level this charge is to take the arguments presented *as arguments,* and to take the making of them as the fundamental purpose of the pieces in which they occur. (Most of the respondents in *The Lives of Animals,* for instance, engage with the arguments in this way.) It is undeniable that the arguments have a certain weight and deserve to be taken seriously. The mistake would be to think that in doing so one had responded to the full ethical force of the fictions themselves.

For the Costello pieces (and I'm including "He and His Man" as a closely related text) are, whatever their generic oddness, works of literature. (We must not miss the irony in the collection's subtitle, *Eight*

"great engine of execution of Halifax" is described in letter 8 (201–3). The man who stays in London during the Great Plague on the strength of a biblical passage is the narrator— himself a fictional persona created by Defoe—of *A Journal of the Plague Year* (12–13), while the same work is the source of the stories of the cloud like an angel with a flaming sword (22–23), the man Robert who feeds his family from a distance (106–9), the man who runs naked into Harrow Alley (171–72), and the man buried alive in the dead pit at Mountmill (90–91).

Lessons: it is Elizabeth Costello as much as the reader who is undergoing these lessons, and what either has learned by the end remains a matter for debate.) As I have stressed, many of these pieces were first staged as public events in which the author was also the speaker; they lose that dimension on the page (though it is a fruitful exercise to attempt to recall it while reading), but as literary works to be read and lived through they remain, in an important sense, events. The arguments within them should more strictly be called *arguings,* utterances made by individuals in concrete situations—wholly unlike the paradigmatic philosophical argument, which implicitly lays claim to a timeless, spaceless, subjectless condition as it pursues its logic. They are, that is, events staged within the event of the work; and they invite the reader's participation not just in the intellectual exercise of positions expounded and defended but in the human experience, and the human cost, of exposing convictions, beliefs, doubts, and fears in a public arena.[10]

One reader—a philosopher, not a literary critic—who sees the importance of this is Cora Diamond. Here is part of her response to *The Lives of Animals:*

> [Elizabeth Costello] is a woman haunted by the horror of what we do to animals. We see her as wounded by this knowledge, this horror, and by the knowledge of how unhaunted others are. The wound marks her and isolates her. . . . So the life of this speaking and wounded and clothed animal is one of the "lives of animals" that the story is about; if it is true that we generally remain unaware of the lives of other animals, it is also true that, as readers of this story, we may remain unaware, as her audience does, of the life of the speaking animal at its center. . . . If we see in the lectures a wounded woman, one thing that wounds her is precisely the common and taken-for-granted mode of thought that "how we should treat animals" is an "ethical issue," and the knowledge that she will be taken to be contributing, or intending to contribute, to discussion of it. ("The Difficulty of Reality," 3–7)

---

10. Costello herself, although she gives lectures of a slightly more conventional sort than those by Coetzee in which they occur, apparently does not publish them. When her daughter Helen asks her if she is writing about brain science she replies, "No. . . . I still confine myself to fiction, you will be relieved to hear. I have not yet descended to hawking my opinions around. The Opinions of Elizabeth Costello, revised edition" ("As a Woman," 13). Coetzee himself seems to have felt no inhibitions about publishing discursive nonfiction pieces, collected in such volumes as *White Writing, Giving Offense,* and *Stranger Shores.*

As Diamond understands, it is not enough to say that Coetzee is trying out positions and arguments as a kind of intellectual experiment, taking them to an extreme he could not himself endorse. This may be accurate, but it omits the crucial fact of the fictional characters and contexts involved, characters and contexts that have their being only as events in the process of reading. Costello herself makes the case powerfully in "The Poets and the Animals" in relation to arguments about human access to animal being: "If I do not convince you, that is because my words, here, lack the power to bring home to you the wholeness, the unabstracted, unintellectual nature, of that animal being. That is why I urge you to read the poets who return the living, electric being to language" (*Elizabeth Costello*, 111). These words themselves, although in Costello's mouth they are an assertion, are part of Coetzee's fictional invention of a character and therefore part of an event which returns the living human being to language.

Coetzee introduced "He and His Man" to his Stockholm audience with a brief anecdote: as a child he read *Robinson Crusoe* avidly, and then later, in a children's encyclopedia (no doubt Arthur Mee's great work, so important to the young John in *Boyhood*), discovered that behind it there was an author, Daniel Defoe. Who was this Defoe, when Crusoe so clearly spoke in his own voice about real adventures?[11] As so often with Coetzee's accounts of his own fiction, this explanation camouflages as much as it clarifies. The piece does indeed play with the reversal of author and character, so that Defoe the novelist becomes a fictional creation of Crusoe's (as Elizabeth Costello the novelist is a fiction of Coetzee's), and, in view of Defoe's own highly successful enterprise of creating fictional narrators who were read as actual authors, the stratagem is an appropriate one. Fiction's uncertain relation to fact has, as we have seen, been a constant thread in the Costello pieces, and in Coetzee's career it goes back to the documentary trappings of Jacobus Coetzee's narrative in *Dusklands* and embraces the engagement with authorial biographies in *Foe* and *The Master of Petersburg* and the self-distanced autobiographies of *Boyhood* and *Youth*.

However, to locate Coetzee in the tradition of postmodern playfulness, teasing the reader with fictional truths and truthful fictions, is to overlook the much more important engagement in his work with the demands and responsibilities of writing and reading, an engagement that runs through

11. Reported by David Attwell (private communication).

these pieces as it does through the novels and memoirs. What "He and His Man" explores is the strange process of fictional writing: the self-division it necessitates, the uncertain origins of the words that one finds oneself writing, the haunting illusion—captured in that image at the end of the piece—that there is an unbridgeable distance between the person who lives in the world and the person, or impersonal force, that produces the words. (Crusoe comments: "Only when he yields himself up to this man of his do such words come.") That Elizabeth Costello is a novelist is not simply a device to generate self-referential ironies in the fictions about her; it is a means toward a profound self-examination on the part of Coetzee, a testing of, and by, the obligations and temptations faced by the literary writer. The reader, moreover, is not a spectator of this process, but a participant, since the event of reading cannot be separated from the event of writing.[12]

It is when we take all the Costello pieces together that their abiding concern with the creation of literary works, with what it means to commit oneself to a life of writing, emerges most clearly. Although individual pieces may appear to focus on issues not particularly related to this question (issues sometimes determined by the nature of the invitation to which Coetzee is responding), such as animal lives or the value of the humanist tradition, the figure of Elizabeth Costello (or in one case Robinson Crusoe) as writer is always central. Coetzee is pursuing the difficult path he broached in *The Master of Petersburg,* with its dark exploration of the cost of fictional creation, and alluded to at the very end of *Boyhood* (written as he was beginning the Costello pieces) when the young John contemplates the burden of the storyteller's vocation.

It is important, too, that Costello is an elderly, successful writer: a writer at the stage of her life at which the big questions, set aside in the rush of an early career, come to haunt her. (She is sixty-six at the start of *Elizabeth Costello;* seventy-two in "When a Woman Grows Older." We may note that there is no mention of any new publication during these six years, and only one reference to work in progress—some short stories referred to in "When a Woman.") She is also at a stage when the demands of the body, also easy to ignore in the healthfulness of youth, complicate the activities of the writer; when the inseparability of mental processes from physical desire and revulsion becomes unmistakable. I don't wish to pursue the question of the degree to which Coetzee is writing out of his own preoccupations as a famous (though not yet elderly) writer, but it is

12. I have argued this more fully in *The Singularity of Literature;* see especially chap. 7.

presumably not for nothing that he and his central character's last names begin with the same letters—even if the counter-figure of her son is given Coetzee's first name.

Elizabeth Costello's opening lesson announces a problem that the entire book both pursues and exemplifies: can the tradition of realism (on which Coetzee's writing in these pieces depends for the readerly empathy that is crucial to its purpose) deal with ideas? I have stressed that Coetzee, for all his experimentation, has always drawn on the stubborn power of realism, on the vivid representation of a world, external and internal, into which the reader is invited. To the extent that we find ourselves treating the Costello pieces as arguments, their realism fails—and to include a long, uninterrupted disquisition in a fiction is to test the limits of realism, as Joyce (in *A Portrait of the Artist as a Young Man*) and Thomas Mann (in *The Magic Mountain*) had already shown. In "Realism," Coetzee demonstrates what has often been demonstrated before, what has, indeed, become one of postmodernism's party-tricks: that the realistic illusion can survive the author's showing of his or her hand. Instead of the unannounced gaps in the narrative upon which the realist tradition relies, the speaker of this text—let us assume it is Professor Coetzee—signals the places where he skips. Moreover, it is made clear that he *is* a speaker: at one point he says, "Unless certain scenes are skipped over we will be here all afternoon" (*Elizabeth Costello*, 16), and notes that these scenes are not skipped in the text he is reading (later he will allude to a gap in the text itself [24]).

The issue of realism's dealings with ideas is raised directly by the speaker—and at the same time the reader of *Elizabeth Costello* receives a hint about the interpretation of this text—in a comment about conversations in which fictional speakers discuss issues: "In such debates ideas do not and indeed cannot float free: they are tied to the speakers by whom they are enounced, and generated from the matrix of individual interests out of which their speakers act in the world" (9). Elizabeth Costello's speech in accepting her award is not so much a presentation of ideas, however, as a revelation of her uncertainties and fears about the status of writing and of language more generally, and by implication a questioning of the value of the art to which she has devoted her life. She will be haunted by this question, in various guises, throughout the book.

In Lesson 2, "The Novel in Africa," the Australian novelist who writes in the European tradition (she has piggy-backed on Joyce as Coetzee has piggy-backed on Defoe and Dostoevsky) is challenged by a novelist who claims to speak for the oral African tradition. (Had Costello been

South African, the connection between this challenge and the criticisms sometimes leveled at Coetzee would have been even more evident.)[13] Her lecture is given only in part and in summary; what is more significant is her lack of conviction in what she is saying about the novel to her shipboard audience. She does not accept the arguments of Egudu, the Nigerian novelist, but there is a sense in which orality comes to complicate her publicly announced, and once-held, beliefs: orality as the power of the voice (Egudu's voice "makes one shudder," says the Russian singer to Costello) and as a marker of the power of sex.

We have noted already, through the words of Cora Diamond, the significance of Costello's suffering in the "Lives of Animals," which constitutes the next two lessons; what must also be stressed is that she is presented (and present in Appleton College) very much as a *novelist*. Part of the burden she is now experiencing is the burden of feeling one's way into other lives, including the lives of animals: the greater one's capacity to enter imaginatively into a different mode of existence, the stronger one's horror at behavior that denies its value. The words that end this section of the book, words of intended comfort spoken by her son as she is about to leave Waltham, are at the same time words that acknowledge, unintentionally perhaps, her death-directed state of mind: "There, there. It will soon be over" (115).

Another challenge to the novelist's vocation is staged in "The Humanities in Africa": Sister Bridget, Elizabeth's sister Blanche, who has devoted her life to Christian ideals, mounts an attack on the humanities in her address to the (presumably somewhat perplexed) graduands of a South African university. The gulf between the two sisters on questions of art becomes most apparent when Elizabeth visits Blanche's mission in Zululand and is introduced to a Zulu sculptor, Joseph. (The fact that he is known only by his first name in the mission hints at the persistence of racist attitudes among the devout nuns.) Joseph, now an old man, has spent his life carving nothing but crucified Christs, the same tortured body over and over in a variety of sizes, and although Elizabeth can think of this only as a stultifying waste of artistic potential, Blanche praises it as true devotion. If anywhere in the book Coetzee is imaginatively entering a mental and emotional region that is deeply foreign to him, this is the place: while Costello fails according to the standards of empathy she has enunciated in "The Lives of Animals," Coetzee—through the power of

---

13. See, for instance, Benita Parry's critique in "Speech and Silence."

his writing—lets us live for a time inside the mind of a dedicated servant of Christ for whom most art is a squandering of human energy. Although the section added to the piece in *Elizabeth Costello* provides Costello with the opportunity to mount a counterattack on Blanche—the story of her sexual generosity to a dying old man—it does not efface the experience she has been through in Zululand, and it is significant that although she imagines her story as a letter to Blanche, she doesn't send it.[14] We see more clearly than ever that this book is far from a celebration of the novelist's art.

"The Problem of Evil" again probes the limits of the novelist's enterprise. As in her lectures in "The Lives of Animals," Costello presents an argument that is less a reasoned case than an expression of an intense response, at once mental, emotional, and physical, to something she has become acutely aware of without having any choice in the matter. In this instance, it is the power of realistic fiction to expose the reader to human evil. Once again, we have no grounds for taking this as Coetzee's position, or even one he is attracted to: what he has done is to imaginatively represent what it might be like to feel this way (or, rather, to come to feel this way at the end of a long career as a novelist). Our rational understanding of the ethics of fictional writing may be unshaken, but it has been exposed to an alternative way of experiencing some of the issues, and to the importance of experience itself in ethical judgments.[15] The fact that Costello's insistence on ethical limits in the practice of fiction clearly arises from her own situation does not reduce the force of what she says, and it may provoke some questioning about the supposedly impersonal positions claimed by those who appeal to reason.[16]

14. Costello's "letter" to her sister omits the final episode in the story, which we learn about only as a private revelation: here the classical image of the woman posing bare-breasted gives way to a decidedly unaesthetic depiction of fellatio. Outside the arena of sibling competition, Costello is not nearly so confident about the heritage of Apollo.

15. James Wood, who was a participant in the conference, reports: "It was a strange, provoking, deliberately self-contradictory tale, which instantly sparked heated commentary. It was hard to figure out Coetzee's meaning. Yet the fictive device had justified itself: one felt that the other participants had been content with their perfected errors while Coetzee, in his new form, had nosed his way towards a battered truth, despite his apparent unwillingness to claim ownership of that truth" ("A Frog's Life").

16. Doubts about the claims of instrumental reason play an important part, as we have seen, in *Disgrace,* and there is a suggestion in "The Humanities in Africa" that this is an area that could provide common ground between Blanche and her sister, and resonate with Coetzee's own concerns: at the end of her graduation speech, Blanche asserts that the impending death of the humanities has been brought about by "the monster enthroned by

The short piece "Eros," which constitutes lesson 7, a meditation on sexual desire between gods and humans, although it continues the engagement with the question of imaginative empathy with other orders of being (not just gods but humans who have been fucked by gods), fails to dramatize Costello's mental wrestlings as fully as the other pieces do. By contrast, the final lesson, "At the Gate," is a moving dramatization of the self-questioning that has characterized Costello's mental and emotional world throughout these sketches of old age. Now, in her dream or fantasy, or simply thanks to novelistic license, Costello is at the gate that leads to a world that we (and she) assume is some kind of heavenly reward. (She is allowed to glimpse the brilliant light beyond, which is disappointingly "not of another order, not more brilliant than, say, a magnesium flash sustained endlessly" [196].) We are immediately reminded of Kafka's fable "Before the Law," and the self-consciously, almost parodistically, novelistic setting lets us know that it is as a novelist that she is in this place. The question of her calling that has run through all the previous episodes now becomes central, as she discovers she has to satisfy a tribunal as to her beliefs before she will be permitted to pass through the gate.

The issue of belief is, of course, what has been at stake in all these fictional representations of positions held and debated. Does Coetzee, does the reader, believe in what Elizabeth Costello, or Emmanuel Egudu, or Sister Bridget have to say about the treatment of animals, the fictional representation of evil, the oral novel, the value of the humanities? Costello's first response is that as a writer of fiction, she cannot have beliefs; she has to be entirely open to those who speak through her. This answer points to the fact that, in Coetzee's fiction, Costello's beliefs, Egudu's beliefs, Sister Bridget's beliefs are what the reader encounters, not Coetzee's. There is no inconsistency between Costello's disclaimer in "At the Gate" and her passionate expression of beliefs elsewhere; the former, she makes clear, refers to her existence as a novelist, whereas the latter arises out of her experience as a human being (200).[17] (Coetzee would no doubt say the

---

those very studies as first and animating principle of the universe: the monster of reason, mechanical reason" (*Elizabeth Costello*, 123). All three would find much to engage them in Derrida's essay, "The Principle of Reason."

17. David Lodge, reviewing *Elizabeth Costello* in the *New York Review of Books*, says that, in reading "At the Gate," "We wonder what has happened to her passionate belief in the rights of animals" (11). Apart from the misleading phrase, "rights of animals," which is not strictly what she is passionate about, this comment ignores the distinction between fiction and nonfiction.

same about his nonfictional prose.) Once again it would be more accurate to use a verbal form, to assert that what we encounter are not these characters' beliefs, but their believings; we undergo their speeches and arguments as events, and we share, momentarily, the process of articulating feelings and ideas. And we cannot escape from the *mise en abîme* in which we are caught: "At the Gate" does not present us with an argument about the place of belief in fiction but enables us to participate in Elizabeth Costello's believing about believing.

Rejected on the basis of this argument, Costello later tries a different tack: she believes, she tells the row of judges, in the frogs that inhabit a particular river in rural Victoria, and gives an impassioned description of their lives. (We have already noted, in discussing Coetzee's use of allegory, that she resists an allegorical interpretation of these frogs.) She has now, of course, emptied the word "belief" of its normal content, so in a way this answer is no different from the first one: she is presenting either a tautology ("The realist novelist believes in the real world") or an instance of extreme arbitrariness, albeit one that continues the exploration of the artist's capacity to enter nonhuman existences. But it does enable her to go on to speculate on the role of belief in the writer's life: "Her mind, when it is truly itself, appears to pass from one belief to the next, pausing, balancing, then moving on" (222). We never learn, perhaps she never learns, whether this second answer is accepted; and although this makes for something of a narrative anticlimax, it leaves us strongly aware that what has mattered, for Elizabeth Costello and for the reader, is the event—literary and ethical at the same time—of storytelling, of testing, of self-questioning, and not the outcome.

Adorno, Theodor W. *Aesthetic Theory.* Edited by Gretel Adorno and Rolf
Tiedemann. Translated by Robert Hullot-Kentor. Minneapolis: University of
Minnesota Press, 1997.

Altieri, Charles. "Taking Lyrics Literally: Teaching Poetry in a Prose Culture."
New Literary History 32 (2001): 259–81.

Ashcroft, Bill. "Irony, Allegory and Empire: *Waiting for the Barbarians* and
In the Heart of the Country." In Kossew, *Critical Essays on J. M. Coetzee,*
100–16.

Attridge, Derek. "Introduction." In Attridge and McDonald, eds., "J. M. Coetzee's
Disgrace," 315–20.

———. *Joyce Effects: On Language, Theory, and History.* Cambridge: Cambridge
University Press, 2000.

———. "Literary Form and the Demands of Politics: Otherness in J. M.
Coetzee's *Age of Iron.*" In *Aesthetics and Ideology,* edited by George Levine,
243–63. New Brunswick: Rutgers University Press, 1994.

———. "On Mount Moriah: The Impossibility of Ethics." In *Questions: For
Jacques Derrida,* edited by Richard Rand. Albany: State University of New
York Press, forthcoming.

———. *The Singularity of Literature.* London: Routledge, 2004.

Attridge, Derek, and Rosemary Jolly. *Writing South Africa: Literature, Apartheid,
and Democracy* 1975–1990. Cambridge: Cambridge University Press,
1998.

Attridge, Derek, and Peter D. McDonald, eds. "J. M. Coetzee's *Disgrace.*"
Special issue, *Interventions: International Journal of Postcolonial Studies* 4,
no. 3 (2002).

Attwell, David. *J. M. Coetzee: South Africa and the Politics of Writing.* Berkeley
and Los Angeles: University of California Press; Cape Town: David Philip,
1993.

———. "The Problem of History in the Fiction of J. M. Coetzee." In Martin
Trump, ed., *Rendering Things Visible,* 94–133.

———. "Race in *Disgrace.*" In Attridge and McDonald, eds., "J. M. Coetzee's
Disgrace," 331–41.

————. Review of J. M. Coetzee, *Boyhood*. *Sunday Independent*, 2 November 1997.

Auerbach, Nina. Review of J. M. Coetzee, *Foe*. *The New Republic*, 9 March 1987, 36–38.

Banville, John. Review of J. M. Coetzee, *Disgrace*. *New York Review of Books*, 20 January 2000, 23–25.

Barnard, Rita. "Coetzee's Country Ways." In Attridge and McDonald, eds., "J. M. Coetzee's *Disgrace*," 384–94.

Barnett, Clive. "Constructions of Apartheid in the International Reception of the Novels of J. M. Coetzee." *Journal of Southern African Studies* 25 (1999): 287–301.

Bastian, F. *Defoe's Early Life*. London: Macmillan, 1981.

Behr, Mark. *Embrace*. London: Little, Brown and Company, 2000.

————. *The Smell of Apples*. New York: St. Martin's Press, 1995.

Benjamin, Walter. *The Origin of German Tragic Drama*. Translated by John Osborne. London: New Left Books, 1977.

Bennington, Geoffrey, and Jacques Derrida. *Jacques Derrida*. Chicago: University of Chicago Press, 1993.

Bhabha, Homi K. *The Location of Culture*. Routledge: London, 1994.

Blake, William. *Compete Writings*. Edited by Geoffrey Keynes. London: Oxford University Press, 1966.

Blanchot, Maurice. *The Space of Literature*. Translated by Ann Smock. Lincoln: University of Nebraska Press, 1982.

————. *The Writing of the Disaster*. Translated by Ann Smock. Lincoln: University of Nebraska Press, 1986.

Boehmer, Elleke. "Not Saying Sorry, Not Speaking Pain: Gender Implications in *Disgrace*." In Attridge and McDonald, eds., "J. M. Coetzee's *Disgrace*," 342–51.

Breytenbach, Breyten. *Mouroir: Mirrornotes of a Novel*. New York: Farrar, Straus and Giroux, 1984.

Briganti, Chiara. "'A Bored Spinster with a Locked Diary': The Politics of Hysteria in *In the Heart of the Country*." In Kossew, *Critical Essays on J. M. Coetzee*, 84–99.

Brink, André. *A Chain of Voices*. London: Faber, 1982.

————. *The Rights of Desire: A Novel*. London: Secker & Warburg, 2000.

————. *States of Emergency*. London: Faber, 1988.

Brooks, Peter. *Troubling Confessions: Speaking Guilt in Law and Literature*. Chicago: University of Chicago Press, 2000.

Bunn, David, and Jane Taylor, eds. "From South Africa: New Writing, Photographs and Art." Special issue, *TriQuarterly* 69 (Spring/Summer 1987).

Bürger, Peter. *Theory of the Avant-Garde*. Translated by Michael Shaw. Minneapolis: University of Minnesota Press, 1984.

Carusi, Annamaria. "Post, Post and Post. Or, Where Is South African Literature in All This?" In *Past the Last Post: Theorizing Post-Colonialism and Post-Modernism,* edited by Ian Adam and Helen Tiffin, 95–108. Calgary: University of Calgary Press, 1990.

Cavafy, C. P. *Collected Poems.* Edited by George Savidis. Translated by Edmund Keeley and Philip Sherrard. London: Hogarth Press, 1975.

Clark, Timothy. *The Theory of Inspiration: Composition as a Crisis of Subjectivity in Romantic and Post-Romantic Writing.* Manchester: Manchester University Press, 1997.

Clingman, Stephen. "Revolution and Reality: South African Fiction in the 1980s." In Trump, *Rendering Things Visible,* 41–60.

Coetzee, J. M. "Against the South African Grain." Review of Breyten Breytenbach, *Dog Heart: A Memoir. New York Review of Books,* 23 September 1999, 51–53.

———. *Age of Iron.* New York: Random House, 1990; London: Secker & Warburg, 1990.

———. "As a Woman Grows Older." *New York Review of Books,* 15 January 2004, 11–14.

———. *Boyhood: Scenes from Provincial Life.* New York: Viking, 1997.

———. "The Castaway." *The Guardian Review,* 13 December 2003, 34–37.

———. "Confession and Double Thoughts: Tolstoy, Rousseau, Dostoevsky." In *Doubling the Point,* 251–93.

———. "Critic and Citizen: A Response." *Pretexts: Literary and Cultural Studies* 9, no. 1 (2000): 109–11.

———. *Disgrace.* London: Secker & Warburg, 1999.

———. *Doubling the Point: J. M. Coetzee, Essays and Interviews.* Edited by David Attwell. Cambridge, Mass.: Harvard University Press, 1992.

———. *Dusklands.* Johannesburg: Ravan Press, 1974; London: Secker & Warburg, 1982; New York: Viking, 1985.

———. *Elizabeth Costello: Eight Lessons.* London: Secker & Warburg, 2003.

———. "Elizabeth Costello and the Problem of Evil." *Salmagundi* 137–38 (Winter 2002–Spring 2003): 49–64.

———. *Foe.* London: Secker & Warburg, 1986; Johannesburg: Ravan Press, 1986; New York: Viking, 1987.

———. *Giving Offense: Essays on Censorship.* Chicago: University of Chicago Press, 1996.

———. "He and His Man." The 2003 Nobel Lecture in Literature. http://www.nobel.se/literature/laureates/2003/coetzee-lecture-e.html

———. *In the Heart of the Country.* London: Secker & Warburg, 1977; New York: Harper, 1977 (as *From the Heart of the Country*).

———. *In the Heart of the Country* (South African edition). Johannesburg: Ravan Press, 1978.

———. *The Humanities in Africa.* Munich: Carl Friedrich von Siemens Stiftung, 2001.

————. Interview with David Attwell. In *AlterNatives: Interviews on Southern African Auto/biography,* edited by Judith Lütge Coullie, Thengani Ngwenya, and Stephan Meyer. Forthcoming.

————. Interview with Claude Wauthier. *Le Nouvel Observateur,* 28 June–4 July 1985, 69.

————. *Life & Times of Michael K.* London: Secker & Warburg, 1983; Johannesburg: Ravan Press, 1983; New York: Viking, 1984.

————. *The Lives of Animals.* With Marjorie Garber, Peter Singer, Wendy Doniger, and Barbara Smuts. Edited by Amy Gutmann. Princeton: Princeton University Press, 1999.

————. *The Master of Petersburg.* New York: Viking, 1994; London: Secker & Warburg, 1994.

————. "Meat Country." *Granta* 52 (Winter 1995): 41–52.

————. *The Novel in Africa.* Occasional Papers of the Doreen B. Townsend Center for the Humanities. Berkeley, 1999.

————. "Remembering Texas." In *Doubling the Point,* 50–54.

————. "The Novel Today." *Upstream* 6, no. 1 (1988): 2–5.

————. *Stranger Shores: Essays 1986–1999.* London: Secker & Warburg, 2001.

————. "Thematizing." In *The Return of Thematic Criticism,* edited by Werner Sollors, 289. Cambridge, Mass.: Harvard University Press, 1993.

————. "Truth in Autobiography." Inaugural Lecture, University of Cape Town, 1984.

————. "Two Interviews with J. M. Coetzee, 1983 and 1987." With Tony Morphet. In Bunn and Taylor, *From South Africa,* 454–64.

————. *Waiting for the Barbarians.* London: Secker & Warburg, 1980; New York: Viking, 1980; Johannesburg: Ravan Press, 1981.

————. "What Is Realism?" *Salmagundi* 114–15 (1997): 60–81.

————. *White Writing: On the Culture of Letters in South Africa.* New Haven: Yale University Press, 1988.

————. *Youth.* London: Secker & Warburg, 2002.

Contemporary Literary Criticism. Detroit: Gale Research. 1973–

Cornwell, Gareth. "*Disgrace*land: History and the Humanities in Frontier Country." *English in Africa* 30, no. 2 (2000): 21–47.

————. "Realism, Rape, and J. M. Coetzee's *Disgrace.*" *Critique* 43 (2002): 307–22.

Cruikshank, Douglas. "Beastly Lectures." Review of *The Lives of Animals,* by J. M. Coetzee. *Salon.com.* www.salon.com/books/it/1999/25/animals.

Darke, Neil. Review of *Foe,* by J. M. Coetzee. *Argus* (Cape Town), 23 October 1986.

Davidson, Donald. *Inquiries into Truth and Interpretation.* Oxford: Oxford University Press, 1984.

————. "Locating Literary Language." In *Literary Theory after Davidson,* edited by Reed Way Dasenbrock, 295–308. University Park: Pennsylvania State University Press, 1993.

_____. "What Metaphors Mean." In *On Metaphor*, edited by Sheldon Sacks, 29–45. Chicago: University of Chicago Press, 1979.

De Certeau, Michel. "Montaigne's 'Of Cannibals': The Savage 'I.'" In *Heterologies: Discourse on the Other*, 67–79. Minneapolis: University of Minnesota Press, 1986.

Defoe, Daniel. *A Journal of the Plague Year*. 1722. Edited by Louis Landa. Oxford: Oxford University Press, 1990.

_____. *The Life and Adventures of Robinson Crusoe*. 1719. Edited by Angus Ross. Harmondsworth: Penguin Books, 1965.

_____. *Roxana/The Fortunate Mistress*. 1724. Edited by Jane Jack. London: Oxford University Press, 1964.

_____. *A Tour through the Whole Island of Great Britain*. 1724–27. 2 vols. Revised edition. London: J. M. Dent, 1962.

De Jong, Marianne, ed. "J. M. Coetzee's *Foe*." Special issue, *Journal of Literary Studies/Tydskrif vir Literatuurwetenskap* 5, no. 2 (June 1989).

De Man, Paul. *Allegories of Reading: Figural Language in Rousseau, Nietzsche, Rilke, and Proust*. New Haven: Yale University Press, 1979.

_____. "The Rhetoric of Temporality." In *Blindness and Insight: Essays in the Contemporary Rhetoric of Criticism*, 187–228. 2d ed. London: Methuen, 1983.

De Voogd, Peter J. "La femme naufragée et le sauvage silencieux: *Foe* de John M. Coetzee." In *L'interprétation détournée*, edited by Leo H. Hoek, 91–99. Amsterdam: Rodopi, 1990.

Derrida, Jacques. *Acts of Literature*. Edited by Derek Attridge. New York: Routledge, 1992.

_____. "Afterword: Toward an Ethic of Discussion." In *Limited Inc.*, edited by Gerald Graff, 111–60. Evanston: Northwestern University Press, 1988.

_____. "The Animal That Therefore I Am (More to Follow)." *Critical Inquiry* 28 (2002): 369–418.

_____. *Aporias: Dying—Awaiting (One Another at) the "Limits of Truth."* Translated by Thomas Dutoit. Stanford: Stanford University Press, 1993.

_____. "'Eating Well,' or the Calculation of the Subject: An Interview." In *Who Comes after the Subject?*, edited by Peter Connor, Eduardo Cadava, and Jean-Luc Nancy, 96–119. New York: Routledge, 1991.

_____. "Force of Law: The 'Mystical Foundation of Authority.'" In *Deconstruction and the Possibility of Justice*, edited by Drucilla Cornell, Michel Rosenfeld, and David Gray Carlson, 3–67. New York: Routledge, 1992.

_____. *The Gift of Death*. Translated by David Wills. Chicago: University of Chicago Press, 1995.

_____. *Given Time: 1. Counterfeit Money*. Translated by Peggy Kamuf. Chicago: University of Chicago Press, 1992.

_____. "Living On/Borderlines." In *Deconstruction and Criticism*, edited by Harold Bloom et al., 75–176. London: Routledge, 1979.

———. *Of Grammatology.* Translated by Gayatri Chakravorty Spivak. Baltimore: Johns Hopkins University Press, 1976.

———. *Of Spirit: Heidegger and the Question.* Translated by Geoffrey Bennington and Rachel Bowlby. Chicago: University of Chicago Press, 1989.

———. *On Cosmopolitanism and Forgiveness.* Translated by Mark Dooley and Michael Hughes. London: Routledge, 2001.

———. "Perhaps or Maybe (Conversation with Alexander Duttman)." *PLI 6* (1997): 1–18.

———. *Points . . . : Interviews, 1974–1994.* Edited by Elisabeth Weber. Translated by Peggy Kamuf and others. Stanford: Stanford University Press, 1995.

———. *Politics of Friendship.* Translated by George Collins. London: Verso, 1997.

———. "The Principle of Reason: The University in the Eyes of Its Pupils." *Diacritics* 13, no. 3 (Fall 1983): 3–20.

———. "Psyche: Invention of the Other." In Derrida, *Acts of Literature,* 310–43.

———. *Specters of Marx: The State of Debt, the Work of Mourning, and the New International.* Translated by Peggy Kamuf. New York: Routledge, 1994.

———. "Structure, Sign, and Play in the Discourses of the Human Sciences." In *Writing and Difference,* translated by Alan Bass, 278–94. London: Routledge and Kegan Paul, 1978.

———. "This Strange Institution Called Literature." In Derrida, *Acts of Literature,* 33–75.

Derrida, Jacques, and Anne Dufourmantelle. *Of Hospitality.* Translated by Rachel Bowlby. Stanford: Stanford University Press, 2000.

Derrida, Jacques, and Pierre-Jean Labarrière. *Altérités.* Paris: Osiris, 1986.

Diamond, Cora. "The Difficulty of Reality and the Difficulty of Philosophy." *Partial Answers* 1, no. 2 (June 2003): 1–26.

Dovey, Teresa. "Allegory vs. Allegory: The Divorce of Different Modes of Allegorical Perception in Coetzee's *Waiting for the Barbarians.*" *Journal of Literary Studies/Tydskrif vir Literatuurwetenskap* 4, no. 2 (June 1988): 133–43.

———. *The Novels of J. M. Coetzee: Lacanian Allegories.* Johannesburg: Ad. Donker, 1988.

———. "*Waiting for the Barbarians:* Allegory of Allegories." In Huggan and Watson, *Critical Perspectives,* 138–51.

During, Simon. "Postmodernism or Post-colonialism Today." *Textual Practice* 1 (1987): 32–47.

Dostoyevsky, Fyodor. *Crime and Punishment.* Translated by David McDuff. Harmondsworth: Penguin Books, 1991.

Easton, Kai. *J. M. Coetzee.* Contemporary World Writers. Manchester: Manchester University Press, forthcoming.

Emants, Marcellus. *A Posthumous Confession.* Translated by J. M. Coetzee. London: Quartet Books, 1986. Originally published as *Een nagelaten bekentenis.* 1894.

Eysteinsson, Astradur. *The Concept of Modernism*. Ithaca: Cornell University Press, 1990.

Fletcher, Angus. *Allegory: The Theory of a Symbolic Mode*. Ithaca: Cornell University Press, 1964.

Foucault, Michel. "The Functions of Literature." In *Michel Foucault: Politics, Philosophy, Culture*, edited by Lawrence D. Kritzman, 307–13. New York: Routledge, 1988.

Frank, Joseph. *Dostoevsky: The Miraculous Years 1851–1871*. Princeton: Princeton University Press, 1995.

Fraser, Robert. *Lifting the Sentence: A Poetics of Postcolonial Fiction*. Manchester: Manchester University Press, 2000.

Frye, Northrop. *Anatomy of Criticism*. New York: Atheneum, 1969.

Gallagher, Susan VanZanten. *A Story of South Africa: J. M. Coetzee's Fiction in Context*. Cambridge, Mass.: Harvard University Press, 1991.

Goddard, Kevin, and John Read. *J. M. Coetzee: A Bibliography*. Grahamstown: NELM, 1990.

Goodwin, Christopher. "White Man without the Burden." *Sunday Times News Review*, 16 January, 2000; http://www.sunday-times.co.uk/news/pages/sti/2000/01/16/stirevnws01014.html.

Gordimer, Nadine. *The Conservationist*. London: Jonathan Cape, 1974.

——. *A Guest of Honour*. London: Jonathan Cape, 1971.

——. *The House Gun*. London: Bloomsbury, 1998.

——. "The Idea of Gardening." *New York Review of Books*, 2 February 1984, 3, 6; reprinted in Kossew, *Critical Essays on J. M. Coetzee*, 139–44.

——. *July's People*. London: Jonathan Cape, 1981.

——. *A Sport of Nature*. New York: Knopf, 1987.

Gorra, Michael. "After the Fall." Review of *Disgrace*, by J. M. Coetzee. *New York Times on the Web*, 28 November 1999; http://www.nytimes.com/books/99/11/28/reviews/ 991128.28gorrat.html.

H., G. Review of *Foe*, by J. M. Coetzee. *The Natal Mercury*, 27 November 1986.

Hacking, Ian. "Our Fellow Animals." Review of *The Lives of Animals*, by J. M. Coetzee, and *Ethics into Action: Henry Spira and the Animal Rights Movement*, by Peter Singer. *New York Review of Books*, 29 June 2000, 20–26.

Hart, Francis R. "Notes for an Anatomy of Modern Autobiography." In *New Directions in Literary History*, edited by Ralph Cohen, 221–47. Baltimore: Johns Hopkins University Press, 1974.

Head, Dominic. *J. M. Coetzee*. Cambridge: Cambridge University Press, 1997.

Heider, Sarah Dove. "The Timeless Ecstasy of Michael K." In *Black/White Writing: Essays on South African Literature*, edited by Pauline Fletcher, 83–98. Lewisburg, Penn.: Bucknell University Press, 1993.

Hesiod. *Theogony; Works and Days*. Translated by M. L. West. World's Classics. Oxford: Oxford University Press, 1988.

Heyns, Michiel. "'Call No Man Happy': Perversity as Narrative Principle in *Disgrace*." *English Studies in Africa* 45, no. 1 (2002): 57–65.

———. *The Children's Day*. Johannesburg: Jonathan Ball, 2002.

———. "The Whole Country's Truth: Confession and Narrative in Recent White South African Writing." Special issue, "South African Fiction after Apartheid," edited by David Attwell and Barbara Harlow, *Modern Fiction Studies* 46, no. 1 (Spring 2000): 42–66.

———. "Houseless Poverty in the House of Fiction: Vagrancy and Genre in Two Novels by J. M. Coetzee." *Current Writing* 11, no. 1 (1999): 20–35.

Hofmannsthal, Hugo von. *The Lord Chandos Letter*. Translated by Russell Stockman. Marlboro, Vermont: The Marlboro Press, 1986.

Holland, Michael. "'Plink-Plunk': Unforgetting the Present in Coetzee's *Disgrace*." In Attridge and McDonald, eds., "J. M. Coetzee's *Disgrace*," 395–404.

Huggan, Graham, and Stephen Watson, eds. *Critical Perspectives on J. M. Coetzee*. London: Macmillan, 1996.

Hutcheon, Linda. *A Poetics of Postmodernism: History, Theory, Fiction*. London: Routledge, 1988.

———. *The Politics of Postmodernism*. London: Routledge, 1989.

Huyssen, Andreas. *After the Great Divide: Modernism, Mass Culture, Postmodernism*. Bloomington: Indiana University Press, 1986.

Ishiguro, Kazuo. "Between Two Worlds." Interview with Bill Bryson. *New York Times* Magazine, 29 April 1990, 38, 40, 44, and 80.

———. *The Remains of the Day*. New York: Knopf, 1989.

Jameson, Fredric. *The Political Unconscious: Narrative as a Socially Symbolic Act*. Ithaca: Cornell University Press, 1981.

———. *Postmodernism, or, The Cultural Logic of Late Capitalism*. Durham, N.C.: Duke University Press, 1991.

———. "Third-World Literature in the Era of Multinational Capitalism." *Social Text* 15 (Fall 1986): 65–88.

JanMohamed, Abdul. "The Economy of Manichean Allegory: The Function of Racial Difference in Colonialist Literature." In *"Race," Writing, and Difference*, edited by Henry Louis Gates Jr., 78–106. Chicago: University of Chicago Press, 1986.

Jolly, Rosemary Jane. *Colonization, Violence, and Narration in White South African Writing: André Brink, Breyten Breytenbach, and J. M. Coetzee*. Athens: Ohio University Press, 1996.

Kafka, Franz. "Before the Law." *The Complete Stories,* edited by Nahum N. Glatzer, 3–4. New York: Schocken Books, 1971.

Kirkpatrick, D. L. *Contemporary Novelists*. 4th ed. New York: St. Martin's Press, 1986.

Kissack, Mike, and Michael Titlestad. "Humility in a Godless World: Shame, Defiance and Dignity in Coetzee's *Disgrace." Journal of Commonwealth Literature* 38, no. 3 (2003): 135–47.

Korang, Kwaku Larbi. "An Allegory of Re-reading: Post-colonialism, Resistance, and J. M. Coetzee's *Foe."* In Kossew, *Critical Essays on J. M. Coetzee,* 180–97.

Kossew, Sue. *Critical Essays on J. M. Coetzee.* New York: G. K. Hall, 1998.

——. *Pen and Power: A Post-colonial Reading of J. M. Coetzee and André Brink.* Amsterdam: Rodopi, 1996.

Lazarus, Neil. "Modernism and Modernity: T. W. Adorno and Contemporary White South African Literature." *Cultural Critique* 5 (Winter 1986–7): 131–55.

Lehmann-Haupt, Christopher. Review of *Life & Times of Michael K,* by J. M. Coetzee. *New York Times,* 6 December 1983, C22.

Leiris, Michel. *Manhood: A Journey from Childhood into the Fierce Order of Virility.* Translated by Richard Howard. Chicago: University of Chicago Press, 1984.

Levinas, Emmanuel. *Otherwise than Being, or Beyond Essence.* Translated by Alphonso Lingis. Pittsburgh: Duquesne University Press, 1981.

——. "Time and the Other." In *The Levinas Reader,* edited by Sean Hand, 37–58. Oxford: Blackwell, 1989.

——. *Totality and Infinity: An Essay on Exteriority.* Translated by Alphonso Lingis. Pittsburgh: Duquesne University Press, 1969.

Lodge, David. "Disturbing the Peace." Review of *Elizabeth Costello,* by J. M. Coetzee. *New York Review of Books,* 20 November 2003, 6–11.

Lukács, Georg. *The Meaning of Contemporary Realism.* Translated by John and Necke Mander. London: Merlin Press, 1963.

Lyotard, Jean-François. *The Differend: Phrases in Dispute.* Translated by Georges Van Den Abbeele. Minneapolis: University of Minnesota Press, 1988.

Macaskill, Brian. "Charting J. M. Coetzee's Middle Voice." In Kossew, *Critical Essays on J. M. Coetzee,* 66–83.

McDonald, Peter D. "*Disgrace* Effects." In Attridge and McDonald, eds., "J. M. Coetzee's *Disgrace,"* 321–30.

——. "'Not Undesirable': How J. M. Coetzee Escaped the Censor." *Times Literary Supplement,* 19 May 2000, 14–15.

——. "The Writer, the Critic, and the Censor: *Waiting for the Barbarians* and the Question of Literature." *Book History* 7 (2004).

McHale, Brian. *Constructing Postmodernism.* London: Routledge, 1992.

Marais, Michael. "Literature and the Labour of Negation: J. M. Coetzee's *Life & Times of Michael K." Journal of Commonwealth Literature* 36, no. 1 (2001): 106–25.

———. "'Little Enough, Less Than Little: Nothing': Ethics, Engagement, and Change in the Fiction of J. M. Coetzee." *Modern Fiction Studies* 46 (2000): 159–82.

———. "The Possibility of Ethical Action: J. M. Coetzee's *Disgrace*." *scrutiny2* 5, no. 1 (2000): 57–63.

Miller, J. Hillis. "Parable and Performative in the Gospels and in Modern Literature." In *Tropes, Parables, Performatives: Essays on Twentieth-Century Literature,* 135–50. London: Harvester Wheatsheaf, 1990.

Moore, John Robert. *Daniel Defoe: Citizen of the Modern World.* Chicago: University of Chicago Press, 1958.

Morphet, Tony. "The Inside Story: Review of J. M. Coetzee, *Age of Iron*." *Southern African Literary Review* 1, no. 2 (April 1991): 1–3.

Moses, Michael Valdez, ed. "The Writings of J. M. Coetzee." Special issue, *South Atlantic Quarterly* 93, no. 1 (1994).

Mpe, Phaswane. *Welcome to Our Hillbrow.* Pietermaritzburg: University of Natal Press, 2001.

Ndebele, Njabulo S. "The English Language and Social Change in South Africa." Keynote address delivered at the Jubilee Conference of the English Academy of South Africa, September 4–6, 1986. In Bunn and Taylor, *From South Africa,* 217–35.

Nicol, Mike. *The Powers that Be.* London: Bloomsbury, 1989.

Nietzsche, Friedrich. *The Genealogy of Morals.* Translated by Walter Kaufmann and R. J. Hollingdale. New York: Vintage, 1967.

Norris, Margot. *Beasts of the Modern Imagination: Darwin, Nietzsche, Kafka, Ernst, and Lawrence.* Baltimore: Johns Hopkins University Press, 1985.

———. *Joyce's Web: The Social Unraveling of Modernism.* Austin: University of Texas Press, 1992.

Ousby, Ian. *The Cambridge Guide to Literature in English.* Cambridge: Cambridge University Press, 1988.

Parker, George. Review of *Foe,* by J. M. Coetzee. *The Nation,* 28 March 1987, 402–5.

Parry, Benita. "Speech and Silence in the Fictions of J. M. Coetzee." In Attridge and Jolly, *Writing South Africa,* 149–65.

Penner, Dick. *Countries of the Mind: The Fiction of J. M. Coetzee.* New York: Greenwood Press, 1989.

Porter, Peter. Review of *Youth,* by J. M. Coetzee. *Times Literary Supplement,* 26 April 2002, 22.

Press, Karen. "Building a National Culture in South Africa." In Trump, *Rendering Things Visible,* 22–40.

Quilligan, Maureen. *The Language of Allegory: Defining the Genre.* Ithaca: Cornell University Press, 1979.

Robbins, Bruce. *The Servant's Hand: English Fiction from Below.* New York: Columbia University Press, 1986.

Rosenblatt, Louise M. *The Reader, the Text, the Poem: The Transactional Theory of the Literary Work*. Carbondale: Southern Illinois University Press, 1978.

Rousseau, Jean-Jacques. *Confessions*. Translated by J. M. Cohen. Harmondsworth: Penguin, 1954.

Sanders, Mark. "Disgrace." In Attridge and McDonald, eds., "J. M. Coetzee's *Disgrace*," 363–73.

Schmitt, Carl. *Political Theology: Four Chapters on the Concept of Sovereignty*. Translated by George Schwab. Cambridge, Mass.: MIT Press, 1985.

Slemon, Stephen. "Post-Colonial Allegory and the Transformation of History." *Journal of Commonwealth Literature* 23 (1988): 157–68.

Sontag, Susan. "Against Interpretation." In *Against Interpretation and Other Essays*, 3–14. New York: Farrar, Straus and Giroux, 1966.

Spivak, Gayatri Chakravorty. *A Critique of Postcolonial Reason: Toward a History of the Vanishing Present*. Cambridge, Mass.: Harvard University Press, 1999.

———. "Ethics and Politics in Tagore, Coetzee, and Certain Scenes of Teaching." *Diacritics* 32, no. 2 (2002).

Strauss, Peter. "Coetzee's Idylls: The Ending of *In the Heart of the Country*." In *Momentum: On Recent South African Writing*, edited by M. J. Daymond, J. V. Jacobs, and Margaret Lenta, 121–28. Pietermaritzburg: University of Natal Press, 1984.

Symposium on *Disgrace*. *scrutiny* 2 7, no. 1 (2002).

Tolstoy, Leo. *Childhood, Boyhood, Manhood*. Translated by Louise and Aylmer Maude. Ware: Wordsworth Editions, 2000.

Tournier, Michel. *Vendredi ou les limbes du Pacifique*. Paris: Gallimard, 1967. Translated by Norman Denny as *Friday*. New York: Pantheon Books, 1969.

Trump, Martin, ed. *Rendering Things Visible: Essays on South African Literary Culture*. Athens: Ohio University Press, 1990.

Van Heerden, Etienne. *Ancestral Voices*. Translated by Malcolm Hacksley. London: Penguin Books, 1989.

———. *The Long Silence of Mario Salviati*. Translated by Catherine Knox. London: Hodder and Stoughton, 2002.

Viola, André. *J. M. Coetzee: Romancier Sud-Africain*. Paris: Harmattan, 1999.

Vladislavic, Ivan. *The Folly*. Cape Town: David Philip, 1993.

———. *The Restless Supermarket*. Cape Town: David Philip, 2001.

Wade, Jean-Philippe. "The Allegorical Text and History: J. M. Coetzee's *Waiting for the Barbarians*." *Journal of Literary Studies/Tydskrif vir Literatuurwetenskap* 6, no. 4 (December 1990): 275–88.

Ward, David. *Chronicles of Darkness*. London: Routledge, 1989.

Watson, Stephen. "Colonialism and the Novels of J. M. Coetzee." *Research in African Literatures* 17 (1986): 370–92.

———. "The Writer and the Devil: J. M. Coetzee's *The Master of Petersburg*." *New Contrast* 22, no. 3 (1994): 47–61.

Wicomb, Zoë. *David's Story: A Novel.* New York: The Feminist Press, 2001.

――――. "Shame and Identity: The Case of the Coloured in South Africa." In Attridge and Jolly, *Writing South Africa,* 91–107.

Wood, James. "A Frog's Life." *London Review of Books,* 23 October 2003, 15–16.

Wood, Philip R. "Aporias of the Postcolonial Subject: Correspondence with J. M. Coetzee." In Moses, "The Writings of J. M. Coetzee," 181–95.

Ziarek, Ewa Płonowska. *The Rhetoric of Failure: Deconstruction of Skepticism, Reinvention of Modernism.* Albany: State University of New York Press, 1996.